GW00760826

GARDA SIOCHANA COLLEGE
20 MAY 1988
LIBRARY
TEMPLEMORE, Co. TIPPERARY.

Managing with INFORMATION TECHNOLOGY

Eric Deeson

First published in Great Britain in 1987
by Kogan Page Limited
120 Pentonville Road
London N1 9JN

British Library Cataloguing in Publication Data

Deeson, Eric
Managing with information technology.
1. Management — Data processing
I. Title
001.5 HD301.2

ISBN 1–85091–271–8
1–85091–272–6 Pbk

Printed and bound in Great Britain by Biddles Limited, Guildford

Contents

Acknowledgements **9**

Introduction **10**

1. Lid Off the Computer **12**
1.1 IT is the basis of modern society *12*
1.2 The computer – basis of IT *14*
1.3 Inside the computer *17*
1.4 There are various kinds of computer *20*
1.5 Computer warehouse *23*
1.6 No computer is an island *24*
1.7 Looking forward *26*

2. Software Matters More Than Hardware **27**
2.1 Running the system *27*
2.2 Mind your language *30*
2.3 Your own purposes *32*

3. Business Software in Action **34**
3.1 What is an office? *34*
3.2 Office software *37*
3.3 Word processing *39*
3.4 Communications *46*
3.5 Databases *57*
3.6 Spreading the sheets *63*
3.7 Graphics software *69*

4. More Software to Manage **76**
4.1 On the right path *76*
4.2 Organisers *et al* *79*

4.3 Integrated software *82*
4.4 Being a wimp *86*
4.5 Relational databases *89*
4.6 Hardware integration – a case study *92*
4.7 A summary of the system *95*

5. Distance No Object **99**
5.1 Spreading the net *100*
5.2 Multi-usage *102*
5.3 Spreading the net wider *107*

6. Choosing Software and Hardware **110**
6.1 Systems analysis *110*
6.2 Why computerise? *111*
6.3 Finding the software *114*
6.4 A case in point *116*
6.5 Hardware checks *122*
6.6 Questions of cost *124*

7. The Reinvention of the Telephone **126**
7.1 Telex *130*
7.2 On to teletex? *132*
7.3 Getting the fax *134*
7.4 Getting the digits out *139*
7.5 Telephone equipment *140*
7.6 Ancillary telephone equipment *144*
7.7 Electronic mail *146*
7.8 Triumphs of technology *147*
7.9 Mobile telephones *151*

8. The Video Connection **154**
8.1 Television background *154*
8.2 Video discs *158*
8.3 Interactive video *164*
8.4 Into space *165*
8.5 Cable tv *167*

9. Desktop Publishing **171**
9.1 Electronic and traditional publishing *171*
9.2 Disc to type *173*
9.3 On to the desk top *178*

10. Databases **185**
10.1 Options old and new *185*
10.2 Prestel *188*

10.3 Other videotex systems *193*
10.4 The compact disc *200*
10.5 Bringing in the expert *203*
10.6 Information in the global village *206*

Appendices

1. Glossary **211**

2. Finding Out More **243**

3. Personal Data Protection **247**

Index **249**

Dedication

I gladly dedicate this book to Jacquetta Megarry, colleague and friend, for the reasons noted elsewhere.

Acknowledgements

As information technology is my business, I cannot possibly name all the people who have helped me form my ideas and have provided hard facts over the last 18 years (since I wrote my first book in the field). There are hundreds of them: authors of books, writers in magazines and journals, speakers at meetings, presenters at exhibitions. There have been (literally) also hundreds of personal correspondents and people with whom I have enjoyed fruitful, perhaps argumentative, lively discussions.

I come down, therefore, to just two names. They are those of the person who induced me to write this book, and the one who helped me write it. Jacquetta Megarry is the first; I have worked closely with her on a number of exciting projects related to IT, and she has contributed in all the ways listed above – as an author of books and of articles I have read, as a speaker at meetings I have attended, and all the rest. Her sharp practical comments have moved me in new directions (including this book) as well as bringing me down to earth about others.

Dragging me along by the other arm has been Jenny Healey. Straight after joining me as a typist, she was thrown into the deep end of IT by having to word process this book. It's a long book with lots of unusual vocabulary, but she kept up, thrived, and by the end was asking for more. At the same time, Jenny was learning the hard way about all the other aspects of keeping my own office running. She held my head above the floods of information at a difficult time.

Such a time is also difficult for a writer's family, especially where (as in this case) there is Christmas and New Year to contend with. Thanks to all of them for shrugging off my too frequent absences as the rate of transfer of information from mind to disc reached a peak during what should have been a holiday.

Introduction

The information revolution of the past couple of decades has radically changed the lives of many millions of people. Among those many millions are the management and staff of companies of all sizes. In particular, few offices remain untouched by the chip and the amazing things it can do. However, at any time of revolution, there are problems. That is as true of the information revolution as of any bloody battle for civil power. The problems always stem from one root in these cases – lack of information.

It may be strange to feel that the problems of the information revolution come from lack of information, but it is so. There are many cases of people losing jobs and of firms going out of business because those concerned were not aware of some aspect or other of information technology (IT). Firms have gone bust because they did not take IT on board when their competitors did, or (more often) because they *did* computerise but went about it the wrong way and, for whichever of these reasons, people have lost jobs.

This book attempts to survey modern IT from the office user's point of view. The office in question may be that of a sole proprietor with few or no staff, or it may be in a large department of a large organisation. In both cases, and in all those between, IT is relevant because information is their business. Think of your work – its concern is information, isn't it? You have information coming in, and you pass it on. You need to store and process information, and you need to transfer it elsewhere. Information technology is concerned with all systems – people, equipment, and real or abstract links – that allow you to carry out these information tasks more efficiently and with less boredom. This book examines how that is so, with the needs of the office, its management, and its staff always at the forefront.

The office is at the leading edge of IT because the office is the embodiment of information handling. What happens in the office in the next few years will show what will happen in every area of human activity in the more distant future. What the office of the 1990s is like will be the world a few decades later. That is mainly why IT excites me so greatly as far as the business environment is concerned. If offers so much that will make the world of the future a better – richer, more relaxed and pleasant – place to live in.

I hope very much that the information in this book will help you to see excitement in such visions too. I have tried to make the content practical without getting bogged down in details that will change before you set eyes on them.

Information transfer, which is what this book is for, should not be a one-way process. I would certainly be very happy to receive your comments, views and ideas (destructive as well as constructive), and will gladly acknowledge the names of those who provide help that reaches the next edition.

Eric Deeson
Harborne
Birmingham
January 1987

1
Lid Off the Computer

The computer is the basis of modern information technology (IT), so that much of this book will be looking specifically at its uses and its links to other equipment. The computer is also the most obvious component of the majority of IT systems, and we need to understand it to the extent of seeing its relevance to the wealth of practical applications and implications. It is important, too, to accept that computers can, and often do, stand alone as useful total systems in their own right.

1.1 IT is the basis of modern society

Information technology concerns the uses of systems that allow the transfer, storage, processing and presentation of information; its aim should be the benefit of society and its individual members. In that computers are information processors and very efficient devices for controlling information storage and transfer, it is a fair claim that IT as we know it depends on them.

It is also a fair claim that society as we know it, in the first and second worlds at least, depends on clear information for its efficient running. We can define information as being that which adds to human knowledge – and knowing what is going on is essential for societies to survive and for individuals to be effective members of them.

The computer has never been an invention looking for an application; its progress has always been led by demand, in that people have at all times been able to ask 'wouldn't it be nice if we could . . .'

In the financial world there has been tremendous change in the past decade or so. Before IT became common in the clearing banks, most customers were resigned to spending lengthy periods in queues to cash cheques, carry out transfers or even just to enquire about the status of their accounts. Transfers could take up to a week to pass through the system, and errors were not uncommon.

Now the queues in the high street banks are much reduced by the ubiquitous 'hole in the wall', the 24-hour-a-day automatic teller machine (atm). This can provide cash on demand and display current balances, as well as offering more and more other information and services. A growing number of customers can obtain such information services with their personal computers through the medium of 'home and office' banking on Prestel, although cash withdrawals are not available – but the many spin-offs of information technology in banking are fast reducing the personal need for cash anyway.

Money transfers now take place much more quickly, and with less risk of error, thus cutting costs in various ways. More and more people and organisations are able to leave a proportion of those transfers entirely to computers; they can buy and sell goods, stocks, shares and currencies automatically and instantaneously, on the basis of continuously updated details of market prices.

Prestel – the world's first public viewdata service – is a splendid example if IT, with its tight relationship between computers and telecommunications. By linking your computer to the telephone network with a modem, you can rapidly access a huge bank of information interactively. Thus, after looking at travel timetables on Prestel, people are able to book seats and holiday packages; they can place hotel and theatre bookings in the same way; and can order deliveries of groceries, flowers and other gifts. Messages to Prestel users elsewhere can be sent free, using the system's electronic mail facility, and to many non-users by linking to the world-wide telex network. News, local and world weather, educational, financial and geographical data – all these and many more areas of information (as well as games) are available to Prestel users at any time of day or night at often little more than the cost of a local phone call.

Information technology helps public transport to provide a better and more efficient service. It allows management to have a clear, up-to-date picture of the position and status of all their vehicles (whether planes, trains or buses) and to keep in touch with the crews. As an appreciation of this continuous knowledge grows, maybe public transport delays will become a dim memory of the past.

Neither is private transport being left behind by the IT revolution. The number of car drivers attached to their office by the invisible umbilical cord of a radio link to the telephone network is growing, while their journeys are speeded by linked traffic control systems, more quickly and efficiently operated roadworks, and warning messages from the in-car computer. Indeed, London is even now installing a route finder system which will give each subscribing driver full information about the best way to any destination, taking account of likely temporary road delays, road closures, and traffic jams.

At work, IT-based information transfers (including word processing and electronic mail) can markedly increase efficiency and job satisfaction. At leisure, Prestel-style squash bookings, details of entertainment programmes and restaurant menus help people to lead fuller lives. At home, the personal computer is starting to take up an essential role other than for playing games; the home is in transition to a unit integrated into a 'global village' society rather than being a traditional castle with closed drawbridge. Prestel-style information transfer is linking with cable and satellite television and video phones so much that there is a marked growth in the number of people ('telecommuters') working with IT from home.

These few examples should convince you, if you didn't already agree, that IT is the basis of our modern society. There are dangers in that as well as huge benefits, but it is a fact.

This book will show how your own professional activities can benefit by introducting or extending computerisation and links to the overall IT network. This applies whether you are a sole trader or freelance, or part of the management team in a department of a large company or organisation. It applies whether your interest is to improve the 'office' aspects of your home or to increase the efficiency of your area of responsibility at work.

Just as information technology is the basis of our society, so the computer is the central focus of IT. Even if computers haven't been mentioned in all the examples above, they are there – quietly getting on with the tasks they are programmed to do.

1.2 The computer – basis of IT

The crucial question – what is a computer? – has many answers, because computers are different things to different people. Some might say that it doesn't matter at all what a computer actually is, for our concern is simply with its place in society and its usage in specific situations. While there is truth in that comment, I think it *is* important to give some kind of clear view. Here then is a definition that can get us started:

A computer is a modern, high speed, general purpose, digital electronic, stored program data processor.

Admittedly, this definition is far from perfect, in that it tends to raise more questions than it answers. Also, there are plenty of computers that don't fully meet the definition, but it will do very well as far as machines discussed in this book are concerned. Below, we consider the sentence term by term.

Modern. The computer as we know it, and as typified by home and personal micros (for instance), goes back in essential concepts only a few decades. In fact the office and home computer systems of the late

1980s do not differ intrinsically from the electronic calculating machines used for research, ballistics, code breaking and so on in the Second World War. Research is currently being undertaken in various countries to develop the next generation of computers, but pretty well all that is said about computers in this book will also apply to them.

High speed. The central processor of even a cheap contemporary computer can carry out millions of operations in a second – and does so all the time it is switched on. The most powerful of modern machines may work a thousand times faster, but the cost will be far more than a thousand times greater, and for most normal purposes there's no need for such speed.

General purpose. With suitable equipment attached to it, and with suitable instructions to guide it, the modern computer could do almost anything one could want. Agreed, in very many cases the trouble and cost may not be worth the results, but almost anything *is* possible. However, this phrase distinguishes between the 'programmable' computers of home and office and the special purpose (dedicated) devices used in a wide range of equipment such as digital watches, calculators, video equipment and cars.

Digital electronic. The tasks of any item of electronic equipment are carried out by small electric currents. Most of a computer's circuitry is in fact microelectronic, the currents involved being thousands or even millions of times smaller than those through a simple light bulb or loudspeaker. However, the current in a light bulb or speaker can take any value between zero and a maximum, but it comes in pulses of a restricted number of different sizes in a digital system such as a computer. In complex situations, digital systems are far easier to design and work with than the others, the analogue ones.

Stored program. A program is a set of instructions which the computer can follow in order to carry out some specific task. Because the machine works so fast, in order to be efficient it *must* be able to store the instructions that it has to follow. The resulting stored program concept is perhaps one of the most crucial aspects of the computer as we know it. This point links with the one made earlier about general purpose as opposed to specific purpose. A special purpose device such as the one at the heart of a pocket calculator has a fixed factory-set program to carry out just a small range of tasks. While those devices too must have their programs stored, in the case of general purpose systems one can change the programs – these systems are programmable.

Data processor. In the same way as a food processor processes food, with the output material in a different and more useful form from that input, so a data processor processes data. Data is the way in which computers and similar devices handle information. However, because this equipment has no intelligence in any human sense, it cannot understand the information that is fed into it, so we use the word data instead. In brief, then, data is information without meaning. All information fed into a computer is converted into data in the form of digital electronic signals, the pulses of electric current mentioned above. In fact computers are *binary* digital systems: everything is based simply on the presence or absence of a pulse of electricity at a given point.

It may be worth saying a little more about information as opposed to data. If you find in a pocket of an old jacket a torn piece of paper saying 420713, it would tell you nothing. The characters have the power to carry meaning, but because they do not, 420713 is data rather than information. If a matching piece of paper now turned up saying 'Telephone Jenny on', 420713 would become meaningful – no longer data, but now information.

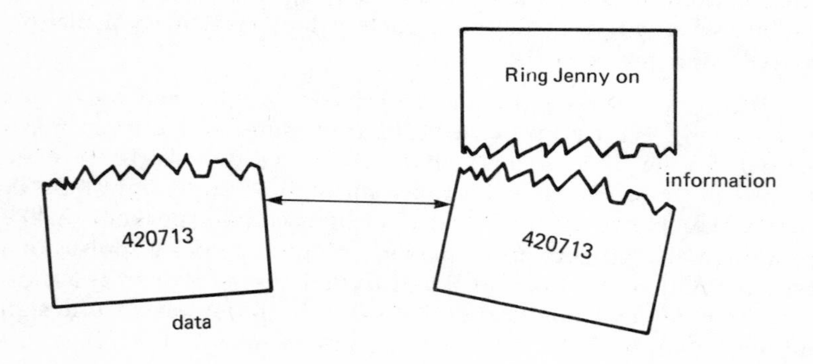

Figure 1.1. Information is data with meaning

Truly, those points about electronics are not of great significance in this context, so the original definition of a computer can be simplified and summarised as follows:

A modern computer is a high speed, programmable information processor.

Nor do we really need to know much about how the computer actually carries out its work of information processing. The essential points are shown in Figure 1.2, a block diagram which gives the functions of the main sections of any computer and shows how these sections are linked together to allow flows of data.

Let's go through those blocks one by one.

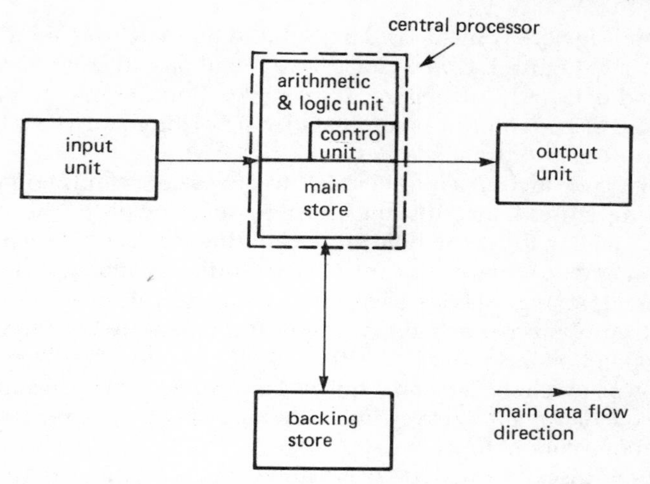

Figure 1.2. Any computer has only a few main sections

1.3 Inside the computer

The part of the system concerned with data processing – the actual handling of data in binary form – has a dashed line around it in the sketch. It is the central processor, or central processing unit (cpu), and we can consider it to be the main unchanging part of the system as a whole. Each step of the processing is carried out by the arithmetic and logic unit (alu) of the central processor; it does so under the overall guidance of the control unit (which includes a sort of clock to keep all the system's activities in step), following the instructions held in the program(s) in the memory.

The work of the arithmetic and logic unit is fairly clearly described by its name. It carries out arithmetical operations, mainly additions, and logical ones, mainly comparisons, on the data it has to deal with from moment to moment.

The computer's main memory (or store) needs to be fairly compact. This is because the control unit must be able to reach (access) any part (location) at very high speed; although electric signals travel fast, the time they take to travel through the store is significant when we are trying to work in tiny fractions of a millionth of a second. In addition, main memory is quite costly even by modern standards, a further reason for restricting the size.

Because of the small capacity and high cost of main memory, and our obvious need to be able to get the computer to undertake an unpredictable but enormous range of tasks, the system has a need for back-up memory or backing store. This can be one of a range of peripheral devices (outside the dotted line that encloses the central processor in Figure 1.2) and must have the ability to store currently unwanted data and instructions. It may take thousandths rather than millionths of a second to access data from backing store, but that is rarely a problem in practice.

People have devised a number of different systems for holding data in backing store. Currently the most popular involves the use of magnetic media; these can hold large quantities of data tightly packed on to a magnetic surface similar to that of audio cassette tape. Indeed, the backing storage device used often with the cheapest home and portable computers is actually a simple audio cassette recorder, with the data kept on a standard cassette. Larger and more costly systems can also use magnetic tape, in a special large, open reel form and used with special large tape drives but, generally speaking, some form of disc is more common.

Magnetic discs, of which there is a huge range of types, have a major advantage in that they are two dimensional, where tape is in effect one dimensional. This means that the system can access any packet of data on a disc far more quickly. High capacity hard discs are rapidly growing in popularity as backing store for small computer systems and their price is falling extremely quickly. At the moment, however, the lower capacity floppy (ie flexible) discs are more common; being replaceable in the drive, they at least offer the opportunity of a theoretically unlimited library of programs and data.

Magnetic discs and tapes have almost completely replaced the previously universal use of punched paper tapes and cards – messy, expensive and low capacity systems that offered very long access times and could not be erased. Other techniques are, however, under development, and it could be that within a few years magnetic media follow punched paper into the history books.

We use bits and bytes to measure memory sizes and related matters. In addition to an ability to store the program instructions and data it is currently working with, a computer must also be able to store the operating system instructions – all the details of how the computer is to carry out the tasks it can be given. All these things are data as far as the computer is concerned, electronic representations in some form or another of binary numbers. The computer's circuits, chips and memory devices follow certain rules to handle strings of binary numbers.

A binary number, called a bit (= binary digit), can take the value 0 or 1 only. A byte is a set of eight bits. The value of a byte can range from 0 (0000 0000) to 225 (1111 1111). In the cheaper, common home micros, the byte is the same as a word, a set of bits of standard length. (You may also come across a nibble, a set of four bits.) Of increasing importance in the home, in education, and in the office are 16-bit micros, machines working on data whose unit (word) is two bytes long. Sixteen-bit machines, and even more so the 32-bit ones that are becoming common, are able to deal with more data more quickly; they are also less restricted in the size of main memory that can be accessed.

Memory size is normally measured in bytes, to indicate how many units of data it can store. The maximum size of a home micro's memory is usually 65,536 bytes, referred to as 64 Kilobytes (64K): the capital letter is used to remind us that, although a kilo represents 1000, one Kilobyte is actually a little bigger, at 1024 bytes. Quite often we need even bigger units than that, and the principal ones are the Megabyte (MB) which, at 1,048,576, is just over a million bytes and the Gigabyte (GB), just over a thousand million bytes.

The main memory of a micro is commonly divided into two parts. The operating software is likely to be fixed permanently in read-only memory (rom); here the system stores data so that it can be accessed (read) but not changed. The contents of rom are truly fixed, even when the power is off. Unchanging and unchangeable, rom is clearly no use for storing the user's current programs and data. We must be able to alter these, so have random-access memory (ram) for this purpose. The contents of ram can be accessed (read) and also changed (written to). Both ram and rom are universally supplied on special microelectronic chips (integrated circuits), though again other techniques are under development.

In discussing the concept of backing store, the term peripheral was introduced to describe a piece of equipment that can be linked to the central processing unit. Figure 1.2 shows two other crucial peripherals, the input and output units which respectively allow data to go into and come out of the system. In particular, a computer must be able to communicate with the people who use it. Communication is a two-way process, and that applies as much to communication between people and computers as to that between two humans. We need to pass information, queries, commands and instructions (all becoming forms of data) into the computer through some kind of input device; it does the reverse for us by way of an output unit.

A standard personal computer provides direct input from a keyboard and supplies direct output to some kind of visual display (tv set, monitor, or flat liquid crystal display (lcd) unit). Without an input device and an output device, no computer is much use, as it will not be able to obtain data for processing, nor will it be able to do anything with the results of that processing. In fact, there are many different ways of getting data into and out of a computer processor. Figure 1.3 shows some common examples of each kind of input and output unit.

1.4 There are various kinds of computer

Figure 1.2 showed a typical small personal computer, or microcomputer (micro). There are various definitions of the term micro, but I can best describe it at the moment as a computer designed for use by only one person at a time.

Groups of micros linked together as a network are becoming very common in offices. Each unit in the network (in other words, each workstation at which someone can operate) acts most of the time as a simple stand-alone micro, like the ones described in the previous section. However, the use of the network can also allow at least a certain level of intercommunication between systems, so that, for instance, one user can send a message to a second, and all can share data and other scarce resources. The sharing of scarce resources by the workstations of a network is of obvious value. Thus a high capacity hard disc is preferable to a number of separate floppy disc drives if there is a frequent need to access complex and/or costly programs and large quantities of common data.

Again, it is usually better to share one or two high quality printers between the users of a network than to provide a cheap one for each user; after all, printing will rarely be required by each user more than about 10 per cent of the time.

Networks come in various styles, as shown in Figure 1.4; each has its own advantages and disadvantages. While the reasons for their use are clear, they can suffer two major problems. First, the data-carrying channels may become overcrowded if too much communication is attempted at a given time and, second, a single fault can put the whole system out of action.

Networks are fairly recent innovations. The more traditional solution to the problems of sharing data and scarce resources between workstations is the minicomputer. While in layout a mini system may look much like the star configuration of networks shown in Figure 1.4(b), a mini is in fact a single processing system able to work with a number of terminals at the same time. A terminal looks very similar to a microcomputer workstation on a network; however, it will normally comprise little more than an input device and an output device (such as a keyboard and a printer or display). Such a terminal is called dumb; in contrast, an intelligent terminal is one that also incorporates some degree of local processing power.

The physical area over which a network as described above can extend is currently fairly limited. Few systems operate satisfactorily if a workstation is more than about half a kilometre from the centre, so such a network is often described as a local area network (lan). As the rate of data transfer between workstation and centre is much lower in the case of a mini, the links can be a lot longer. In that case, it is quite

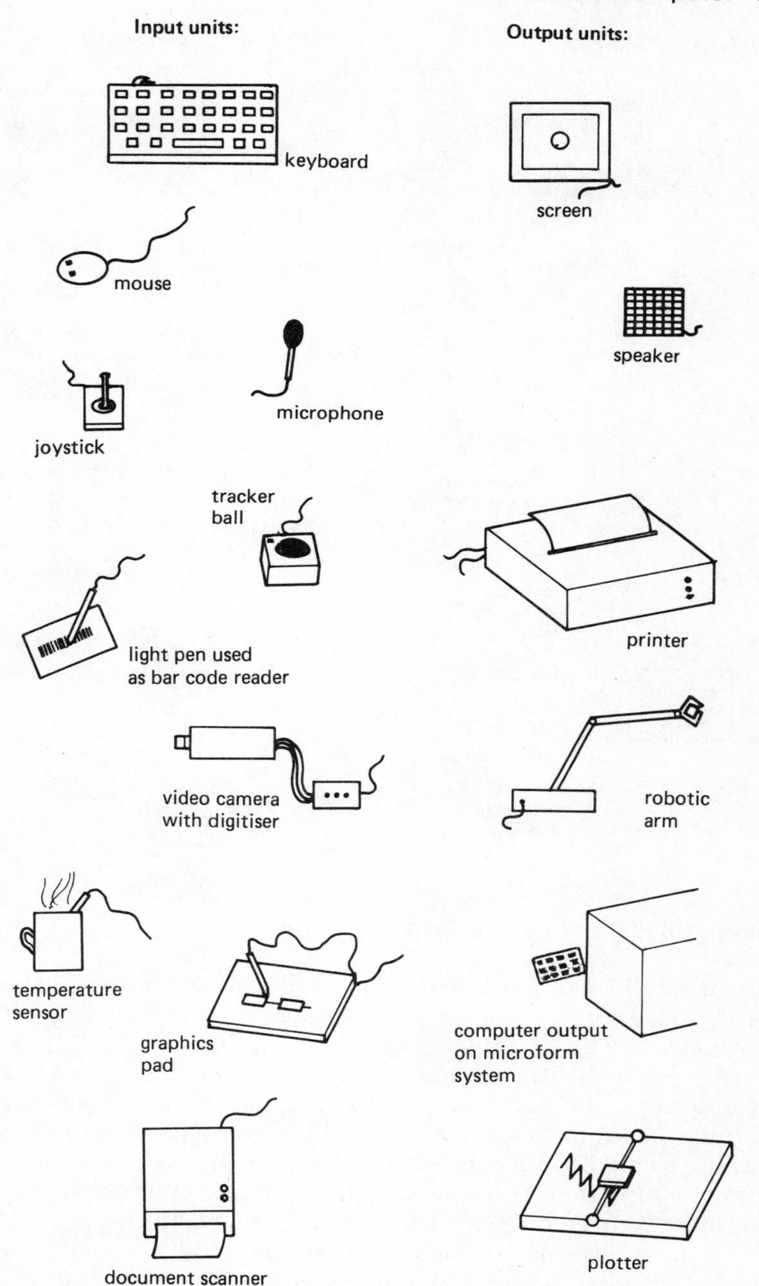

Figure 1.3. There are many common input and output units

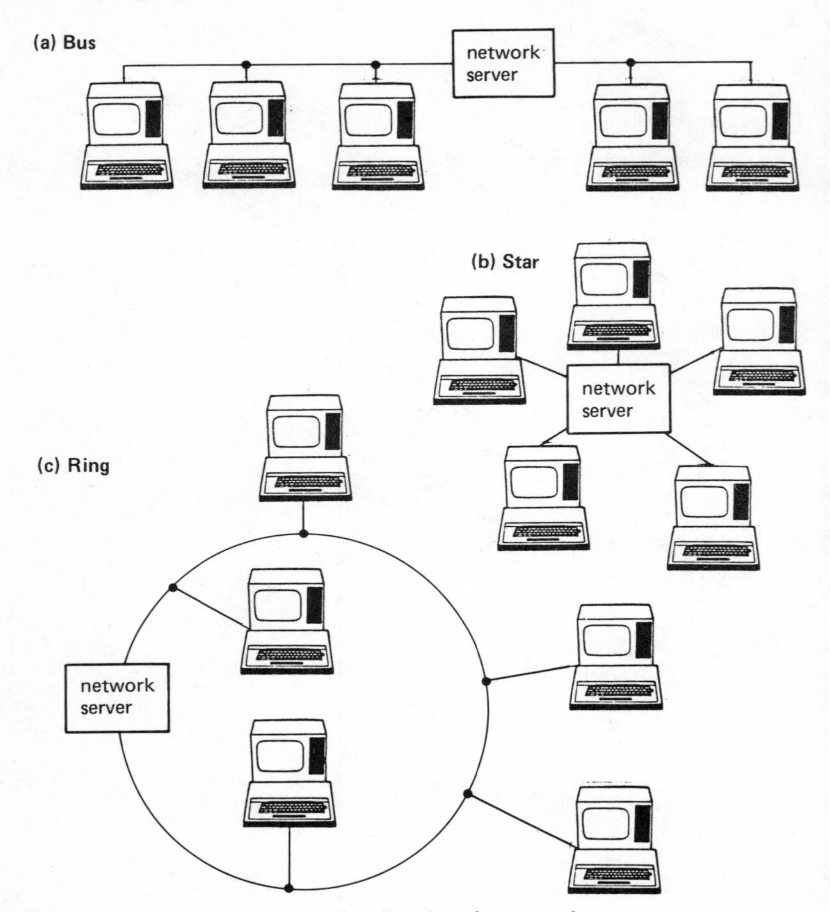

Figure 1.4 There are various kinds of network

common to join terminals in different buildings or even on different sites using a fairly simple private cable or even a microwave channel.

The limit on the size of a minicomputer system is in fact the number of terminals it can supervise. The operating software of the mini's central processor must continually scan all the terminal cable links for incoming data, and keep meeting the needs of the various users. As a result, most current minis are able to handle no more than about a dozen terminals – but they can do so efficiently and cheaply.

Where an even larger number of geographically separate users need to access a single central computer through terminals, they must turn to a mainframe computer in order to cope.

Mainframe is the traditional word to describe the largest types of computer, those that offer great computing power and processing speed as well as the ability to supervise the use of a large number of terminals. The word originates from the steel frames or racks on which the banks of circuit boards and valves used to be mounted to make up the then necessarily large central processor. We also use the word mainframe to describe the large computers found in the data processing departments of major organisations (such as banks, insurance companies and government departments). Often, as well as having a fairly large number of terminals connected to them, such systems may handle dozens of other peripherals, such as disc drives and printers. A major difference between any kind of mainframe computer and the others is that permanent staff are needed to keep the former system running.

For completeness I also ought to mention the term supercomputer, sometimes applied to the very largest and most modern mainframe systems. Supercomputers characteristically offer extremely high processing speeds; thus they are able to handle the huge quantities of data involved in the work of, for instance, a meteorological office (weather bureau) and spacecraft control. However, all this terminology is now in the melting pot as the marketing people invent new names – like mini-micro and super-micro – in an attempt to imply that their products are truly new.

1.5 Computer warehouse

The use of the terms hardware and software has so far been avoided, but I ought to mention them briefly now, as you will inevitably meet them.

By hardware we mean all the physical equipment within a computer or other IT system. This will include a central processor and its various parts as described above, plus the peripherals that the particular user will need to be able to work with it. In effect, then, it is what comes in the boxes when one decides to purchase a 'computer'.

A 'computer', however, is no use until it has instructions to follow and data to work on. The programs needed to turn an empty and ineffective machine into a useful working system can be bought separately on disc (or tape) as required. So, games on cassette may be purchased for a cheap home computer, or databases and graphics programs on disc for an office machine. The programs used by computer hardware to carry out a specific purpose are called software. Software, consisting as it does of programs, is in fact intangible, although it must be carried in some form of medium readable by a backing storage device: discs or cassettes, for instance. However, those discs and cassettes are not the software itself, they simply carry the software that the computer uses.

In fact, few (if any) computers nowadays are completely empty when viewed as a set of hardware; they are all able to do something when you switch them on, even if it is only to look for software on disc. This means that certain programs must reside permanently inside the hardware. Those programs are software (by the above definition) but are an inherent and crucial part of the hardware. They will often be provided in chips (integrated circuits) plugged permanently into the computer's main circuit board and in that these chips carrying programs are neither truly software nor hardware, we use the word firmware for them. Firmware is software held on chips (rom chips); the term will also include programs that the user may later decide to add to the system if those programs are on chip and if the chips can be used by the particular hardware.

Some people have been rather carried away by these different types of computer ware, and have devised similar names for other parts of a computer system. You may come across liveware, for the staff required to run a large computer; paperware, to include all the manuals that have to be struggled through in order to understand some aspect or other of operation; and even underware to describe the special furniture and other such equipment that may be added. A full computer system also requires the purchase of various types of consumable, but so far (fortunately) no one seems to have coined a ware word to describe them. Consumables include blank discs (or tapes) for data and back-up copies of programs to be stored on, paper for the printer, and the special forms that may be associated with certain usages of the system.

1.6 No computer is an island

We have already emphasised the fact that the central processor, the main part of any computer system, is entirely useless without peripherals, and therefore must have the ability to transfer data outside itself. A stand-alone micro involves data transfers between the peripherals and the central processor, but in many contexts its usage can be much enhanced by allowing communication with systems elsewhere.

Unless we are dealing simply with data transfers between the different parts of a local area network (or even using a long lead between a stand-alone micro and a printer in the next room), we at last return to the realms of telecommunications and IT in general. To see the true value of communications between separate computers we need to remember some of the ideas raised in the general descriptions of IT systems early in this chapter.

When personal computer users access a viewdata system such as Prestel in order to explore public transport timetables and make bookings, they are explicitly using IT by integrating computer systems and a telecommunications network (the telephone system in this case).

Figure 1.5 shows the main Prestel menu (choice page) to give you some idea of the overall facilities available if you are not already aware of these. It is very easy to access and use this database from your computer, if you have the right software and a hardware link to the telephone network.

While large companies will have so much data to transfer, perhaps even 24 hours a day, that they will need their own special data communications links (such as private telephone lines, called land lines), the personal micro user will almost always be content to use the public telephone network. Plenty more will be said about this in later chapters, but at this stage it is worth noting that a special piece of equipment called a modem is needed to interface the computer with the telephone line. The main reason for this is that, as we have seen, computers are digital devices that transfer data in the form of pulses of electric current. Current telephone lines are not able to handle digital signals effectively, so the prime task of a modem is to convert the digital output of a computer to the analogue form required by the telephone line and to do the reverse for the data that comes in.

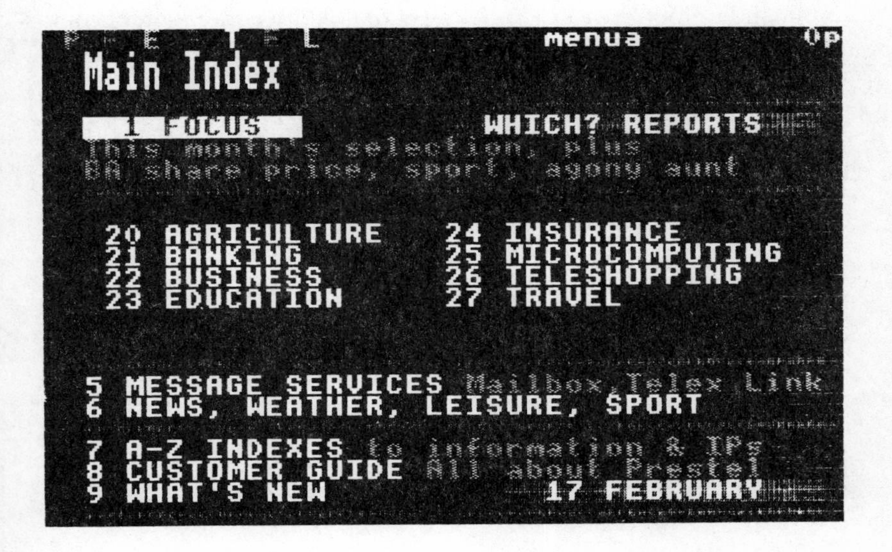

Figure 1.5. Prestel offers a huge range of information and services

If one is working from home as an employee of a large company, or has other reasons to transfer data more effectively than can be done by electronic mail, the use of communications links and communications software in the computer is very exciting and can be very cost-effective. We shall return to this theme later in the book, just noting here that this important aspect of IT is certain to become an integral part of all computer systems within only a few years.

1.7 Looking forward

It is worth emphasising again that the description of computer hardware and software given in this chapter is not likely to date very fast. Although significant advances in IT and computer technology are announced almost daily, the basic principles are fairly fixed. The cost and complexity of computer systems have fallen fast over the last few decades and will continue to do so. Progress in microelectronics is the main reason for this, as chips become more complex yet cheaper. We can see the same rate of advance in the case of electronic calculators, digital watches, and broadcast receivers. Thus personal computers the size of credit cards are beginning to appear, as is a variety of systems the user can carry on a watch strap.

Miniaturisation is not, however, the only objective of the computer industry. As far as peripherals are concerned, people expect voice input and output to be crucial features of the fifth generation of computers of the early 1990s, while as for the central processing unit, we can look forward to systems which involve a number of processors working as a team on a range of different tasks simultaneously.

It may not be long, therefore, before the 'traditional' picture of a computer as consisting of keyboard, screen, and various hidden bits and pieces of hardware and software will disappear. We shall consider later what types of system may replace this, but you can be sure that the basic concept as outlined in Figure 1.2 will still be able to describe them.

2

Software Matters More Than Hardware

Various points in Chapter 1 should make it clear that this title is serious. A computer without software is as much use as a car without anyone who has knowledge of driving, and world-wide more and more effort is going into software development than into hardware development.

Applications software – software designed to enable a computer system to carry out tasks that the user wishes to assign to it – is only the outermost layer of the computer's many-tiered software structure. In this chapter we need first to take a look at the lower levels.

2.1 Running the system

The innermost tier in any computer's software hierarchy is the program (or suite of programs) that keeps the hardware working properly. This software goes by the name of operating software (or monitor, supervisor, control program, or executive – all near enough the same, as far as we are concerned). We can define a computer's operating software as being the program(s) that the hardware needs to carry out the instructions of the next tier without too much human supervision.

The purpose of an operating software is not just to give the user an easy life – after all, the designer of every aspect of a computer should have that aim in mind. At least as important is to keep the computer working as close to full time as possible; only then can its huge power fully be realised. As every part of the whole hardware/software/liveware unit costs money, it is not cost-effective to leave any of it idle for long periods.

In particular, the processor – able to carry out millions of actions a second – is not used to the full when there are data transfers to peripherals. Thus it is not economic for a processor to concentrate full time on keyboard input at a couple of characters per second. Similar processing time losses can occur during the preparation stages for any particular job, or when something goes wrong that the user must investigate. In any context humans are far more intelligent than computers, but on the whole they are far, far slower.

Thus a major task of the operating software is to ensure that at any moment the tremendous power of each part of the system is being used most effectively. This task itself uses computer processing effort; it also reduces the amount of memory available for the current application. However, overall there is a very significant gain in efficiency.

Here's what a mainframe computer's operating software will handle:

- Transfer of programs, subprograms and other data to and fro between main memory and backing store as they are needed.
- Scheduling of how the system carries out the various jobs in hand, with the aim of continuous processing.
- Control of the use of peripherals, including monitoring all lines from terminals.
- If more than one program is being carried out during a period, the supervision of the tasks of each program in turn, to aim for continuous processing and efficient data transfer to and from peripherals, while all the time bearing in mind the priority of each of the programs.
- Automatic handling of problems and errors as much as possible.
- Arrangement of temporary storage (eg sending to a disc data that is to be printed if no printer is available, and getting it back later).
- Keeping the operator informed as to what is going on and what actions he or she may need to organise.
- Every so often (eg at the end of a shift) or on demand, printing out a log of all jobs undertaken, their progress and any problems met.

At the start of a typical session with such a mainframe, then, the operator will instruct the system software as to the programs to be carried out. All necessary details will be supplied, including the priority of each job, and then the system will be left to look after itself. The operating software will sort out the details of the jobs and their priorities, and will check the resource needs of each one (including the proportions of tasks involving input, processing, transfers to and from backing store, and output).

For the rest of the session, the operating software will carry out all the tasks described above. From moment to moment it has to try to keep the processor busy and to arrange data transfers as and when needed. On occasion it will need to send a message to the operator asking for a certain disc to be put into a certain drive, noting that a printer needs to have its paper changed, or indicating when a particular job is complete and what should be done with it next.

Clearly a large system like this needs complex operating software. It also requires a fairly large staff to look after it; the shift's chief operator, the people looking after the needs of the peripherals, a data librarian to supervise the issue and return of discs, and so on.

All those staff are rolled into one in the case of a stand-alone micro or network station, that one being the actual user. The user's concern is to get on with specific applications rather than to bother with operations and control. The operating software of a small system must therefore be prepared for this, but even so its tasks do not differ greatly, except in scale, from those described for the mainframe.

In this context there is currently another significant difference between microcomputers and mainframes. The latter offer multi-programming, the ability to share time between several programs in memory at the same moment. Much of a mainframe operating software's effort is therefore spent on scheduling the interleaving of the tasks of these programs. Figure 2.1 shows how the work of processor and peripherals may be shared between three programs in a multi-programming context.

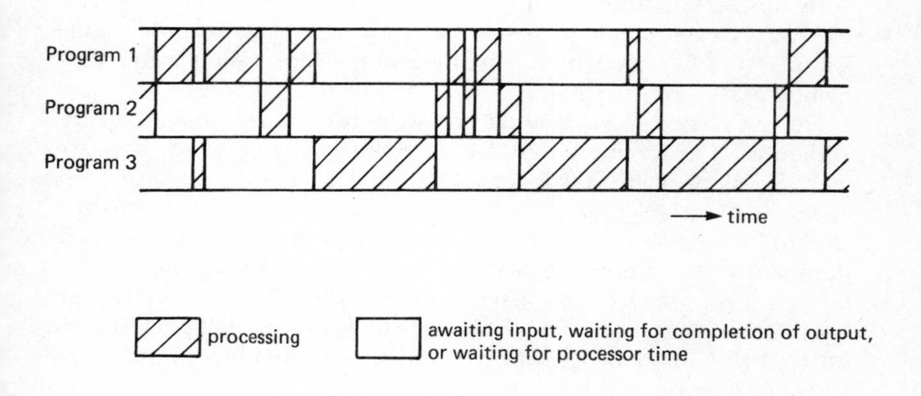

Figure 2.1. Multi-programming is when a large computer shares its time between the tasks of different programs

Few micros yet offer much in the way of multi-programming, though progress is bound to be swift in the next few years. At the moment, however, microcomputer operating software (the most common standards being cp/m for eight-bit machines (explained below) and MS-DOS for 16-bit hardware) does not need to be particularly complex. Indeed, it is left to the authors of applications programs to cover such needs as messages to the user to change discs and printer paper.

All the same, micro users need to be aware of some aspects of their operating software so that they can gain maximum benefit from it. A beginner's course (perhaps even given by a friend) of a couple of hours or so is usually the best way to obtain this awareness; after that the previously incomprehensible operating software manual will become somewhat easier to use.

2.2 Mind your language

Earlier we met the concept of the layered nature of a computer's software. The operating system must occupy the layer (or, in practice, several layers) in closest contact with the hardware; that is because in essence its task is to control the hardware. Normally, therefore, the operating software is machine specific and supplied with the computer on purchase.

As noted above, cp/m and MS-DOS are particularly common suites of operating software for micros. Control program for microcomputers, or cp/m, is the older. It became a major standard for the eight-bit machines that were the norm a few years ago and as such was fairly universal. (Interestingly, Britain is a big exception; its own hardware development at the time was so active that most of its large manufacturers created their own operating systems rather than follow United States' practice.)

However, because operating software must be machine specific, and because every micro must differ from the rest in detail, there are many versions of cp/m. All versions should appear the same to users as far as messages and procedures are concerned; all versions too should be able to work with the full range of higher layer software designed to be compatible with cp/m. These ideals are not always borne out in practice – the user must beware of possible individual variations between computer models that may mean that books aren't fully correct in their descriptions and that compatible applications software may not work properly.

Much the same is true of MS-DOS, the more modern operating suite for 16-bit micros (although 16-bit versions of cp/m have been produced as well). It cannot be emphasised too much that the existence of non-standard varieties of standard software makes systems development more tricky than it should be. While it would be wrong to insist on full compatibility, for that would stifle progress, it is a real pity that the end user suffers so much.

All those comments apply just as much to the next layer in the software ladder, the layer that carries program language software. The large majority of applications programs do not access the operating software directly; rather they depend on a language program to convert them into a form the operating system can work with. Figure 2.2 shows all these layers.

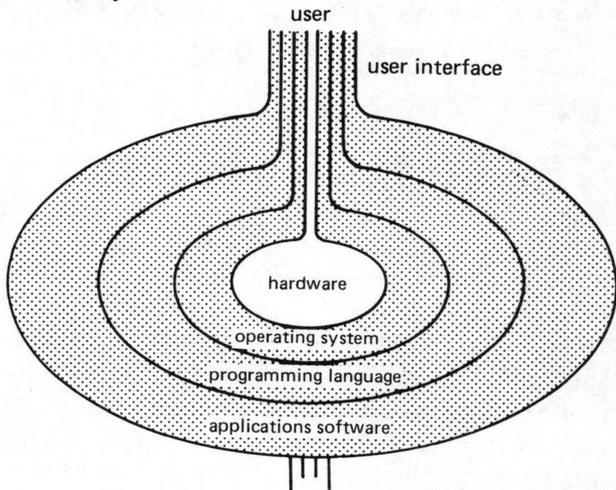

Figure 2.2. The software of a computer is rather like an onion

It is possible – and in computing's early days it was essential – to write computer programs in binary digital (bit) form so that the system can at once 'understand' each instruction. To program like that is extremely difficult, for it needs a great knowledge of how each part of the hardware works and must take account of the transfer and processing of every single chunk of data. The rows of machine code 0s and 1s are very hard to follow and check; you can imagine how tricky it would be to instruct computers with hundreds of lines of code like those in Figure 2.3.

Because computers should make life easier for programmers as much as for any other user, over the decades better and better software has been devised for computers to translate clear instructions into the binary form they need. These translating programs go by the name of program language software, or programming languages. Their function is to convert each instruction received into the sequence of 0s and 1s with which the system will be able to work.

Hundreds of programming languages have been devised over the years to meet the specific needs of different markets or the specific ideas of different programmers. You may have heard of Cobol (common in commerce), Fortran (fine for formulas, in mathematical contexts) and Logo (for programming logical thinking).

By far the most common programming language for micros at the

```
0011010111010100
1011010100100101
1100010010110111
1001001011100110
1110101011001101
0001011100100100
1001001000110101
```

Figure 2.3. A fragment of binary machine code from history; all computer programming was once done like this

moment is Basic; indeed Basic is provided as the only standard programming language in most cases. It was originally devised to help people learn programming skills, and as a result it was (and is) easy to grasp and use. Most people with the need and the interest find that, in a few hours, they can gain enough of the essentials of Basic to allow them then rapidly to pick up the other skills and concepts they may want to use.

Programming in Basic is great fun and a very popular hobby. As a hobby it has led many people in the past to some degree of fame and fortune. However, it is important to make clear that the vast majority of computer users need to know even less about program languages than about operating software. Programming knowledge is essential only if you want to write your own applications software or to tailor other people's to your own specific purpose – and even then it is really wiser to commission a specialist rather than try to learn all the concepts yourself. I repeat – you need know nothing about programming to be able to use a computer effectively for your own purposes.

2.3 Your own purposes

Using a computer effectively for your own needs is what you really want to know, so the next two chapters in particular deal with the applications of computers in the environment of the small business and the office. In these contexts a selection of applications programs, the outermost layer of the software onion, is used.

People devise applications programs with a particular task in mind, and also (in theory, if not always in practice) with a particular range of contexts in mind. Much (but not all) applications software depends on particular program languages, thus a lot of the programs designed to run on home and school micros are written in Basic. Don't forget, however, the point made about language versions.

In just the same way as operating software like cp/m differs to some degree or other with each different system it works on, so too does language software. This is especially true of Basic, the language of the personal computers, because progress in the features offered by these machines has been astounding. Thus we have moved in half a decade from monochrome upper-case (capital letters) text as the only output to text using large character sets, with full colour, high quality graphics and multi-voice sound.

The point to make most strongly is that if you decide to buy some software you must be sure that it will run with your particular hardware system.

However, software matters more than hardware, as the title of this chapter says. If you want a computer to carry out certain tasks for you, it is better to start in the market-place by looking at the software. Only when you've found the particular applications programs you want, should you start building up the hardware system to suit.

Looking at various computer applications is what we need to do now, and that's the subject of Chapters 3 and 4.

3 Business Software in Action

This is the longest chapter in the book. It explores, in breadth and in depth, the major types of business software that are relevant to the needs of any office, however small or large and whatever its aims. Chapter 4 goes on to other types, before looking at the most modern kinds of office program packages.

In each case, a generalised package will be described, meaning that I shan't go into detail about one particular system for one computer or group of computers. There are several reasons for this. The first is the huge range of styles of handling information in any particular context. As far as word processors are concerned, for instance, there may be dozens of packages available on the market for any given computer system. Even if this book concerned computing with a particular machine, it would not necessarily be wise to describe a single package.

The second reason for not using the more specific approach is that nothing stands still in this field. Even well established programs need to be updated and improved fairly often; so, in the lifetime of this book – from the time of writing early in 1987 – no package specific account could hope to remain current.

3.1 What is an office?

Any office has always embodied the basic features of information technology. That is because it explicitly handles information. Each office takes in information and puts it out; it also has the need to store, access and process information.

Figure 3.1 shows the point in block form; you will see at once that it is very much like Figure 1.2, which showed what a computer system does with data. The only difference between the two block diagrams (apart from some of the labels) is the new 'access' feature, ie the need

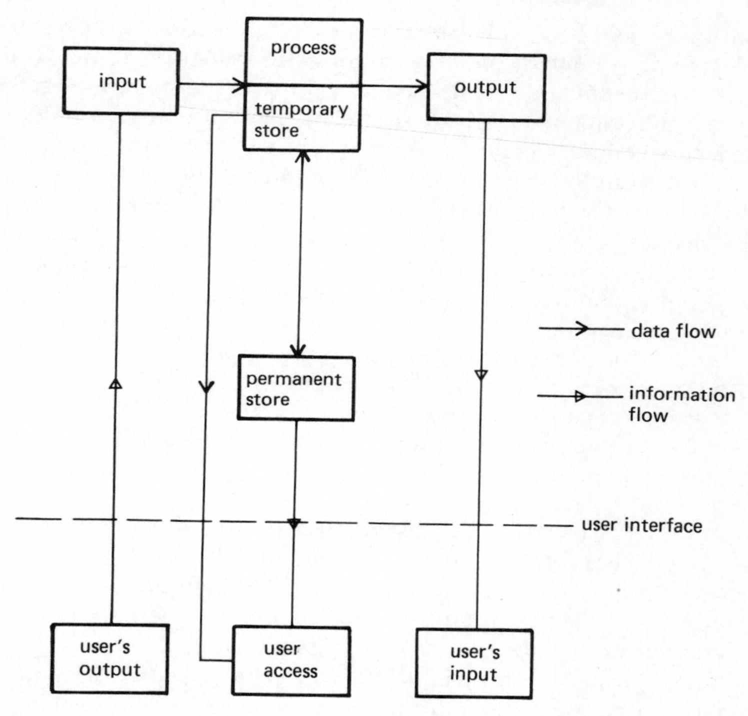

Figure 3.1. An office is in essence an information handling system

for the people who use the office to be able to lay their hands on information stored there in some form or other.

A brief look at a couple of common office usage scenarios will help make clear what is meant by the different aspects of the office as an information handling system.

It is a typical morning in the office of Charley's Cocoa Factory. The first major job of the day is to deal with the mail, a bundle of enveloped items that has just arrived. There is information on the envelopes, as well as inside them. The addresses are the most obvious of course (but they may include the names or titles of the staff who should deal with them); however, there is also information in the stamps, the postmarks, the franking impressions, and perhaps an extra message such as the name and address of the sender or a note added after the envelope was sealed.

A large office may receive hundreds or thousands of items of incoming mail each day and it will need a number of staff specially to deal with it all. Even in a small office with only a few dozen letters a day, the same type of processing of this input information is involved.

In this information processing stage the items of mail that come to

Charley's Cocoa Factory will be sorted into bundles for each person or department – management, accounts, stores and so on. If the envelopes are opened, it will be necessary to clip the contents together in the right order, and to include the envelope if it bears significant extra information. (Of course the envelopes will have to be opened if it isn't clear from the outside where the contents should be passed.)

In some traditional offices it is even considered necessary to record a line of notes about each item of post received, using a great incoming mail ledger – a form of information storage, that is. So too is making and keeping photocopies, as is done in some places. Finally, the new bundles of mail pass on to the people who have to take the necessary action.

You may or may not view these people – all of course information processors – as part of the office. It doesn't really matter, though if one has an IT attitude one can readily see ways of improving efficiency by integrating as many information handling tasks into the office area itself.

Later on, the results of processing that information will be back in the office. There will be letters to type, phone calls to make, records in files to check, papers to collate, items to file, figures to compile, accounts to work on, outgoing mail to prepare (and perhaps record in yet another great ledger).

Thus the day comes to an end. Every aspect of the office of Charley's Cocoa Factory, seen as an information processing system as in Figure 3.1, will have been involved. The better planned the system is, the more content the staff and the more efficient the company.

Now let's look at a simpler task, but one which still involves the office's information handling roles of input, process, temporary and permanent storage, and storage access.

The phone rings on Charley's Cocoa Factory switchboard. It is a supplier who wants to know why her invoice of a couple of months ago hasn't been paid. The call is put through to an accounts clerk at a nearby desk. He jots down the caller's name, company, number and invoice details on a pad – temporary information storage – and promises (output of information) to explore the situation and call back. His next step is to check the card index file of suppliers; that will give him the relevant reference number. He then goes to his filing cabinet to take out the right folder. Both tasks involve access to permanent information storage.

In the folder the accounts clerk finds the invoice and sees that there's no record of payment having been made. The goods are reported there as having been received, so the clerk decides to send a memo to the stores department asking if there's any reason for not approving payment.

He therefore makes a note in the file of the problem and the action he took, and puts it back in its place. The clerk makes another note in his (temporary storage) list of things to do; this will (all being well) remind him to follow up his memo if he doesn't have a reply within three days. His final task for the moment is to ring the caller back and tell her what's happened with her enquiry.

Again we have seen how the office's various information handling tasks (as shown in Figure 3.1) all tend to be involved as someone carries out a given task, however minor.

The point is an important one. An office may consist of one part-time secretary, or there may be hundreds of people with various specialist roles. Whatever the case, the office – the rooms, the people, their equipment, storage systems and furniture – make up a complex information processing system that can be described by the block diagram.

Information technology concerns the analysis and improvement of any information handling system. Although offices have evolved over a period of several hundred years – and have therefore become (in theory) highly efficient – there is room for huge improvement by the use of modern IT. This is because the traditional office is based on information on paper; the use of the telephone doesn't make much difference to that. Paper is bulky; it is messy; it is open to loss, abuse and damage; and it is very costly both in itself and as far as associated working time, equipment and furniture are concerned.

New information technology does not rely on paper, although it can of course link with paper-based systems if need be. IT is electronic: it offers an office the chance to input, output, process, store and access information electronically 100 per cent of the time. This can lead to great savings in costs of all kinds, including those that relate to storage space, security and the time spent on individual tasks.

At one time people called the IT-based office the 'paperless office'. This name is rarely used nowadays – too many people have seen how computer printout and old manuals overflow the scrap paper cupboards of their young children's schools.

All the same it is true that the users of an electronic office could manage entirely without paper. The barrier is, as much as anything, that they are used to paper, and in many contexts prefer it. It is, after all, simpler for most of us to jot a message down on a pad than to enter it into a computer; we find it easier to scan and learn from a report in booklet form than from one viewed on a screen.

3.2 Office software

As compared with games or robot control software, for instance, this category of computer package directly concerns the handling of information in its own right. Traditionally – ie from the mid-1980s – there are five categories of business software:

Word processing software has the task of making a typist's work much simpler. A word processor allows the entry and easy editing (amendment) of text into a computer's memory and on to its screen rather than just out to paper. It allows the user to code the material in memory for layout and for special effects such as highlighting certain sections. It allows a printout (some people call it hard copy) to be made at any stage. And, most important of all, a word processor lets you save the text on to disc whenever you wish, for access, amendment and further use in the future.

Communications software is designed to enable a computer user to get information from, and send information to, a second, distant computer. It involves joining the systems via a telecommunication network. Thus a telephone link can be made with a public database, such as Prestel or Telecom Gold in Britain; alternatively, the system can send data to another private computer if the two are linked and fitted with the right software.

Database software allows particularly flexible access to the user's files of data stored in a suitable electronic form. It offers all the features of a sophisticated paper-based filing system or card index, but does so electronically. As a result, a computer-managed database can be very speedy and versatile in use, as well as saving a huge amount of space.

Spreadsheet software at its simplest usage level is for dealing with accounts. A spreadsheet is a grid of small screen 'boxes' into which labels, numbers and formulas can go. The formulas act on the numbers in other boxes, so that as soon as one number is added or changed, the contents of the grid change to suit.

At the level of the simplest balance sheet, you can use a spreadsheet to keep automatic totals in the various rows and columns. It is also, however, easy to devise grids which let you see the effect of possible, rather than actual, changes. In this way, spreadsheets can offer great predictive and planning power.

Business graphics programs have the function of working on sets of data to produce user-designed line graphs, bar charts, and pie diagrams. It is, for instance, easy to obtain graphs showing how sales vary from month to month or how they split into different categories.

Other business programs include packages to handle payroll, stock control needs, the ledger aspects of accounts work, and appointment diary and task lists. We shall look at those briefly later, for the five types of software package listed above are the most important. In Chapter 4 we shall find a detailed consideration of various types of integrated software. Packages in that group allow information to be transferred as required from, for instance, a spreadsheet grid to graphics form, with the obvious benefit that a given set of data need not be entered more than once.

Figure 3.2 shows all the flows between the functional areas of a company like Charley's Cocoa Factory. Apart from the factory itself (the production sections) and the warehouse, all the departments shown – personnel, accounts, purchasing, sales, goods in, and goods out – are offices as we have described them. Indeed in a small company, one person may carry out all these roles.

The function of the firm is to obtain raw materials, and to process them into finished goods; the goods then pass out to the customers. These movements are the firm's various flows of materials. However, you can see clearly from Figure 3.2 that, in order to support that function of movement of physical items, there are far more flows of information (or flows of paper in the traditional office). In the 'paperless office' each such movement can (in theory anyway) be replaced by electronic data transfer; as we have already seen, that offers many advantages for the efficient and cost-effective working of the firm.

The information flows include the three cashflows: payments to suppliers, payments from customers, and wages and salaries to the staff. As far as office working is concerned, and indeed in the economy as a whole, money is information. Because of this, financial movements are open to handling by IT just as much as the other types of information transfer in Figure 3.2.

3.3 Word processing

In the days before communication by paper involved anything more than quills and parchment, it was very costly and hard to use, and the skills of scribes were rare. The appearance of cheaper materials, wider literacy, and mechanical aids (such as better pens and typewriters) haven't really changed the basic problem in committing words to paper: editing is difficult and time-consuming, so that errors once made tend not to be remedied.

Computer-based word processing changes the situation completely. Original thoughts are committed to a display screen in a form in which they can easily be edited and moved around. Only when the author wishes is there any need to commit the text to paper, enabling near perfect documents to be produced without much trouble.

A second important aspect of word processing is that the documents produced can be stored (normally on disc) for future re-use. Later, you can take the original text, change it as much as you wish, and print it again.

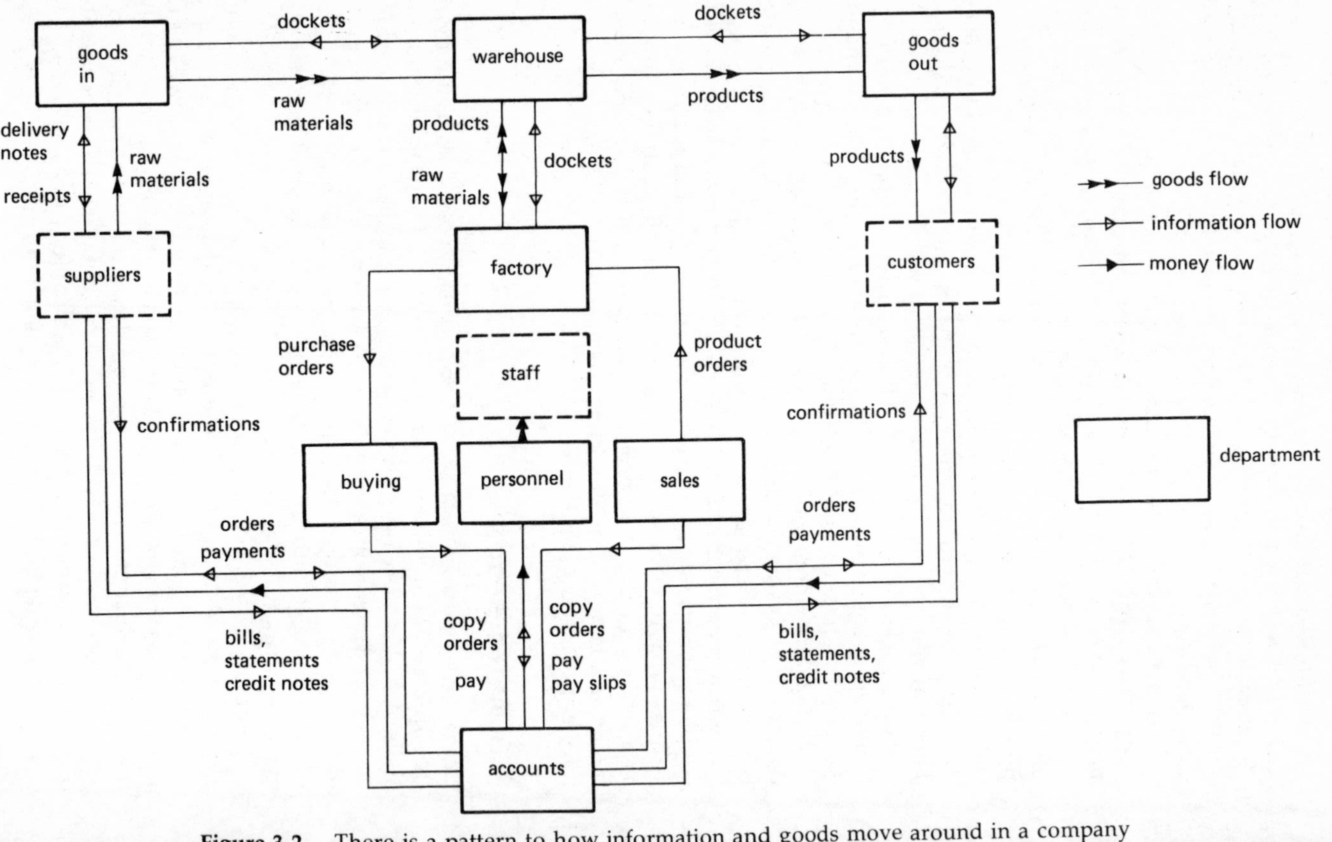

Figure 3.2. There is a pattern to how information and goods move around in a company

In the office, therefore, word processing is extremely useful. Also, the hardware/software systems are cheap and easy to use, the techniques are not difficult to learn, and the results can be far superior to those produced by traditional writing or typing. For people in an office environment, the system is ideally suited to the preparation, editing and saving of documents like worksheets, discussion papers, minutes of meetings, letters, notes, circulars, notices and reports.

For material that is to be properly printed, the output of a word processor can be sent on disc or through a communications link to a typesetter, or printed out for use as a direct master. We shall return to this matter in Chapter 9 when discussing desktop publishing.

Extra work *is* involved in the production of material this way – it's quicker to scribble a quick series of notes on a pad than to produce properly processed text. On the other hand, the finished product is of higher quality and it's easy at any stage in the future to pull it out again and amend it. So word processing is well worth considering.

I prefer to call it text processing, in that its function is to allow you to produce and mess around with chunks of text (rather than individual words). The document that you type in forms an enormous string of characters in the system's memory (and perhaps also on the disc in the computer's drive at the time); it then offers you a wide range of simple techniques in order to produce a wide range of complex actions. As a result, when you display the text or send it to a printer, it doesn't appear just as a series of words, but as a nicely laid-out document.

A word processing program organises that by inserting control codes within the text string at the right places. So if you want material highlighted in bold type **like this**, you must tell the system to insert a code for bold printing at the start of the material concerned, and at the end of the material that's to be in bold type, another code must appear in the string to tell the system to switch the effect off.

With some text processors, the insertion of codes can be quite a complex operation. Not only that; the codes may not be hidden, but rather appear on screen to mess up the look of the material. Most current systems, however, are called wysiwyg – 'what you see is what you get'; the codes are hidden, but the effects appear on the screen.

To start using a text processor, you must first enter the text to be processed (or at least part of it). That requires the use of insert mode, indicated perhaps by a suitable symbol at the top or the foot of the screen. Many programs will put you in insert mode when you first access them.

At the bottom and/or top of the screen may be more items of information telling you where you are at any stage (ie your status). There may also be little boxes giving you the options you can use at any time (these are prompts). An alternative approach is to let you access this kind of information by various key presses, each of which will cause a little notice or menu to roll down the screen.

The main part of the display, the text area, is currently empty except for some kind of marker, perhaps a flashing line or square. That is the text cursor; it exists to tell you where you are, where any new character types will appear. So let's get typing.

Entering text into a word processor's text area differs little from the use of a standard typewriter. There's only one major difference: you don't need to return the carriage at the end of each line of text, only using that action (with the computer's <RETURN> (or <ENTER>) key) to indicate the start of a new paragraph.

There is nothing else you need to know when you enter text. In particular you don't need to worry about errors, and you certainly don't need to start again if you see you've done something wrong. One of the major advantages of text processing systems is that there's no need to correct mistakes as soon as you observe them. That means you can type as fast as you wish without staring at the screen – bad practice, I know, but it's what all we untrained typists prefer.

Figure 3.3 shows the letter that might result (a printout rather than a photograph of the screen, but much the same as what you would actually see in the text area apart from the horizontal/vertical scale factor).

```
Dear Sales Manager

Charleys Cocoa Factory is a mjor user of raw cocao produtcs, as you
may well know.  We have annula sales of over $10000 000 and our tae of
growth has averged 23 % in the last five years.

We understand that you have recentlyy entered the busines of
importaiong related raw materails from the revelent countries, and we
would be most grateful if you would be kind enough to supply us wiyh
fill details of your services.
We would of course ;ike to know your prices for all products and all
qantty discounts, delirevy detials, and payment tersm.
Please be goog enogh to provide these ful detailils as soon s possible
in order yhat we can asses the potntial of your company before our
next round of bul purchase.
Thanks very much.  We look forward very much to hearing from you.
```

Figure 3.3. Enquiry letter, version 1

Actually, that's not a bad letter already, is it – or are my standards lower than yours? There are some mistakes but not too many, and the layout's quite good. Still, with text processing we can improve anything – and we don't need to start again as with a typewriter. Let's first correct the typing slips.

Different processors have different methods of dealing with errors, but the techniques you can expect to find are as follows. You'll need to get used to moving the cursor around your text, and you'll find ways of doing that at various speeds.

- To replace a chunk of existing text with another, either by overwriting the former or by doing a search and replace operation.
- To insert new text where the cursor is.
- To delete old material, character by character, word by word, line by line, sentence by sentence, or even in longer chunks, by using special keys or by marking a block to be removed.
- To change the case of letters.

Using all these editing techniques on our letter gives the new version shown in Figure 3.4.

```
Dear Sales Manager

Charley's Cocoa Factory is a major user of raw cocoa products, as you
may well know.  We have annual sales of over £10 000 000.

We understand that you have recently entered the business of importing
related raw materials from the relevant countries, and we would be
most grateful if you would be kind enough to supply us with full
details of your services.

We would of course like to know your prices for all products and all
quantity discounts, delivery details, and payment terms, as well as
analytical data.

Please be good enough to provide these full details as soon as
possible; then we can assess the potential of your company before our
next round of bulk purchase.

With thanks - we look forward to hearing from you shortly.
```

Figure 3.4. Enquiry letter, version 2

Of course, our letter is not perfect yet! In particular there are no address details at the start, or closing lines at the end. And maybe the third paragraph would be better set out to a smaller line length (indented both right and left). Your word processor will allow you to incorporate various kinds of layout technique in some way or another–tabulation, indentation, hyphenation, justification (aligning at right), centring, and so on. There may be a 'ruler' on screen to help with this. There may also be a spelling checker available with the text processor that will tell you if it doesn't recognise a word you've typed.

You may also want to use the highlighting techniques available with your printer, showing some material (such as a heading) in heavy (bold) style, putting in some italic or underline effects, and so on. You could end up with what's shown in Figure 3.5. The wysiwyg ('what you see is what you get') feature, if offered, will ensure that the screen shows a fairly accurate representation of all those effects.

A major advantage of text processing software, then, is that you can

13 Jul 88

The Sales Manager
KOKOMports
Cokeville
CK19 91KC

Dear Sales Manager

Request for product information

Charley's Cocoa Factory is a major user of raw cocoa products, as you may well know. We have annual sales of over £10 000 000.

We understand that you have recently entered the business of importing related raw materials from the relevant countries, and we would be most grateful if you would be kind enough to supply us with full details of your services.

We would of course like to know your prices for all products and all quantity discounts, delivery details, and payment terms, as well as analytical data.

Please be good enough to provide these full details as soon as possible; then we can assess the potential of your company before our next round of bulk purchase.

With thanks - we look forward to hearing from you shortly.

Yours truly

Melanie Brown
Assistant Buyer

Figure 3.5. Enquiry letter, version 3

work on the polishing separately from the text entry. There is no need to attempt to reach a perfect result from the start, because the text appears on screen rather than permanently on paper.

You can print the document out at any stage. This may be because you prefer to think about polishing and correction from a draft on paper, or because you need to consult other people about what you are writing. At any stage too you can save the text on disc, pass on to some other task, and return to the word processing later.

Stephen – a word processing case study

Stephen works as a junior manager at Charley's Cocoa Factory, and uses a text processor for the preparation of his management reports. A typical session runs like this.

After checking that the system is properly connected and switched on, Steve inserts his disc into the drive and 'boots' it to start things moving. The main menu appears on screen, followed by a list (catalogue) of all the documents ('files') held on the disc.

One of those, called **setupr**, is the one Steve uses to give a standard style and look to his reports. Pressing a couple of keys causes the system to transfer a copy of that file into memory. The process takes just a few seconds.

The next stage involves typing in the actual material of the report; Steve has prepared this mentally and knows pretty well what he wants to say. So he types with fair confidence, despite using only two or three fingers.

Editing is a fairly straightforward task too. A quick key press lets Steve jump back to the start of the document; he works through it on the screen, inserting extra material, deleting stray characters as required, and laying it out better. Sometimes he moves a whole paragraph from one part of the text to another.

After a while, Steve turns back to the menu and asks the system to preview the text, ie to show it on the screen as near as possible to the way it would look on paper. This allows him to take a close look at the overall layout of the document. One or two more errors come to light, and Steve quickly edits those as before.

The menu also provides him with the option of using a key press to print out a copy of the text in the computer's memory. The printer at Steve's workstation is common in British offices – a fairly quiet dot matrix machine that churns out text at high speed and with high quality. Charley's Cocoa Factory also has a page printer on the network that can silently produce extremely high quality material at several dozen pages a minute, but this report doesn't need that quality.

Steve carefully checks the paper draft now produced for final errors and possibly opportunity for further polish; he also takes it to a colleague to look at in case of further ideas. Before leaving his desk to do that, Steve instructs the system to save a copy of the current version of the document, just in case of accidents. After a bit more editing, Steve is satisfied, and saves his work as a final file on disc for use in the future.

All that took no more than a few hours. During it Steve typed in and carefully edited a 10-page report. Since he learned how to use the word processor, he has transferred a number of his earlier reports on to disc, realising that he can quickly print any of them out at any time in the future, with or without changes. Already he has had some proof of this: he has been able to produce related reports at great speed for purposes other than those he wrote them for.

A major benefit of this system is not so obvious: even after a few more years, Steve could carry the saved masters of all his reports, papers and other such documents around on no more than two or three cheap floppy discs that take up less room and cost less than a small paperback book. The benefits of that to office organisation are enormous– a box of 10 floppies can carry as much information as a filing cabinet drawer. All he wants kept will also be in store on the hard (Winchester) disc at the centre of the network; however, the material on a floppy disc is portable. Anyway, it is wise to keep back-up copies in case of problems with the system.

3.4 Communications

In the business (office) context, there are two types of electronic computer-based communications we need to consider. The first is internal– internal to the computer system itself; the second is external – information transfer through links between separate computer systems.

In Charley's Cocoa Factory, different people handle the office functions set out in Figure 3.2. Those functions are personnel, accounts, purchasing, sales, goods in, and goods out. In each case, one or more of the staff work in their own area of the large open-plan office on particular tasks. They have their own equipment, filing cabinets and furniture; they process and store their own files and records.

In addition, the shop floor (factory) and the warehouse have office needs too and have office staff in their own physical spaces. Charley's Cocoa Factory has a reception area as well, close to but separate from the main office and the managers' rooms. It provides the telephone switchboard service; this too is an office in the sense in which we use the word here. There is yet another office in the catering area: its functions relate to many of those in the main office, so it is sensible for them to use the same systems.

As we have seen, information flows in quantity between these different office areas. The links shown in Figure 3.2 are simplified in Figure 3.6, this time giving only the information flow lines internal to the company's operations.

While each member of the office staff is likely to gain a great deal from having the use of a computer, it will not help the operation of the company overall if information cannot pass between the machines. The best way to achieve the electronic transfers required is to link all other units together as a single computer system. Otherwise traditional methods of information transfer will be needed, with delays, errors and other problems as a result. Those traditional methods include the use of an intercom, internal mail, or even shouting.

In Chapter 1 we looked at different types of computer system. These range from the single-user micro to various arrangements in which one or more linked processors handle the needs of several, or many, users at the same time.

There are two intrinsically different approaches that can be taken. The first is to install a large minicomputer or small mainframe, and issue each member of staff with a terminal. The other is to integrate the individual micros into a network. In either case, internal electronic transfers of data and messages should be allowed, as well as the sharing of information files as appropriate. Either can be represented as in Figure 3.7.

Networking allows the linking together of workstations up to about half a kilometre apart. That presents no problems of office integration for a single-site company like Charley's Cocoa Factory. For dealings with other branches, other companies (including customers and suppliers) and other organisations, external communications are needed: these involve data transfers over distance between separate computer systems.

The information transfers can be through one or other of the normal telephone networks, through special private lines or radio type links, or through data networks run in a similar way to the telephone system. These are all set up with computers at each end; thus they do not include such techniques as traditional telex, videoconferencing and facsimile transmission, which are dealt with in later chapters.

Here we shall concentrate on the use of the standard telephone system (not even wanting to distinguish between the services of British Telecom and Mercury).

There are two fundamentally different ways of passing information between computer A and computer B (in either direction) using the telephone system. They are shown in Figure 3.8. In the one case, a direct link is set up through the exchanges between the two telephone lines. In the other, use is made of a central data storage or host computer (C) to which very many users may have access.

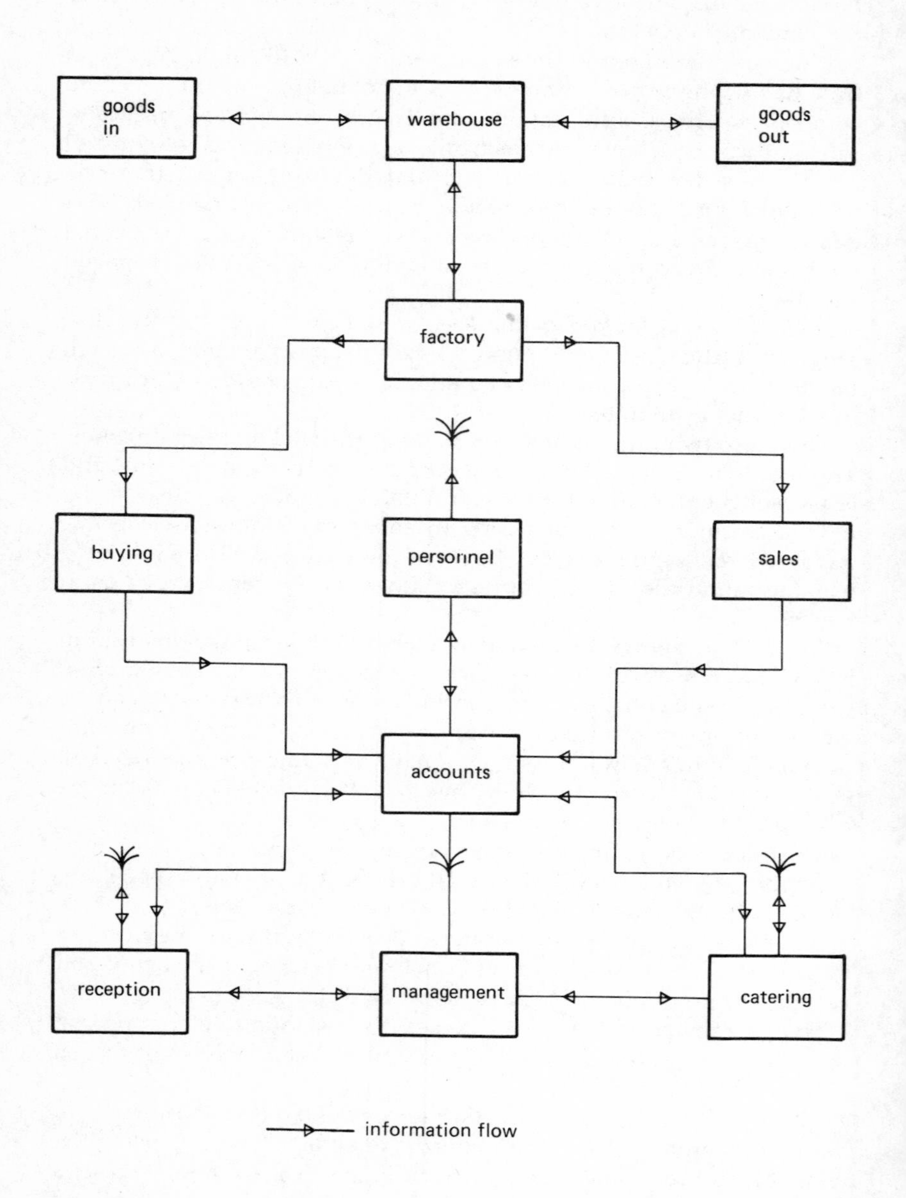

Figure 3.6. There are many information flows within a company

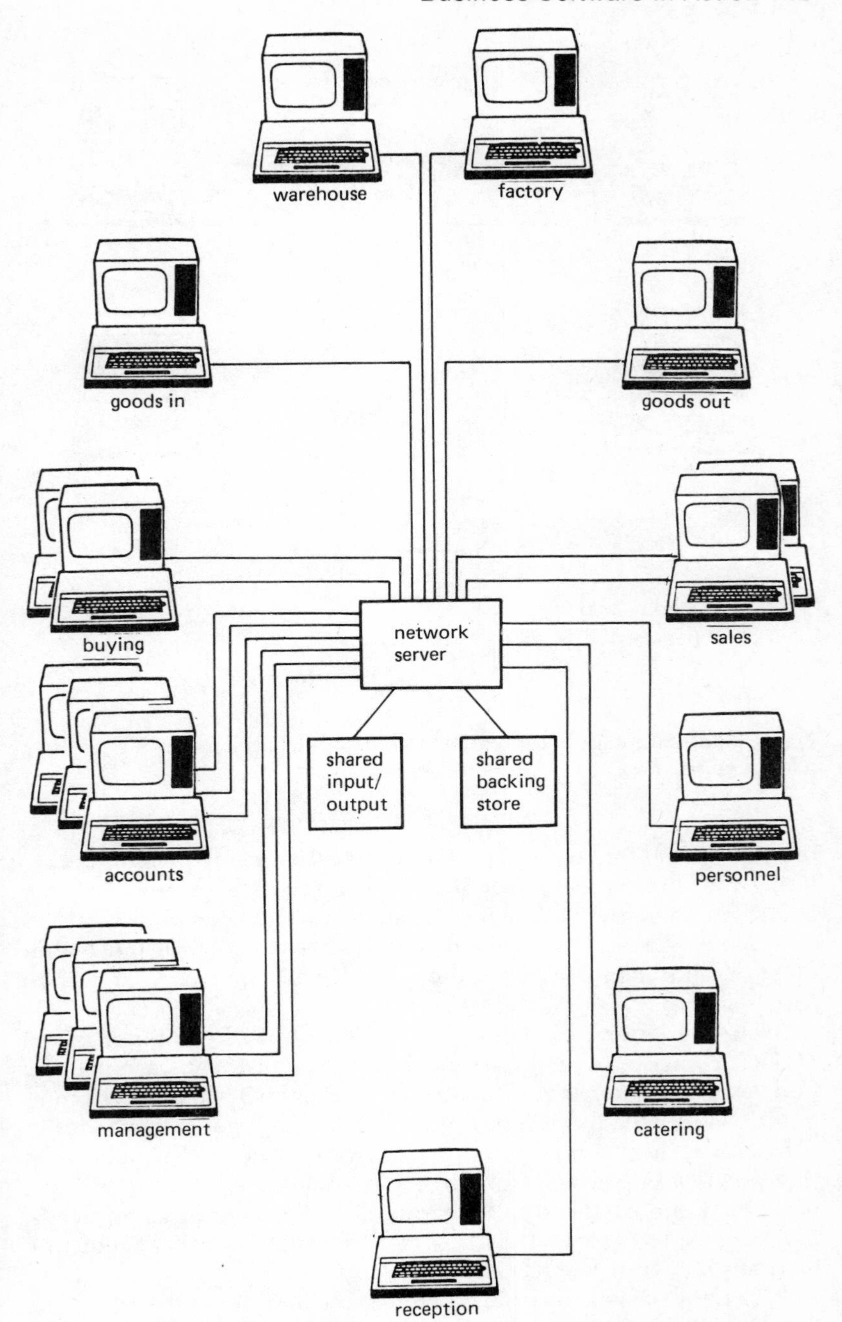

Figure 3.7. A star network or minicomputer system on a single site

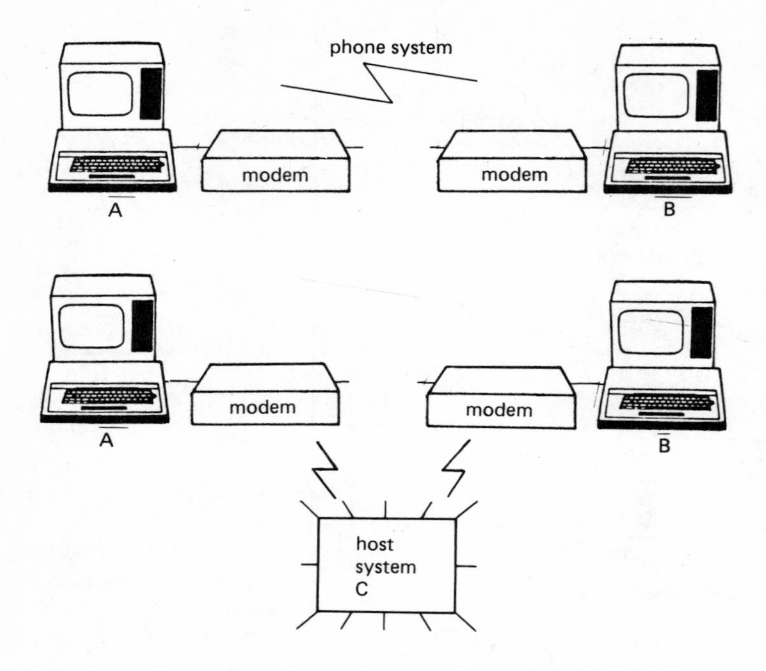

Figure 3.8. Information can pass between two computers through the telephone network

The company using computer A wishes to send a document (a message, order, or report, for instance) to the firm with computer B. Using the direct link, someone on the former's staff must dial the latter's number; there computer B either has its own telephone lines so can accept calls automatically, or a switchboard operator must complete the link manually. Only then can the machine communication take place.

Using the second system, with the data storage computer in the middle, company A will transfer the document there, in much the same way as before. At some later time, company B will dial in to computer C and have the material transferred into its own computer.

In either case, communications software is needed to allow the transfers to take place. The end results are the same, but time and cost patterns differ and need to be explored in the light of given needs. Before considering this, though, something ought to be said about the modems shown in Figure 3.8.

A modem is an essential link between a computer and a telephone line. The reason is that a computer is a digital electronic device, while the current telephone system mainly carries only analogue signals. A modem converts the digital signal from the computer into an analogue version to go down the telephone line; analogue signals coming into the modem through the telephone are converted the other way, into digital data the computer can handle.

Figure 3.9 shows how analogue and digital signals differ. Both are (in this context) varying electric currents in a wire; however, analogue signals vary smoothly between their extreme values, while digital ones come in pulses of only a small number of possible values – often just high and low. That is in fact the type shown in the diagram.

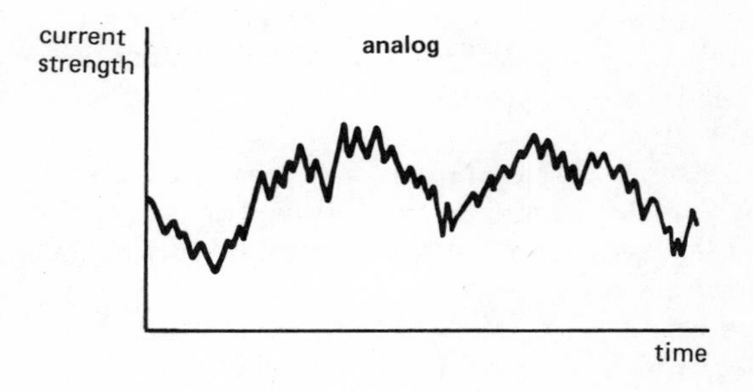

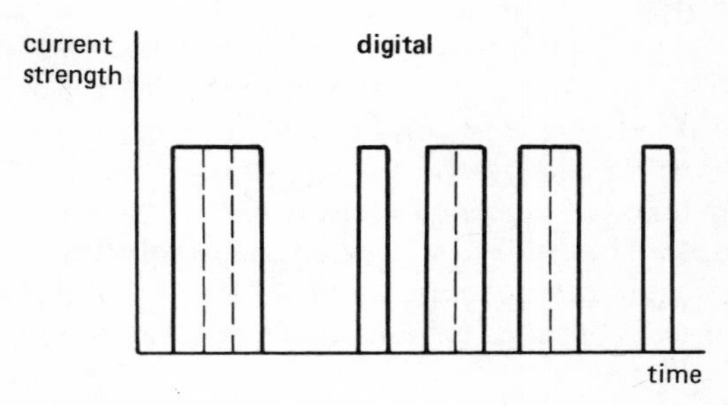

Figure 3.9. Analogue signals are wavy; digital ones are steplike

Communications software looks after as much of the data transfer as possible; the aim is that the user need not trouble with the details, so can concentrate on the information. In particular, the program must be able to transfer information from your screen or disc to the modem in the right form and at the right speed; for communication the other way it must translate the arriving signal into a screen display, a chunk of data stored on disc, and/or a printout.

Typical communications software can also handle the following tasks for you:

- Connect to the telephone system and call the number you want.
- Send logging on codes (passwords and such) for the particular system accessed (especially if it is a public data storage computer like Prestel or Telecom Gold).
- Adjust the data transfer procedures, speeds and so on, to match a new target system.
- Control the usage of special keys (so you can move to and fro in an incoming document or through an accessed database, for instance).
- Display 'help' information when required.
- Pause data transfer.
- Allow printouts of sections you select to be produced.
- Tag interesting material for later re-examination.
- Download software (program files) from the other computer, or upload software to it.
- Provide a 'chat' mode, allowing people at each end to communicate by transfer of text conversationally.
- Leave the system gracefully (sending proper logging off codes and disconnecting the line).
- Disconnect automatically after, say, 10 minutes, if there is lack of activity, in order to save telephone charges.
- Detail costs incurred during a given transfer.

To summarise, then, suitable communications hardware and software allow you to send documents to people elsewhere with access to similar facilities. The documents may be long (like reports), shorter ones (letters, orders, invoices), or very short ones (notes, memos). If your information transfer needs are bigger than any of those, other systems exist to help you, and we'll come back to that later. (An example would be if a distant branch office needed frequently to access material used in your headquarter computer files.) Figure 3.10 gives a summary of the use of communications hardware and software.

Angela – a communications case study

Angela has the grand title of communications officer at Charley's Cocoa Factory, and, unlike some other people with such a title, she does more than look after the main switchboard. Certainly she does have turns of duty on the telephone switchboard, but there is always someone else there and most of Angela's time is associated with more modern means of telecommunications.

The work of a switchboard operator is fairly straightforward: incoming calls are to be answered sweetly and promptly and then routed to their proper destination. Politeness is always essential in dealing with callers, but at least Angela avoids the sing-song voice that some people

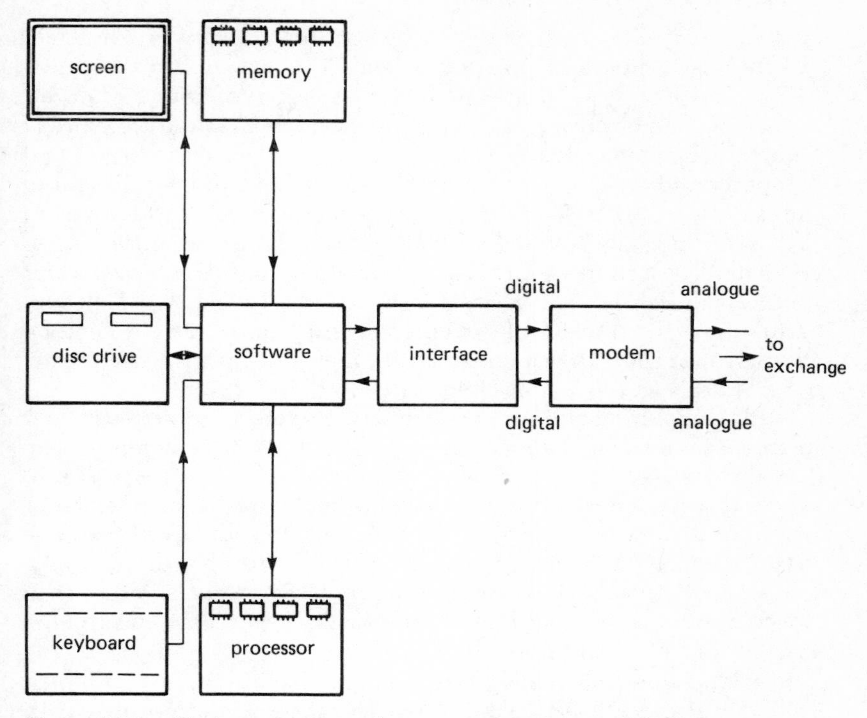

Figure 3.10. Communicating using a computer system involves controlled data flows

seem to put on in this situation. The politeness is particularly important when the extension called is engaged, or when the person wanted can't be found. The switchboard operators at Charley's Cocoa Factory don't need to spend much time with outgoing calls, as most of these are routed automatically from the extensions.

A somewhat more modern item of equipment in the same area is the telex machine, which is covered in detail in Chapter 7. A telex machine is a sort of automatic telephone system which can leave messages on paper at any time of day or night. It needs a separate line to the exchange, and indeed there is a whole separate international telex system with its own directories, directory enquiries, and so on.

When Angela arrives in the morning, her first task is to take out of the printer all the messages that have appeared on the telex machine since she was last at the office. In the same way as for incoming mail (Section 3.1), these messages need to be passed on to the people that are to deal with them. Sometimes telex messages will print out during the day (particularly from companies in other countries), and Angela deals with these in the same sort of way.

Electronic mail messages also accumulate overnight, and another of

Angela's early tasks each day is to check through the firm's mail boxes on the host computers. Charley's Cocoa Factory subscribes to two main electronic messaging systems (and is always exploring more).

Each of these electronic communications networks fits the picture of Figure 3.8(B), namely that messages from any subscriber go to a central computer and are stored until the intended recipient later logs on to the system, when the waiting messages can be picked up for action. (The term 'message' should be taken to refer to communications of any length, eg a short enquiry, a substantial report, or a complex order for raw materials.) Prestel is best for short messages, whereas Telecom Gold allows the transfer of extremely lengthy documents if need be (though at a cost). Angela finds that, on the whole, people use Prestel for enquiries and Telecom Gold for orders.

At the beginning and end of each day, therefore, Angela uses her microcomputer workstation to log on to each of the systems in turn. That involves setting the communications software in the network into action; through this she can tell her computer to call the main (storage) mainframe, and pass through to it the logging on codes that have to be used. The passwords needed could also be sent through automatically. For security reasons, however, this is not done – Angela, rather than the computer, is the guardian of the passwords, and she has to type them in herself each time.

In each case, when one logs on to a mail system, a notice on screen will state if there is any mail to 'collect'. If there are no messages, Angela logs off at once (saving telephone time), but if there are some, she proceeds to:

- Scan each message on screen to see whether she can answer it straight away or it needs to be passed on to someone else.
- Make a printout of the message if it is important enough.
- Copy the message on to the firm's own computer system.
- Readdress the message to one of her colleagues for action; then that person can see at once that there is something waiting when logging on to the network.

Angela repeats the whole process at the end of the day. There is one major difference, however, in that now there may well be outgoing messages to deal with. It is much more efficient to send these all out as a batch; thus such material appears during the day, it is stored on the network so that Angela can collect it at the right time. (Of course important messages can be sent at any time, but Angela – like a signals officer – still has to be the person dealing with them.)

Therefore, towards the end of the day Angela gathers together the electronic mail that has built up ready to go out. She then accesses each mail system in turn, and automatically sends the messages from the network disc through to the storage computer. It is only copies of these items that go out from Charley's Cocoa Factory, for the originals remain on the disc. It is then Angela's task to check which can be deleted and which files she should use to hold the others for future reference.

There is a lot of sense in letting a firm's own network computer act as the storage computer in a Prestel-like way. That means that other people using computers can phone through and automatically access information. There is not actually much call for this as far as the activities of Charley's Cocoa Factory are concerned, but all the same it is a small service that the firm provides to its customers.

Customers using their computers to phone into Charley's Cocoa Factory system see on their own screen the simple menu shown in Figure 3.11. All they need to do is press the key that corresponds to the option that interests them; the system then sends information from the corresponding part of the tiny database that services this function. To the Cocoa Factory computer each such caller becomes just another workstation on the network, though with access to only a very small range of information. There has been no attempt so far to provide more than one line for this purpose, but very few people have complained about getting an engaged signal.

Figure 3.11. If you contact Charley's Cocoa Factory viewdata base, this is what it greets you with

As the company's communications officer, Angela has the task of keeping this information up to date. This involves checking for messages daily, dealing with the suggestions that appear (and acknowledging them), updating the news feature each month, and making sure that the people fixing the prices and organising the special offers keep her informed of what's going on. This is one of the aspects of her work that Angela enjoys most.

The firm is thinking vaguely that one day certain of the staff may be working from home. It is this kind of feature within the communications aspect of Charley's Cocoa Factory that would need serious thought should that ever come about. However, in essence this provision for telecommuting would mean that the network would recognise a number of extra stations. The fact that some of them would be a good distance away would not be relevant to the way the system itself worked.

Figure 3.12 gives a summary of the areas of Angela's work as communications officer. Also included is the facsimile (fax) machine which is under her care as well. In many ways this is a kind of modern

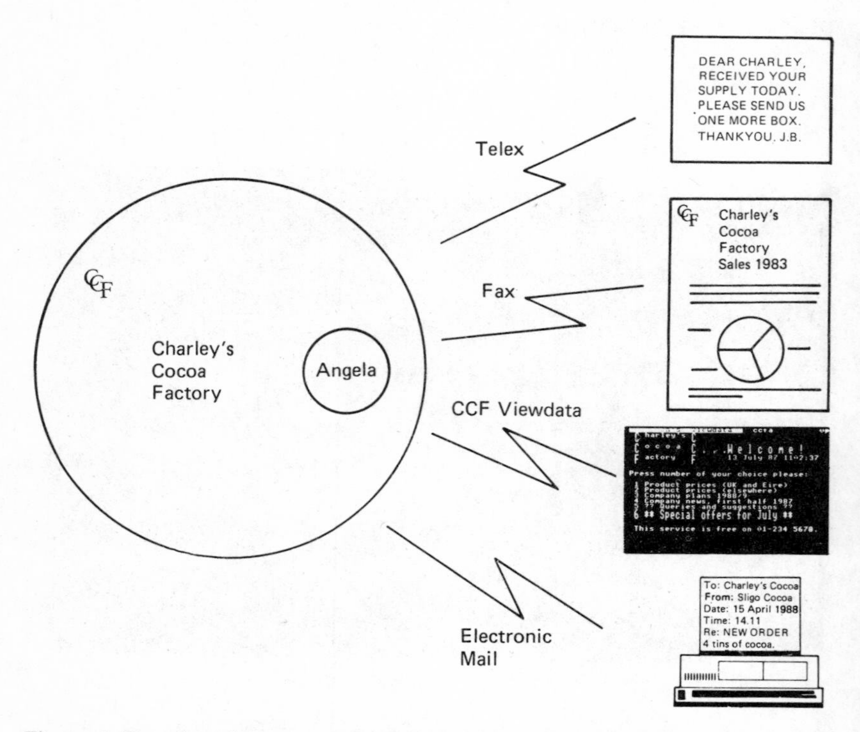

Figure 3.12. Angela represents Charley's Cocoa Factory at the centre of a web of modern communications

telex; it allows the transmission of copies of documents very quickly around the world, and is discussed further in Chapter 7.

3.5 Databases

Any firm, however large or small, must maintain records of what it is doing. Thus an estate agency needs to know what properties are at the moment in their hands, and how far each has progressed towards complete sale. A builder or a consultant must have the same kind of record about each job he or she goes for. A mail order company will need to maintain up-to-date records about the customers, and an office staffing firm the same about each person and employer on their books.

The traditional way to handle these needs is to use paper. At the simplest level one would use piles of papers clipped together; a little more organised is to maintain a card index; a filing cabinet system is the next step up.

After centuries of use, each of these paper-based systems can be fairly efficient in its way. All, however, suffer from certain problems. Not only is paper costly, bulky and dirty, but individual pieces can get damaged, lost or misplaced. A major problem, however, is that traditional record systems are hard to use in unforeseen ways; the information stored is very hard, if not impossible, to collate flexibly.

Take the case of a builders' merchant who, at the end of each month, needs to know how much money is outstanding. To find the answer would involve physically looking at every record in the customer files and adding the total of unpaid bills. That is a lot of extra work; it would also be extra work if the merchant decided to keep a separate file (list) of bills sent out, because now there would be two separate systems to update each day. However, if the merchant's customer records are kept on a computer in the form of a database, it would be a simple task to produce a printout of debts as required.

Another example would be a travel agent wanting to announce a number of special skiing holiday offers. Rather than advertising generally, it would be much more effective to send a leaflet to all past customers. If customer records are stored on paper, producing all those envelope labels would be a mammoth task. If, on the other hand, there is a customer database, the computer can be told to print the labels out automatically. The agent could even go further, and produce an apparently individual letter for each customer, as people addressed by name are more likely to respond positively to the approach.

Tasks like these – producing reports and mail shots – are handled very easily by even a cheap and simple computer system. The database software package lies behind them.

It is just as easy to convert a microcomputer for the time being into an automatic flexible filing system (database manager) as it is to make it act as a word processor. The software may be held on disc or in a special chip in the machine; in either case just a few key strokes will call it into action.

In the same way as a librarian can maintain a number of different card indexes, a database program can handle a number (almost unlimited) of different 'files'. Thus a given firm may have computer-based files for customers, suppliers, staff, products and competitors: each one is handled the same way by the software, and the user can quickly jump between them. The whole collection of files is the actual database (or databank).

In turn, each file consists of a number of records (the data on a single member of staff, for instance) and each record is built up of fields. The database structure is shown in Figure 3.13, but using a card index to help you get the picture.

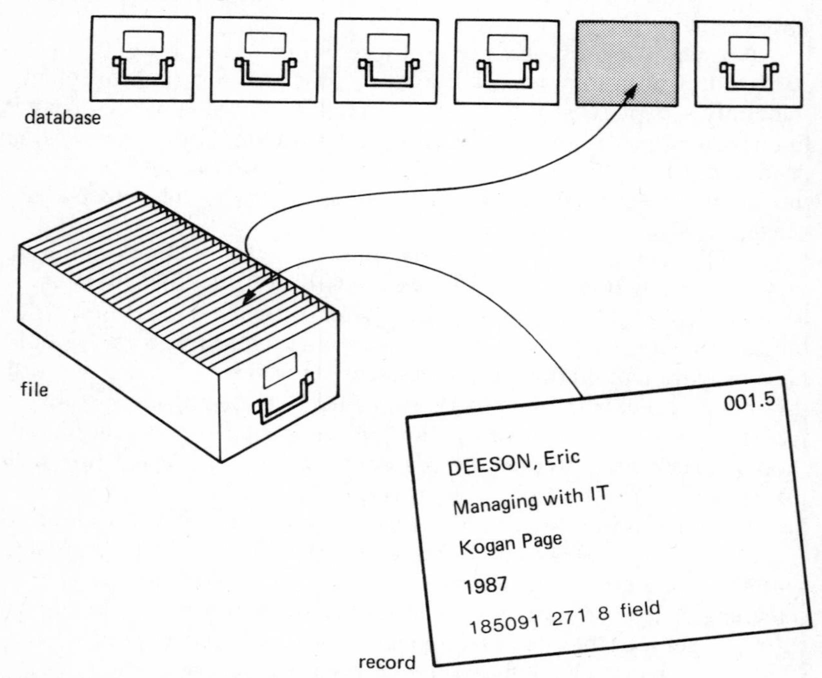

Figure 3.13. A standard computer database has a structure of files, records and fields, much as a set of card indexes

When you wish to look at details of one book in a library card index, you find and scan the corresponding card. In the same kind of way you can ask the database to show you such and such a record and it will appear on the screen. Actually, some modern database systems allow very large individual records, each too large for the screen; here, a suitable block appears on display and you can scroll to other parts using special keys.

However, though important, that kind of usage is not what makes a database exciting. The strength of a database software package is that it can do automatically all the tedious manual tasks required of a card index, as well as others one could never attempt.

Let's think again of the builders' merchant and the monthly debt collation exercise. Now that the customer file is held on a computer database it is a simple task to ask for that printout of people owing money, with dates and totals. Before making the final printout, the program can take the records of the debtors out into a temporary sub-file and put them in order, perhaps of date of debt, or of size of debt, or of postcode, or of almost anything you can imagine. In turn a sub-sub-file can be created from those records of all customers owing over £100 for more than two months and special letters can be produced to send to them in envelopes bearing their personal names and addresses. The merchant can now relax over a welcome cup of tea while thinking of better ways to handle the business.

Ah! How about sending a letter with an offer of a free gift to all customers who pay promptly if they place another order over £100 in the next month? That's a simple task with the computer-based customer file. So too would it be to send a similar offer letter to all clients of more than five years' standing who pay promptly and have placed orders of total value of at least £1000 in the past 12 months. And so on.

Sorting records into different orders and searching them on the basis of criteria relating to the different fields are the tasks that a database software package is particularly good at. Sorting and searching will need only a few key presses and a few seconds' time – and the results are ready for scanning or further exploration.

Earlier I said that you need no knowledge of programming to use a computer system to help your business. It is only fair to say, however, that the ability to devise simple programs is required to achieve the full power of a modern database manager. You can manage without, but it is not in fact a major task to produce a program like that in Figure 3.14.

That example, typical of the sort of thing I mean, is used to show that writing a database program is not a task you need much study or training for. The program is in fact what the builders' merchant could use to carry out the last bonus offer task mentioned above. Skip the details that follow if this doesn't interest you at the moment.

The program opens the *customer* file and warns the system that some data will be put into two new files. It then searches the customer file as requested. The search involves looking at the *first order-year* field of each record to see if the value is less than 1982. If it is, the program will

```
program loyalty-bonus

open customers
create labels, who

repeat
    find
        first-order-year less than 1983
    and
        payment-record "prompt"
    and
        years-orders greater than 1000

    then
        send to labels: person, firm, address1, address2, address3,,
"SPECIAL OFFER!!"
        send to who: (labels),,"Dear "+person
until end of file

end of program
```

Figure 3.14. A simple database program can select the recipients of a special mailing

see if the word 'prompt' appears in the *payment-record* field, and, if so, whether the value in the *years-orders* field is more than £1000.

By this means the program matches records against the search criteria. It then goes on, each time it finds a match, as follows:

Send a copy to the newly created *labels* file from the matched records for contact person, company name, and address; also send a blank line (the double comma) followed by the 'SPECIAL OFFER!!' message.

Send a copy to the new *who* file of the same data, a blank line, the message 'Dear' and the addressee's name.

This whole process of sending data to the new files for each matched record goes on until the search reaches the end of the customer file. And that's the end of the program. Our merchant could then send the labels file to the printer to produce the address labels or the addressed envelopes. In conjunction with a suitable standard letter and the data in the *who* file, the word processor could prepare all the letters. Figure 3.15 shows the result.

The main point to be made is that using a database program makes the software's action even more automated – and database programming is easy to learn.

Kuldip – a database management case study

Kuldip is a trainee junior manager who has only just joined the staff of Charley's Cocoa Factory. It is always important that new staff find out about a firm's business as quickly and pleasantly as possible, so Kuldip has been given a new project of his own to handle as part of that exercise. He has to find out as much as he can about the products of companies that compete with Charley's Cocoa Factory, then he is to enter the details into a specially designed database on the firm's net-

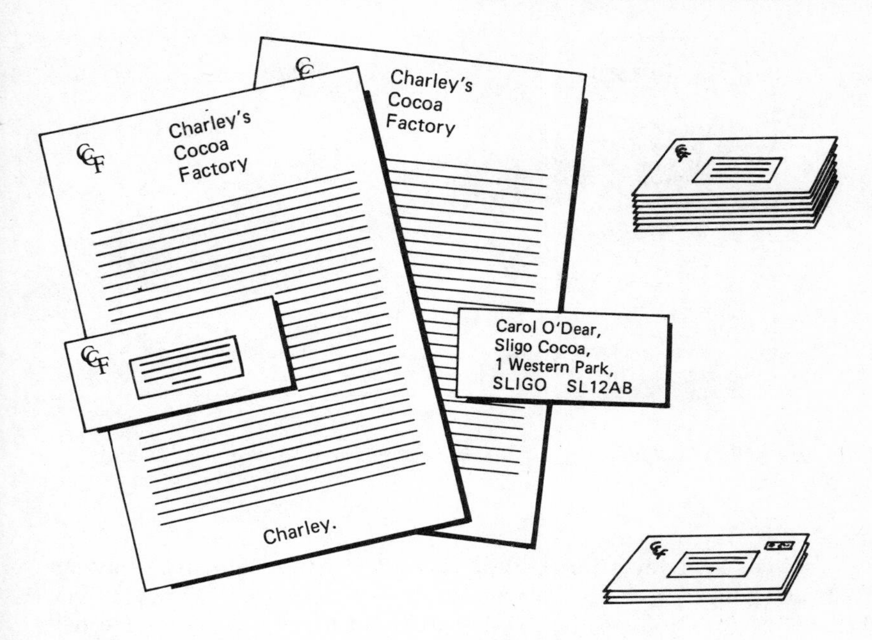

Figure 3.15. After processing, the user has a pile of 'personalised' letters

work. The aim is that, within a month or two, Kuldip will be able to produce a report from the database covering the competition and making recommendations to management. The hidden agenda is that by this means Kuldip will learn a great deal about the industry he has chosen to work in, as well as about the firm's computer system and its use.

After a lot of discussion with various colleagues in the firm, Kuldip is able to plan the structure of the records in his database, there being one record per competitor. It is actually quite a problem with this kind of software that one must carefully plan fairly exactly how one intends in the future to use the information stored; it is not always very easy to change the structure of a database once information has been entered.

Figure 3.16 shows the rough layout of each record that Kuldip has in mind at the moment. He will still need to work on this, as for sure there are fields missing; however, the outline principles are taking shape.

Each record contains (as well as the obvious details of company name, address and so on) space for a list of product names, constituent codes, and prices. It is naturally useful for Charley's Cocoa Factory to

```
Name                                                    MD
HQ address                                              Phone
                                                        Telex
                                                        Fax
Postcode                                                Research
Date founded                                            No.staff
Product Name       Date   Type codes    Price code
1 CocoSplash       1982   A C G H       14
2 Dreamboat        1984   A B C G H     16
3
4
5
6
7
8
9

Cocoa from: WHSmith grade D price 9
Sugar from: Brantson grade F price 4
```

Figure 3.16. Planning the layout of a record in a file requires careful thought

know what products their competitors supply and as much as they can about those products; however, information that is not public knowledge is going to be rather harder for Kuldip to obtain. He will need, for instance, to organise chemical analyses of competitors' products. The results will be coded both to assist with confidentiality and to fit them into a fairly small field on screen.

What will be even more difficult – a sort of industrial espionage – will be Kuldip's attempts to find out where these other companies get their various raw materials from and at what prices. The information he finds out in this context will be coded too, at least in part. As much as possible, the plans for the whole of Kuldip's campaign need to be laid before he starts work; otherwise a lot of time could be wasted reorganising the database structure. (The same is true when doing this kind of work without the help of a computerised database management system.)

Adding the data to the file is not likely to be a methodical process – new information will appear in all sorts of forms at various times. However, the program now starts to come into its own, as it makes it easy for Kuldip to add new records or new items of information within the fields of existing records, and to change and rearrange the stored material.

The database, once completed, should be able to offer valuable information in a number of different forms to the managers of Charley's Cocoa Factory. Sorting and searching are the two special features such a program offers, both in a range of sophisticated ways. If Kuldip is able to code product types in a suitable form, an enquirer will very easily be able to pull out from the file a list of, for instance, prices and compositions of all caffeine-free, low-fat, unsweetened cocoa products available in the country. Another of the many possibilities would be to list the suppliers of sugar to cocoa firms around the country, in order of increasing wholesale price.

If Kuldip succeeds in this exercise, he and his database will be more knowledgeable about Britain's retail cocoa industry than any other person. Keeping the details up to date, however, will be another matter.

3.6 Spreading the sheets

In the account of word processing and database software, I used quite a lot of ink in comparing them with traditional paper-based methods. Any such comparison does not apply to spreadsheet programs, however, because they are an example of how computers can lead to almost totally new kinds of activity. (The only other example that crosses my mind at the moment are the 'arcade' games, like Space Invaders and Defender!)

On a very simple level, a spreadsheet is a two-dimensional table, as shown in Figure 3.17. We call each box in the table a cell. One is shown shaded in the table; it is in column B and row 003, so we refer to it as cell B3 (or B003). Each cell, therefore, has its own reference, just as each square in a map grid has its own map reference. When you switch this spreadsheet on, the top left cell, A1, is highlighted (in colour perhaps); you can move to any other cell by pressing special keys. The highlighted cell at a given moment is the one in which your next typed data will go.

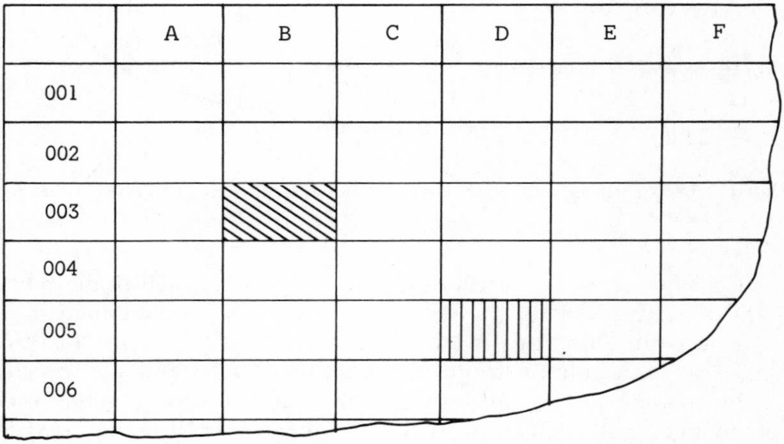

	A	B	C	D	E	F
001						
002						
003						
004						
005						
006						

Figure 3.17. A spreadsheet is a two-dimensional table made up of a number of cells

The cells in the grid can each hold up to about 10 characters (numbers or letters) in a single row, as indicated in cell D5 in Figure 3.17. However, you can make columns wider or narrower, to suit your needs in any given case.

Spreadsheets on the market vary greatly in size. Some have a couple of hundred or more rows and columns, giving you several thousand cells to work with (although it is unlikely that that many cells would be used at one time, except if holding several separate tables of data at once). The screen can show only a part of this great grid, but as you move the highlight the screen 'window' will move to suit.

Each cell starts off empty; in use it can hold a number, a word or two (such as a row or column title, or a short message), or a formula. It is this formula feature that gives real power to speadsheets.

For instance, you may want your spreadsheet to hold the sales, outgoings and profit for each of the last three months. You will start your grid by putting titles for the rows and columns as in Figure 3.18, moving the highlight from cell to cell as required.

	A	B	C	D	E	F
1		January	February	March	TOTAL	
2	Sales					
3	Outgoings					
4	Profit					
5						
6						

Figure 3.18. Putting labels for rows and columns is the first step in using a spreadsheet

Next, type in the sales and outgoings figures for each of the three months. Figure 3.19 shows the sort of screen display obtained.

If you were doing this exercise on paper, you'd now subtract the figures in each column to get the monthly profits and add up the figures in each row to get the totals in column E. Using a computer spreadsheet, with that formula feature, means you'll never need to stand by your balance sheet with a calculator again. Here's how.

Put into cell B4 the formula **B2 − B3** (ie, profit for January is that

	A	B	C	D	E	F
1		January	February	March	TOTAL	
2	Sales	123456	234567	345678		
3	Outgoings	78901	89012	90123		
4	Profit					
5						
6						

Figure 3.19. Next, add the data

month's income minus its outgoings). Like magic, instead of the formula appearing on screen, the answer – 44555 – will appear.

Tell the system to repeat the corresponding formulas along row 3 up to column E. Exactly how you do that depends on the spreadsheet program. The February and March profit figures now appear.

Highlight cell E2 and insert its formula: **B2 + C2 + D2**. This gives the total sales for the quarter. Repeat the formula down the column, and the balance sheet is complete, as in Figure 3.20.

	A	B	C	D	E	F
1		January	February	March	TOTAL	
2	Sales	123456	234567	345678	703701	
3	Outgoings	78901	89012	90123	258036	
4	Profit	44555	145555	255555	445665	
5						
6						

Figure 3.20. The spreadsheet completes the balance sheet automatically

That was a very trivial example. However, it was enough to give some idea of the power of a spreadsheet software package. It would not have taken much longer to work through the procedure to obtain a full annual itemised account, with VAT and so on as well.

Perhaps the main use of the spreadsheet is in financial costings and estimates. It is, for instance, very easy to change one figure (such as the cost per tonne of raw cocoa) and see the effect of that change on all dependent values. This forecasting aspect of spreadsheet usage is crucial for management's planning. We call it carrying out a 'what if' exercise: 'but what if the price of cocoa went up 10 per cent?' or 'what if we tried that packaging that costs £3 less for 50 cartons?'

Carline – a spreadsheet case study

Carline is a food scientist who works in the quality control department of Charley's Cocoa Factory. Her role is to ensure that all the firm's products meet the required standards, are nutritious and pleasant to the taste, and are produced as cheaply and profitably as possible.

Currently she is involved, with a couple of other people, in the development of a new product called OvoMalt, a malted cocoa drink. Her knowledge of food constituents and some market research indicate that the product will need eight constituents. These are low-fat cocoa, dried egg powder, malt and barley extract, dried skimmed milk, fine-ground sucrose (white sugar), glucose syrup, salt, and flavouring. The flavouring to be used is one of the firm's secrets so it's not spelt out in more detail.

The company has decided to market this new product in 500g packs, and Carline's job is to devise the best mixture of the constituents. She will use a spreadsheet to help her with this task. When she loads the spreadsheet from the network into her personal workstation, she sees a blank grid of cells much like that of Figure 3.17. Her first task is to decide what column and row headings to use, and to change the widths of the columns to suit. After Carline has done this, and entered the text in the various cells required, the result is as shown in Figure 3.21. Carline spends a fair amount of time making the layout as good as possible, because the final material, when printed out, will go into reports to management.

Rather than adding data now, Carline's next step is to insert the formulas into those cells that will need them. This is a sensible planning approach: the data should be the last thing to come into the table, as it is not fixed.

Figure 3.22 shows how Carline's spreadsheet grid looks now. Here the formulas are the material in bold (apart from the heading, of course); in normal practice the formulas would be invisible, but to show what Carline has done a printout with them on, is produced.

OvoMalt - Product 87/X3 - cp870123

Constituent	Code	Quantity/g	Price £/kg	Cost/£
Cocoa, low fat	22			
Egg, dried powder	4b			
Malt/barley extract	Xfel			
Milk, dried skimmed	M14			
Sucrose, ground	S3g			
Glucose, syrup	G3s			
Salt, ground	A+			
Flavour	Cx4			
TOTAL				
	Production			
	Packaging			
COST PRICE OF 500g OvoMalt:				

Figure 3.21. After the column widths are adjusted, text can be entered into spreadsheet cells

OvoMalt - Product 87/X3 - cp870123

Constituent	Code	Quantity/g	Price £/kg	Cost/£
Cocoa, low fat	22			c4*d4/1000
Egg, dried powder	4b			c5*d5/1000
Malt/barley extract	Xfel			c6*d6/1000
Milk, dried skimmed	M14			c7*d7/1000
Sucrose, ground	S3g			c8*d8/1000
Glucose, syrup	G3s			c9*d9/1000
Salt, ground	A+			c10*d10/1000
Flavour	Cx4			c11*d11/1000
TOTAL		sum(c4/11)		sum(e4/11)
	Production			sum(g28/36)
	Packaging			sum(c43/47)
COST PRICE OF 500g OvoMalt:				sum(e12/14)

Figure 3.22. A spreadsheet ready for data requires text and formula cells to be complete

Carline has done this kind of work before; it is one of her main roles to run spreadsheets daily as part of product development and quality control. She finds it very easy to move around from cell to cell, and knows the 'programming language' to use for writing formulas. Thus to produce the formulas in the first six rows of the last column, all she needed to do was to enter the first one (**c4*d4/1000**), and then to send a command to the system to replicate the formula in the rows below, but with the row numbers changed to suit.

What the formula **c4*d4/1000** in box E4 means is that in that cell should go a figure derived by multiplying the data in cells C4 and D4 and then dividing by 1000 (as there are 1000 grams in a kilogram). The 'programming language' used for formulas in this particular spreadsheet is shown by a very simple example in box C12 – **sum (c4/11)**.

This formula indicates that in that cell should go the sum of the contents of the cells in column C, rows 4–11. There are similar formulas in column E; those in the production and packaging rows are in fact being devised elsewhere in the spreadsheet – Carline is running several separate grids within the same spreadsheet for different purposes.

Entering the data is no particular problem, and (as you will be aware from the earlier text), as the figures go in the formulas will automatically cause the corresponding calculations to be carried out and the results displayed. There is no point in showing the end result as a figure.

The important thing with a spreadsheet is what follows after text, formulas and data are in the grid. Now is the time for the 'what if?' exercises. What if we cut out the expensive malt and barley extract and replace it with a suitable flavouring? What if we improve taste and nutritional value by having more dried egg at the expense of dried milk? What if we take less note of the wishes of the diet-conscious, and use ordinary cocoa rather than low fat? The latter is a lot more costly and also requires more fiddling to get a good taste.

To explore many kinds of query, what Carline has to do is to change the type of constituent; change the code and the price. No spreadsheet is currently intelligent enough to allow the price automatically to change with the code; this would require an interesting merging of database style with spreadsheet style. All the same, Carline is able to call the relevant data from the database on to screen as required, and she makes manual changes to the spreadsheet in order to investigate effects.

Maybe she wishes to consider the implications of using coarse salt rather than ground salt: all she has to do is to look in the database for the relevant new code and price and to replace those values in the spreadsheet table. The software will look after the rest automatically.

One or two other commands within the spreadsheet language are worth mentioning.

There is *grid* to let Carline insert an extra row or column if she realises that there is a need for it. She can change the table to have the constituents in alphabetical order with the *order* command. Using *justify*, she can place text and/or numbers in cells aligned from the left, from the right or round the centre.

A particularly powerful command is *copy*. This lets the user set up a duplicate of all or part of the table in another section of the spreadsheet grid to allow experimentation without damage to the original data, or to save time if there is a lot of repetition.

As well as using *sum*, Carline has other functions she can call on, including the very useful *min* (giving the lowest value in a column or row) and *max* (the greatest value in a column or row). Finally, there are various commands for layout during printing, causing certain cells or groups of cells to be highlighted (underlined or printed in bold), and allowing various forms of background grid lines to be reproduced.

3.7 Graphics software

Much of this book concerns information and its handling in various contexts. Information as output by a word processor or a spreadsheet is intended strictly to inform; it is information for presentation (to others or perhaps to the originator at some later time).

Graphics programs also present information in this way. Rather than doing so in text (like a word processor) or in tables of figures (like a spreadsheet), their output is in picture form. Information as graphics is a very powerful method of communication – there is much truth in the old saying that a picture is worth a thousand words. Traditional graphic forms of representing information are the line graph, bar chart (or histogram), pictogram (a form of bar chart), and pie chart. See Figure 3.23, but note that three-dimensional versions are common.

Graphs of these kinds, suitably selected and prepared, aid com-

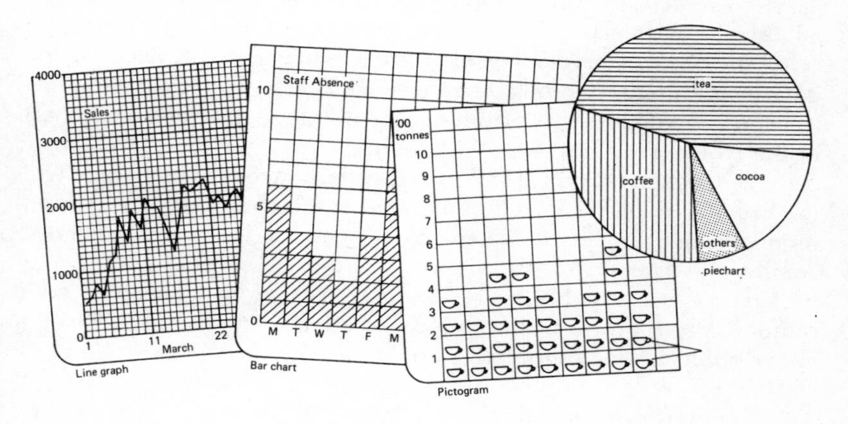

Figure 3.23. Various types of graph are of value in business communication

munication in such contexts as reports to management, shareholders, staff and public; advertisements and sales literature; handbooks and manuals. In the last context in particular there is also a place for line diagrams, with or without shading, of buildings and other structures, equipment and parts; it is straightforward to prepare pictures like these using special artwork software.

Art (or painting) programs are great fun to use; however, their importance in most offices is very low. What they do is to let you use the screen as a sheet of paper or, in the more complex versions, as a window on to a much larger sheet. On this space you can draw lines or coloured bands freehand; put in a variety of standard shapes (like straight lines, rectangles, ellipses, arcs) of any size; call on standard shapes (eg little people); and add text in various typefaces in a number of different orientations. The range of colour and stipple effects can be breathtaking, and the most complex packages in this field allow you to produce computer graphics, with or without animation, as good as any you can see on tv. On the other hand, there are many cheap programs around that will let you draw, for instance, good neat block diagrams, flow charts, and circuits. Using this kind of software is best with a mouse or other such input unit (see page 88), while if you want good hard copy output, you'll need a high quality printer, perhaps with colour.

Here, however, we'll concentrate on business graphics work, using a computer and a graphics package to produce material like that in Figure 3.23.

Considering the splendour of the effects, it is really amazing how easy most business graphics software packages are to use. In essence, all one has to do is to enter the data to be put in to graphic form, and select the particular type of display one would like to use. Entering the data is admittedly tedious, but most packages of this nature allow selection of type of graphic from a visual menu, so that at least that part of the work needs only a few moments.

It goes without saying that the displays produced on the screen will use colour, though this is optional and somewhat more costly than monochrome; in many cases colour makes for very effective communication of information (not always, because quite a number of packages, especially the less recent ones, use colour for its own sake rather than for proper communications effect). The comments made above about colour output also apply here.

Alan – a graphics case study

Alan is not an artist, but he has been on a couple of courses on the use of business graphics software and has become acquainted with the attitudes and styles involved. Currently he is helping Lynne to work on the annual report for Charley's Cocoa Factory; his particular task is to produce meaningful graphics to illustrate various parts of the text.

There are two aims in the presentation of the material on which he is working at the moment. The first is to represent the growth of the company's business over the previous 10 years, while the second is to show how the past year's sales are distributed among the different types of product.

Any of the first three types of graphs shown in Figure 3.23 would suit the first case, while the pie chart is best for showing how the sales 'cake' divides into slices for the various products.

Alan's first task is to enter into the system the data for the sales and profits over the last decade. For this purpose he opens a special file within his section of the computer network, and sends an electronic message to the accounts department for the data he needs. There, of course, the data already exists on the network disc, and it is a simple matter for the staff to pass him the figures required. It is for security reasons that the system will not allow him direct access to the figures. They are shown, in table form for ease of reference, in Figure 3.24.

Year	Sales/£	Profits/£
1978	1 234 567	123 456
1979	2 345 678	345 678
1980	2 678 345	234 567
1981	3 456 789	333 333
1982	3 789 456	321 321
1983	3 219 876	234 567
1984	3 654 987	312 312
1985	4 321 987	432 198
1986	4 111 111	398 765
1987	4 567 890	567 890

Figure 3.24. It is often convenient to think of data for a graphics package as being in a table

Alan now accesses the graphics software. On the menu page that opens the display the action *Import data* is on offer. Alan presses the corresponding key and on request types in the name that he has given his new data file. The data appears on screen for him to check, in much the same form as in the figure. He types <Y> (for 'yes') to show approval, and the program now offers a new menu of types of graphic display.

In turn, Alan selects the line graph, bar chart, and pictogram options, and works through several different styles of each until he finds the ones he like best. These are shown in Figure 3.25.

Alan suspects that it will not be worth going on with the pie diagram, but isn't really sure whether the line graph or the bar chart is the better way of showing the data. The former appears more scientific, which

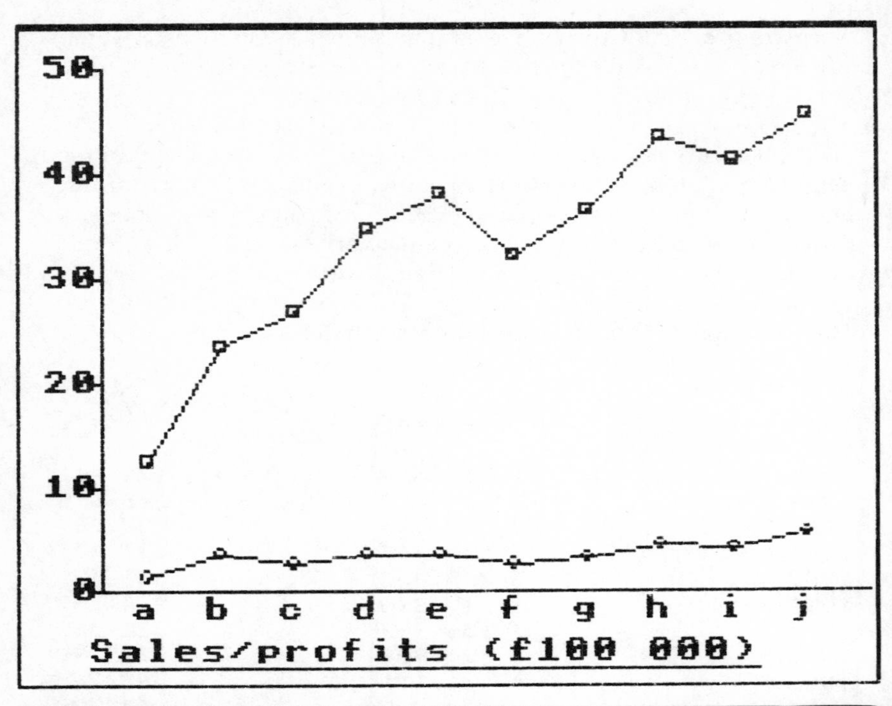
50
40
30
20
10
0
a
b
c
d
e
f
g
h
i
j
Sales/profits (£100 000)

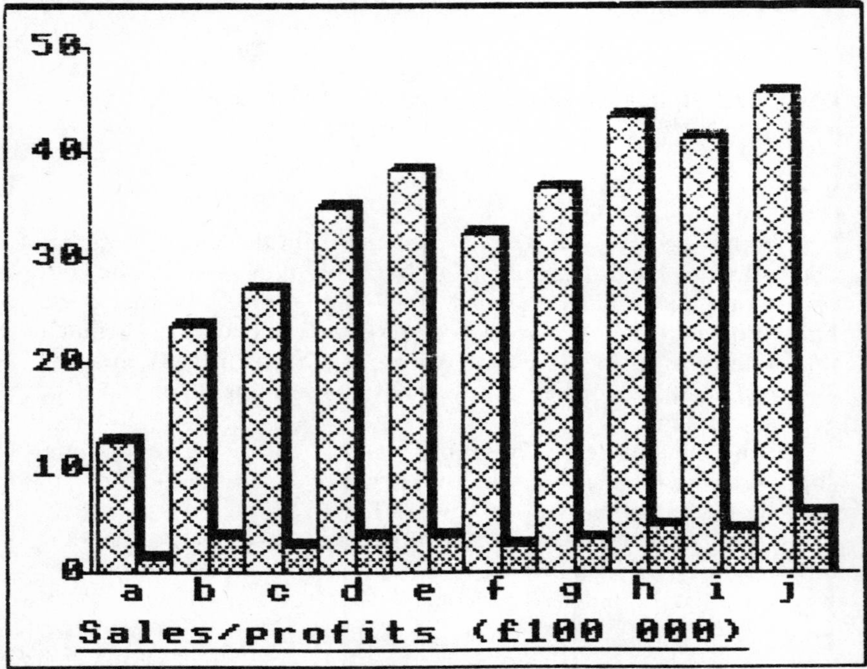
50
40
30
20
10
0
a
b
c
d
e
f
g
h
i
j
Sales/profits (£100 000)

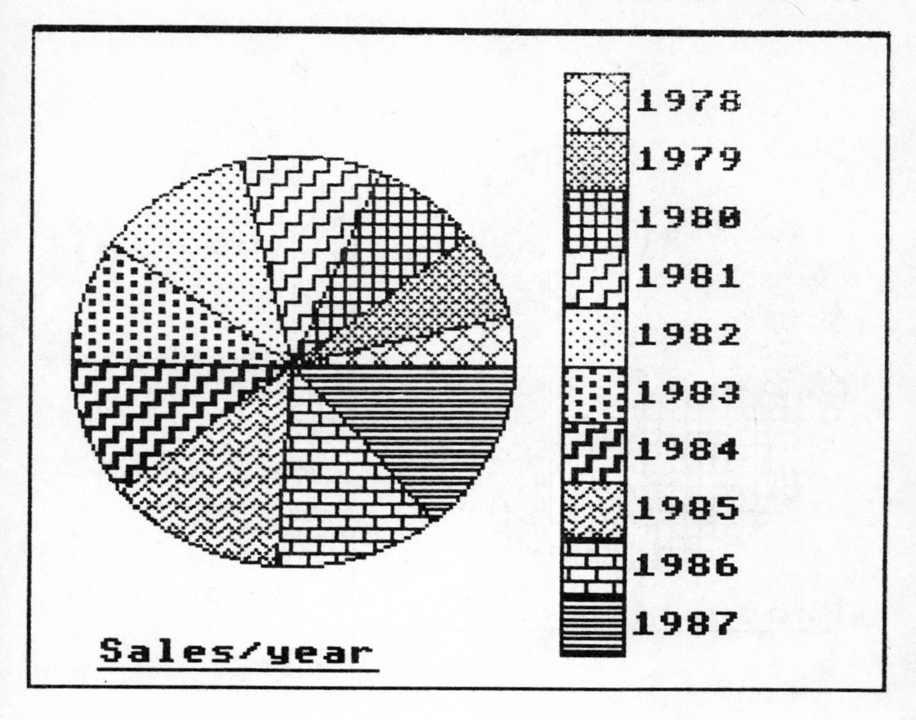

Figure 3.25. A graphics program gives plenty of choice of methods for displaying information

may impress people; but on the other hand, it may put readers off for the very same reason. Alan prefers the bar chart himself, but is not quite sure of his motives, and will need to ask a few of his colleagues.

Much the same stages are followed in order to produce the pie chart showing the product mix in the sales of the year just ended. The same data could certainly be shown in the form of either a bar chart or a pictogram, but this time Alan is certain that the pie chart is the best approach.

Alan has to get the data he needs this time from the sales department, but imports it into the graphics program just as quickly as before. He then tries a number of different pies before ending up with the one shown in Figure 3.26. Beneath the pie chart are the figures he used so you can compare these two methods of communication.

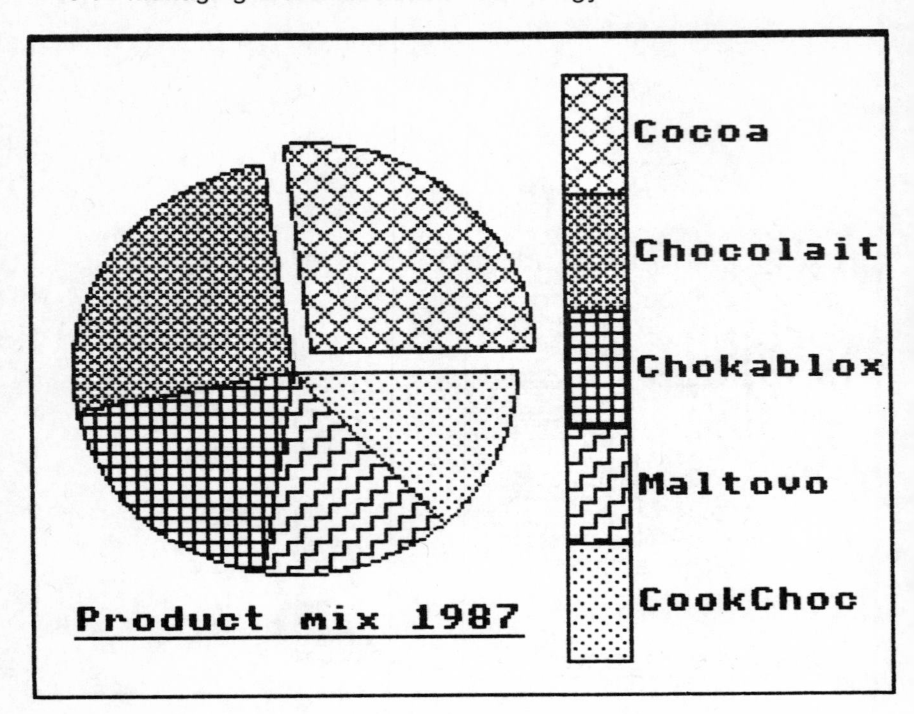

Product	Percent
Cocoa	27.3
Chocolait	25.8
Chokablox	19.6
Maltovo	14.2
CookChoc	13.1
	100.0

Figure 3.26. Perhaps this is the best pie for the data shown

Charley's Cocoa Factory doesn't have a colour printer of its own. However, for an annual report it is clearly valuable to have colour output to give the print shop. Alan has to save his final graphs on to a floppy disc, and takes it to a local university where high quality colour printing is offered. He will then pass the output to Lynne for final checking and inclusion in the materials being collected for the annual report.

4
More Software to Manage

The five types of computer package we have looked at so far are the most important by far in the armoury of the modern business. They are:

- *Word processor* for the flexible handling of text information.
- *Communications software* for the transfer of information between systems.
- *Database manager* for the flexible handling of files and records of information.
- *Spreadsheet program* for the flexible handling of numerical information.
- *Graphics software* for the flexible handling of graphic information.

In passing, one or two other types of program that people in business find useful have also been mentioned. In this chapter, we shall start by noting the existence of those that you may need in your particular context, or may come across and wonder about. Then we shall turn to integrated software.

4.1 On the right path

Critical path analysis (cpa) is a technique whose aim is to allow the efficient planning of a project over time. The technique is not new, but the advent of computers has made a tremendous difference, as they can carry out the tasks involved so well and so fast.

A typical project handled well by cpa is a large construction job, such as the new warehouse that Charley's Cocoa Factory is planning to erect. To complete such a project means that a large number of separate tasks needs to be done. Each task requires certain materials, labour and length of time; also, it cannot be started until certain other tasks have been finished. For example, plastering walls needs certain raw materials and specialist labour to be on site and will take two weeks. This task can't be started, however, until the walls are up and someone has installed the electrics and other services. Equally, the decorators can't move in until the plaster is on and dry.

A cpa program allows the builder to produce a complete list of all tasks and their requirements in terms of materials, labour, completed tasks, and time. The program will also need to know how long materials take to be delivered once ordered, and such restrictions as the use of the plasterers on other sites. In some cases weather conditions will be relevant too.

Once all this information is in, the program will build up a master plan for the project. An outline for a sample case appears in Figure 4.1. This shows a small number of tasks, each of which is part of an overall project. The tasks are in boxes, and the line coming out of each one gives the number of days it needs for completion. The diagram also shows the sequences; thus we can't start task E until both B and D are done.

The program next works out and shows the critical path for the project – it is the heavy line in the figure. By adding up the times

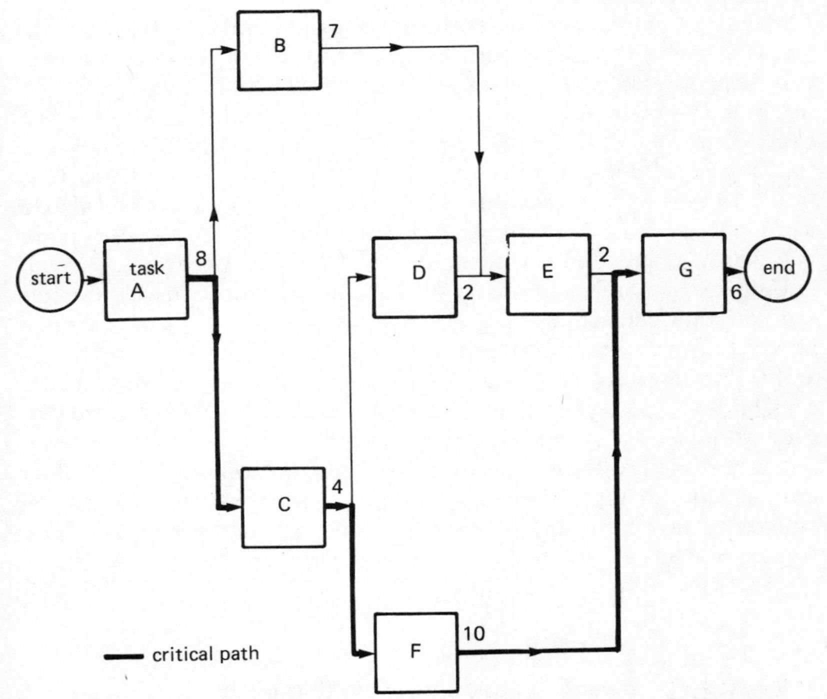

Figure 4.1. A project control program shows the critical path to be kept to in order to complete the project on time

required for each task along that particular path from start to end, the number of days needed to finish the project is obtained. Only by cutting the times along the critical path can the project finish sooner (and cutting times may change that path itself as other tasks become critical).

A printout of the chart (best made on a large plotter; Figure 1.3) is of great help to project management. If things go wrong on site, it is then much easier to see what steps to take in order to keep the project on schedule. Things that go wrong could include incorrect or late deliveries of supplies, bad weather, sickness, and errors in the plans.

A good cpa program (often called a project scheduler) will allow the user to interact with the diagram every so often so that the true picture can be maintained. Such a program will even allow you to add tasks you forgot before, or to change a sequence. It will keep track of resources (materials and labour as well as time), provide a list each day of things to do, and allow post-mortem analysis. It will even sympathise when you get an apologetic phone call from a supplier or hear the glad news of a flu outbreak among the brickies– and then list your possible courses of action and their implications.

Programs of this type currently on the market vary in style and features. In particular, some start by asking for a task list while others commence work by allowing you to draw and extend a draft network on the screen with a mouse or light-pen. Features to look out for (if needed) are the ability to incorporate dynamic budget keeping, the tracking of labour and other resources, report provision of various types, and (as with any software package) ease of use. You need also to be able to estimate the number of tasks in the largest project you are ever likely to have to handle, so you can be sure to get a package with enough capacity for your needs. A final question is how many projects the program can handle at a given time, at least as far as resource allocation and tracking are concerned.

It is important to make clear that a project scheduler is not available on Charley's Cocoa Factory computer network – this is software that they would expect their building contractor to have and use. However, interested as they are in the use of new information technology, they have asked the person liaising with their contractor to get to know the software. Maybe one day they'll start using cpa themselves. Here are some projects for which it could be most useful:

- To schedule and track the tasks leading to the launch of a new product.
- To introduce, test and start up a new assembly line.
- To work towards an autumn marketing push.
- To ensure that the annual general meeting is prepared for without a hitch.

These items are put in reverse order of difficulty, you may notice.

4.2 Organisers *et al*

Organisers include various types of battery-driven electronic diary as well as software designed to run on the office computer. The former group is rapidly becoming common, although it is probably fair to say at the moment that many of these products are more gimmicks than thoroughly useful items. Only the day before writing this, I saw a report about a new credit card sized diary that can carry dates up to the year 2200. That definitely seems to me to be a gimmick.

Organiser software is meant to provide the flexibility of combined diary, appointments system, address and telephone record, and 'things to do' book; in effect, almost to be a computer-based personal assistant. It may be worth thinking about a package of this nature if:

- You spend a lot of time at a desk with a computer available.
- Your computer is left on all the time (or keeps accurate time when switched off).
- The package you have in mind is easy to access, whatever else you are doing with the computer at the time.

Stock control packages became popular and important early in the history of business computing. As long as they are updated properly, they keep accurate records of stock levels. A typical inventory program (as it is sometimes called) can do more than just monitor the stores situation and give reports on the need to reorder certain items, however.

A good system should aid management in all sorts of related decision-making exercises. For instance, it should be able to recommend reorder levels on the basis of supply and demand, storage costs (including capital tied up), delivery delays, depreciation, deterioration, and relationships between items in practice. It goes without saying that a program in this field should be able to put a value on stock held at any moment.

Accounting is the reason for that last statement. Any firm must be able to keep track of the money flowing through it (as in Figure 3.2). At the crudest level, this means keeping accounts (lists) of all incoming and outgoing sums of money; the difference between these credits and debits during a period gives the firm's financial balance. In practice there are different kinds of both credit and debit.

Keeping accounts based on more detailed categories provides further information about the firm's position. Then too there are tax (including VAT) and other such things that you will need to include.

In the good old days of information based on paper, companies used three main books to hold the details of their accounts. In the sales ledger went notes about each invoice, including the receipt of payment. The purchase ledger carried similar details about expenditure. The third, the nominal ledger, was to hold both these sets of details in various categories, in such a way as to make the end of period accounting fairly straightforward: statement of position, balance sheets, profit and loss accounts, lists of debtors, and details of how long each bill was left unpaid.

Most computer accounting software packages follow the same structure and principle, and allow the same well-tried approach. Much of the work to be done could involve the spreadsheet, however, so if you want to computerise your accounts, think of that possibility too. A major problem, all the same, is keeping such programs up to date in the light of changing government requirements.

Payroll software, in much the same way, is like a database. This is because a firm has more to do with its staff than just paying them. Personnel administration would be a better description of a suitable program – can it list all the staff on a certain grade or tell you national insurance numbers, for instance?

A simple payroll program will do the following for each member of staff:

- Work out the gross pay, including overtime, commission and bonus.
- Deal with the various deductions to be made (such as tax, union dues, pension fund and so on).
- Provide a statement of gross and net pay and deductions.
- Pay out, meaning that where a firm pays in cash, the software should also analyse the numbers of each note and coin to be put into each wage packet. If cheques are the means of payment, it should print these out ready for signature. If instead there is direct transfer between bank accounts, the file needed by the firm's bank should be prepared. The wider type of personnel administration software would cover these needs, of course, but this also involves a staff database.

There are implications here for the accountants: all the tax deducted from gross wages and salaries has to be paid to the Inland Revenue, with a proper statement. What we need is to integrate the payroll and the accounts software so that this task is also automated. Perhaps we can then also update the software more easily as legislation changes.

That brings us to the whole field of the integrated software package. This is software which provides some of the functions discussed in this

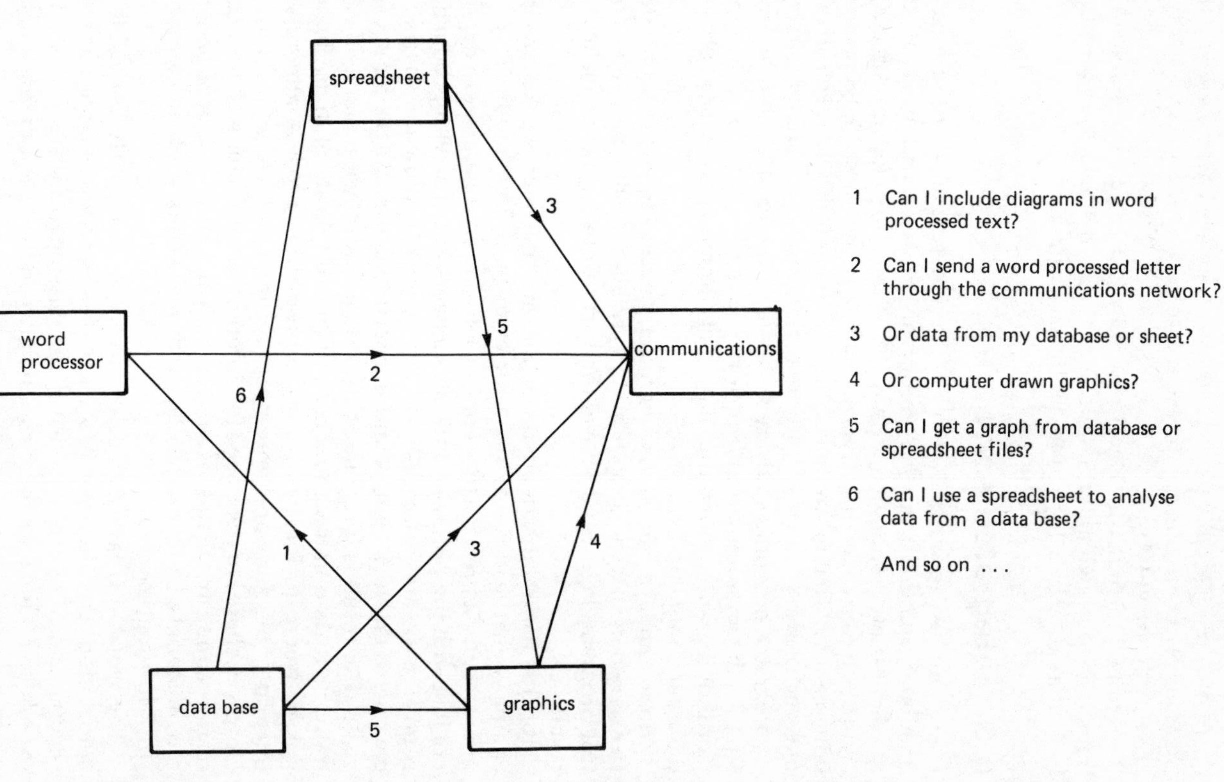

Figure 4.2. How far can the function of the various types of business software be combined?

chapter or the last, and also allows easy transfer of data between the separate programs. In Figure 4.2 are some common questions that arise in this context.

Figure 4.2 includes, for simplicity, only the five main program functions covered in Chapter 3. One could draw a similar one for those looked at above, or indeed for both sets combined.

4.3 Integrated software

It was implied towards the end of the last section that the idea of integrating different business programs relates most clearly to the needs of the accountants. Originally an accounts software package comprised separate programs to maintain the three ledgers mentioned above. That meant that users had to enter the same sets of data into each ledger – a waste of time and a powerful source of error.

Integrated accounts software suites came along to avoid that problem. They can automatically post details between ledgers. In other words, integration allows the sharing of common sets of data between different programs.

More modern integrated accounts packages also allow data transfers between the ledgers and payroll, job costing and stock control program. Figure 4.3 shows the sort of links you can make as a result.

It is the natural information relationships between work areas in a company that lead to the need for even more integration. Thus, as indicated in Figure 3.6, stock control software shares data, to a degree, not just with the purchase and sales ledgers but also with production control. Software designers have been trying to allow the sharing of data between stock control and financial ledger packages for several years. The result is integrated business software, with data held centrally, up to date, and without redundancy (duplication). In the logical link between stock control and the production process, attempts to integrate the software are more recent (and therefore fewer). However, there is a clear need for different departments to share information about the factors of production (including stocks of parts or raw materials), process yields, and the status and efficiency of work in progress.

The work of Charley's Cocoa Factory is particularly amenable to automation and the firm has used process control computers for several years now. They have just commissioned a systems analyst to explore the transfer of information between those computers and the office network.

This means that the process control computers will have to do more than analyse the conditions along the production lines (temperature, flow rates and such); they will need also to report those conditions in a

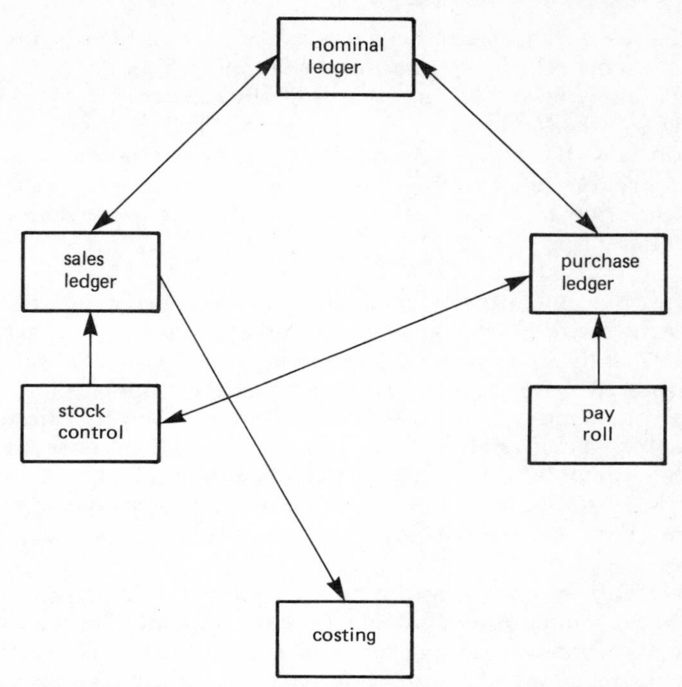

Figure 4.3. Integrated accounts software suites allow the ready flow of information between programs

meaningful way. Then the firm's marketing, financial and planning functions will become more efficient.

A fine example of integration between process control and other software is provided by a system being introduced into Britain's electricity boards. The staff in control of the supply and routeing of power use special graphics software that can show a high detail plan of the grid in their region. A user can zoom into the smallest part of the plan, such as a sub-station, and then by pressing keys on the keyboard open and close switches in the system as required. The software can also show where each engineer is and allow communication, show the position and nature of faults, and suggest the best course of action if any problem should arise.

This kind of integration goes further than we need to think about at length in this book. So too do other kinds of integration that will be mentioned later. (Here I am thinking of the integration of storage of information in such forms as voice and video. These are just as important as information held as text and simple business graphics.)

What we'll stay with here are integrated business packages offering standard programs, that can handle the following needs:

- To share information between tasks, avoiding the need to key the same set of data into the system more than once.
- To allow instantaneous switching between programs without loss of data.
- To have the same style of operation, screen layout, and key sequences in each program so that the user does not have to learn how to do the same things in different ways when using different programs.

Packages like this are fast becoming common, partly because the manufacturers of business computers are getting into the habit of 'bundling' software in with hardware. The users expect that software to include word processor, database manager, spreadsheet, and graphics generator, so the software designers ensure these are compatible. You'll notice that communications software is not included in that list – it is still not the norm to bundle that in with a business system, although that situation is sure to change soon.

Here, very briefly, is how an integrated system works in practice.

Lynne is busy preparing the annual report for Charley's Cocoa Factory; the annual general meeting is coming soon. The report will consist of sections, each a page or so long, from the main department heads, opening with the usual flowery prose of the chairman. The accountants' report will lead into the balance sheets and statements of income and expenditure. While the various people concerned are working on their sections, Lynne is arranging for a photographer to tour the site and for a printer to produce the final document.

The word processor software is humming round the network as the managers get on with their reports, while over in the corner of the office a clerk is busy feeding data from the nominal ledger into a spreadsheet to provide the accounts in nice tabular form.

Gradually the pieces come together. Reports start reaching Lynne's workstation for her to edit, tidy up and merge. The photographer leaves a pack of prints on her desk so she can start to think which pictures to use and where to place them. The spreadsheet summaries reach their final form and Lynne gets in a huddle with the PR people to discuss which information to put in graphic form and what are the best formats. Printouts start piling up for people to check.

Running off the final document is not too much of a problem: Lynne has been on an integrated software training course and has tried smaller tasks of this nature already. The processed text is the backbone of the final booklet; codes inserted within it are able to call on spreadsheet tables and graphic representations where appropriate. The text also includes notes referring to the photos.

The report is to be offset-printed by a local firm; they are not able to handle material on disc, so Lynne has to produce high quality output for them to make the printing plates from. She therefore gets the computer to send the output information to the page printer. The local printer will then work with her to cut and paste the material to the final layout required. They will make photocopies of this to give to people to check, and then go ahead with the print run.

When the printed reports come back to her, Lynne will have to mail a number of them out to the press, to shareholders who can't attend the annual general meeting, and to friends of the firm. She will again call on the features of the integrated software, producing a mailing list out of the database files, word processing a letter, personalising the letter for each recipient, and running off the envelope labels. It's all a lot of work, even with the computer system, but at least the report makes it clear that Charley's Cocoa Factory has done well this year.

Lynne's exercise as a whole is a good example of the use of integrated business software in practice. She and her colleagues on the network have used many of the packages effectively – effectively because absolutely no retyping of text or other information was required. External communications software was admittedly not involved. (It could have been if any of the authors were working from home, but this company isn't likely to have staff telecommuting for a good few years yet, as we saw at the end of Section 3.4.)

The most obvious application of communications software could have been to send the text and graphics to the print shop. However, not only does the printer not have the necessary hardware and software (some do), but for this kind of work it is essential that the people involved work closely together to discuss layout and so on. Perhaps in the future a videophone link or teleconferencing system may come to their aid? (We'll look at these concepts later in the book.)

Lynne thinks not. She would much rather keep the report more fully under her control and is now thinking about desktop publishing as the way forward. With desktop publishing software at her fingertips she would be able to integrate all those items of information even more, and do the layout on screen before sending it to the page printer. A chapter on this subject comes later.

Electronic publishing is another system she has in the back of her mind for the more distant future. That would involve the current recipients of the reports phoning in, using their computers to access Charley's (this kind of approach was discussed in Section 3.4). Each one could scan the report quickly while leaving it stored on disc, or arrange for a copy of all or part of it to come into his or her computer – all through the telephone system. At the moment, however, electronic mail (for this is a variety of it) is not good with graphics and pictures. Maybe by the time this approach makes publishing paperless, office information handling will at last be paperless too.

Clearly, integrated software packages offer massive advantages. There are problems too, of course. The main difficulty is the cost of coming to terms with them. While the cost of purchase is not high (a few hundred pounds perhaps), the staff using them have to put a lot of effort into familiarisation. The user interface is the major problem, this being jargon for how (easily) the user can interact with the package by way of keyboard and screen. The big reason for the problem here is that integrated software packages are still fairly new, so the designers haven't much to go on as far as making their products friendly to the user is concerned. No doubt packages of this nature will quickly become easier to use, but there will remain a long learning process, however simple it is to switch between programs and transfer information between them.

At the moment though, usage of integrated software packages is similar to the reported usage of the human brain – in nearly all cases as much as 50 per cent of the power available is never tapped.

Perhaps the best course of action when thinking about getting into this field of software use is to consider modular suites. These still consist of the five (or four) essential programs that link together properly, but you can buy and learn about them one at a time. However, I am not entirely sure about this advice: for a start it could raise the total purchase cost; and more important is the common belief that modular suites are not as good at information transfer as fully integrated packages. Also, if you take the modular path step by step, you may stop after a couple of steps.

4.4 Being a wimp

A wimp operating environment is probably the best one for the user of integrated business software. The rather horrid acronym stands for windows, icons, mice and pointers (or pull-down menus). These business software environments are offered by new operating systems such as that of the Apple Macintosh, GEM from Digital Research and Windows from Microsoft.

The wimp user interface is carefully and cleverly designed to maximise friendliness. Indeed, the term operating environment is used to imply that a wimp system is a mix between a suitable operating software suite (generally a most unfriendly creature) and an applications program (within which one tends to be able to work much more happily).

Again, we'll go through the terms in order.

Windows let you split the screen into different sections for the different jobs you want to carry out during a given period. You may be word processing one document while referring to a couple of others, using three windows to do so; you should then be able to pull chunks out of the old documents and drop them into your new one. You may be trying to prepare graphics from data in a spreadsheet while jotting notes into a word processor file and running a calculations program, using four windows. And so on.

When you have several screen windows open at once you can normally actually work with only a single program at a given moment; the contents of the other windows are frozen. Thus you can't scroll through two texts at exactly the same time. However, it takes only a moment to move from one to a second. Actually, true concurrent multi-tasking – true simultaneous operation – is possible in some systems, but as human attention cannot be split usefully between different jobs, the point is to some extent academic.

Icons are little sketches on a screen that represent different options open at a given time. The idea is to select an icon and thus access the option concerned. This is supposed to be simpler and less open to error than typing in commands at the keyboard; 'supposed to be' for some people don't agree. Some typical icons appear in Figure 4.4.

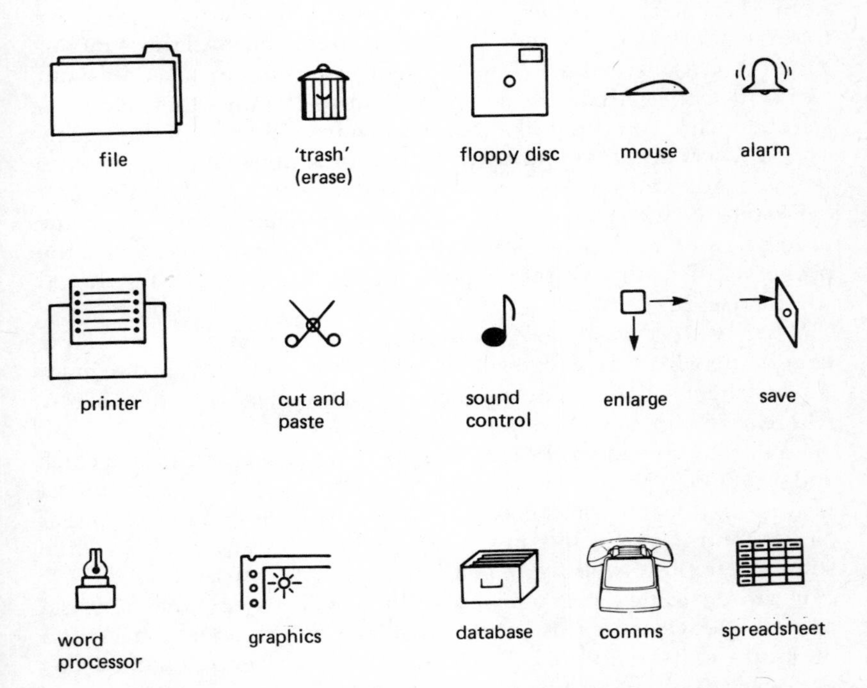

Figure 4.4. Icons are screen graphic symbols that represent options you can select

The *mouse* first appeared in Figure 1.3. It's a kind of joystick in effect (the sort of thing you may have come across with computer games), a small box that you roll around on your worksurface to move the cursor around the screen (or around a window). Actually I prefer joysticks to mice – my work surface rarely has enough space for running a mouse – though a tracker ball, really just a mouse upside down, is almost as good.

Mice have grown rapidly in popularity in the last few years. This is because it is very easy to roll the mouse around so that the screen cursor comes to an icon, then to press a button on the top in order to select the option the icon stands for. If you haven't a mouse, joystick or tracker ball, you can use the keyboard almost as well.

A *pointer* (one reading of the 'p' in wimp) is the name given to that screen cursor. It is normally in the shape of a small arrow. However, it doesn't strictly point: rather than pointing at an icon to get the effect you want, you have to place the pointer actually within the icon image before you can access it.

Instead of a pointer, we can take the wimp's 'p' to stand for *pull-down menus.* A menu, you recall, is a screen list of options you can choose from. Many software packages use menus a lot, to save the user having to remember a large number of different commands. All these menus can't be on screen all the time, as there would be no space for your work. Instead, perhaps by using the mouse to move the pointer to select an icon, you can pull a menu down from the top of the screen. This will of course temporarily cover part of your workspace, but once you've made your choice, the menu will smartly vanish again.

Despite the name, a wimp operating environment is easy to become used to – and then to become addicted to. Wimps greatly reduce the problems of using integrated business software. Figure 4.5 should summarise this section.

What is (or was) your paper-based, pre-computer operating environment like? It is a worksurface with your current task in the centre – a few sheets of paper and a pencil. There's a telephone there somewhere, a row of reference books, in- and out-trays, piles of files you need to refer to and work with, various other sheets of paper, a clock and a calendar, and maybe an intercom, a calculator and a picture of nearest and dearest on the ski slope. On the floor is the wastepaper basket (and if you're like me, more papers, files and books), while somewhere out of the scene is a filing cabinet or two.

In an ideal integrated software system with wimps, that physical operating environment is entirely matched by the screen image of a desktop and its peripherals. You can use the mouse to drag the icons you want to places you want them. Then you can drag material between them and the windows that represent the parts of your real

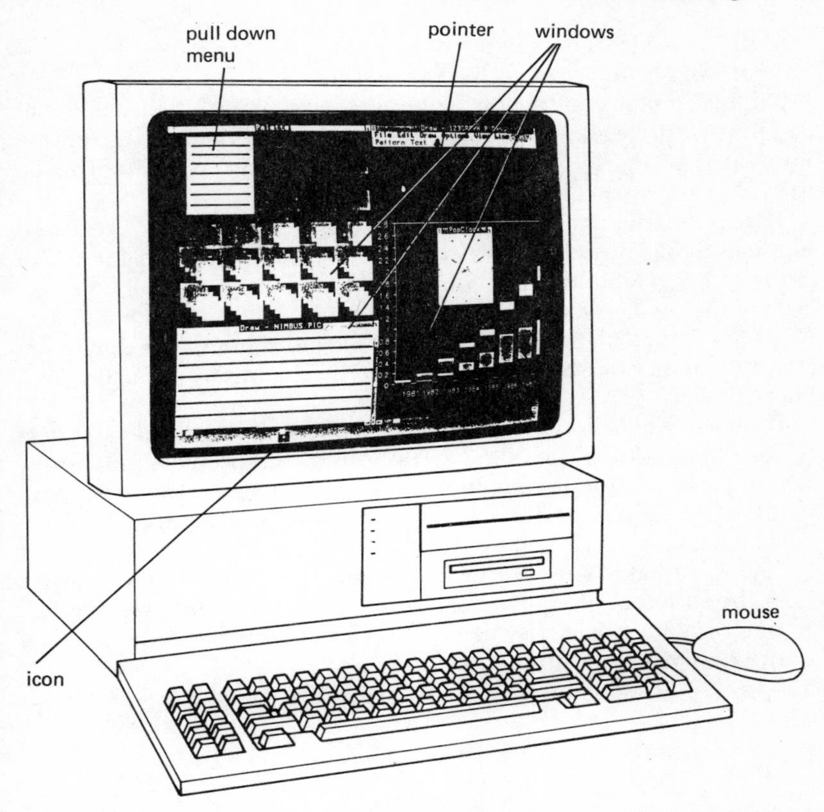

Figure 4.5. Here is a typical wimp operating environment – windows, icons, a mouse, a pointer and a pulled-down menu

desktop. Thus a 'page' from this word processed document can be pulled out, edited, and popped into that text. Figures from this table can be turned into a nice shaded pie chart and put into that file. This set of accounts can be dragged over to the wastepaper basket icon and thrown away. And so on.

4.5 Relational databases

If it is true that few users of traditional database software learn enough about their systems to be able to take full advantage of their power, it is even more true of the newer relational databases.

That paragraph must be taken as an implied warning that if you are in the database market-place you shouldn't automatically plump for a relational package just because it (a) is more costly and (b) offers more power. This kind of software is indeed not cheap – the price range is at least as much as that of integrated software suites; it is certainly powerful, but do you really need the power?

On the other hand, most commentators expect that relational databases will become the norm. As they can in many cases replace integrated business software packages, their existence ought to be mentioned in this context.

The traditional database management system (dbms) is organised in a hierarchical way. The structure (as outlined in the card index of Figure 3.11) is a bit like the biblical 'beget' business – a database consists of files, each of which contains records, each of which contains fields for the actual data items. Much the same as an upside down tree (but still called a tree by computer buffs), this hierarchy is illustrated in Figure 4.6.

To work with this kind of structure, the dbms has to add extra data (pointers) to all the data items. The role of the pointers is to show where the data items belong in the overall structure; they relate them particularly to the nodes of the tree. This is restrictive in three ways:

1. The dbms has to spend quite a lot of effort reorganising the pointers as the structure of a given file changes. As soon as the user puts in a new type of data (a new field, say) a lot of work has to be done on the pointers throughout the file.
2. The size of the computer's memory limits the size of the file.

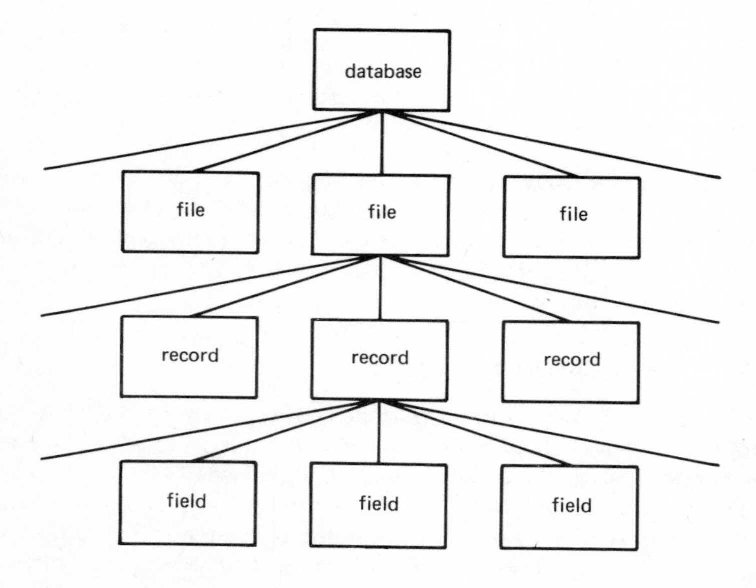

Figure 4.6. The hierarchical structure of a conventional database is much like a tree

3. Programming sets of instructions into the system is not as straightforward as it should be.

A relational database management system (rdbms) throws off that rigid tree-like hierarchical structure in favour of a more realistic set of relations between data items. The value of this is that, in reality, chunks of information relate to other chunks in all sorts of ways that a tree could not hope to model.

The structure of a traditional (paper) encyclopedia is like this, except that the user provides, in effect, the software. By using the encyclopedia's cross-references, it is easy to slip from one data item (paragraph) to almost any other in only half a dozen or so jumps. In the same kind of way, one can reach a given data item in a modern database from many others without much difficulty. Rather than seeing the data items as leaves at the end of the twigs on the branches of the trunk of a tree, we can visualise this data structure in detail as in Figure 4.7.

Relational databases use a number of different techniques to store the relationship between data items. To us the importance of that is as follows:

- The rdbms does not need to spend time on frequent reorganisation of the structure.

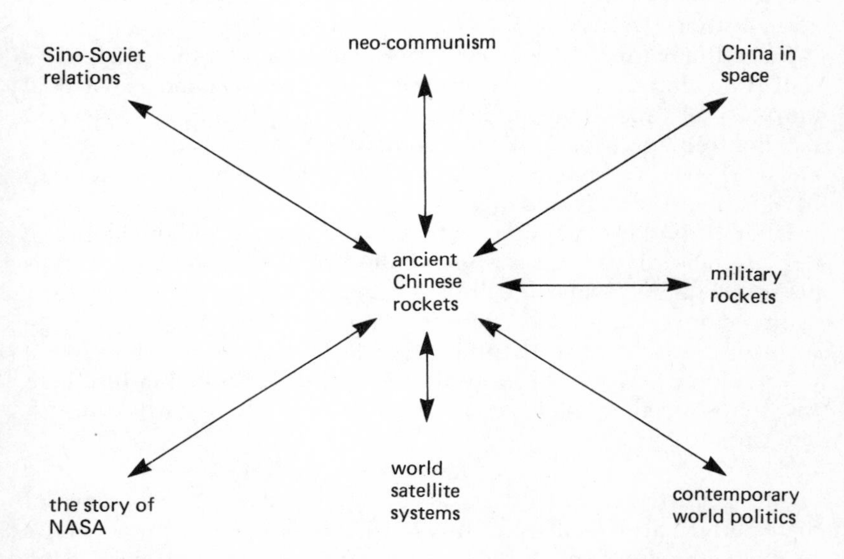

Figure 4.7. The relationships between data items in an encyclopedia form a complex network

- There is no theoretical limit to the volume of data held.
- Programming instructions can be much more flexible.

To the manager, the significance of this is that an rdbms can be programmed to allow full and efficient integration of the software handling of all the company's records. Accounting, tax, payroll, stock, personnel, customers, suppliers, and so on – one can set up all these apparently separate files with a relational database. Then (taking expert advice) it is no great task to define all the user's relevant relationships. As a result, any new data item entered will lead to the updating of all related data items within the whole system. It's a bit like a huge multi-dimensional spreadsheet.

Some of the pitfalls should now be obvious. Not only has all the information concerned to be typed in, but so too have the relations – and the relations need very careful thought even if programming them is easy. Less obvious is the opposite effect: the company now fully converted to relational databasing may have more information on tap than its staff can cope with. You may be able to get a graph relating the sugar content of biscuits to the price of cardboard in Sweden – but will that help Charley run the cocoa factory better?

4.6 Hardware integration – a case study

Charley's Cocoa Factory has a sales force of four people who cover the whole of the British Isles. June is one of them, her territory being Eire and Northern Ireland.

Since the company introduced portable computers for their sales staff, June's job has changed markedly. She can now spend a great deal more of her time in actual selling (rather than handling paper and making frequent trips back to headquarters). As a result, she enjoys her work even more than before, and because she makes more sales her income has increased.

In the back of her car, along with the samples case and the literature displays, she carries a hand-held, battery powered intelligent computer terminal not very much bigger than a calculator.

She is now just driving up to the car park of Sligo Cocoa, a large wholesaler who has been handling Charley's products for a number of years. After parking, June types the key word **sligo** into her terminal; she then scans the liquid crystal display (lcd) screen for what the system can tell her.

The display shows current information on her customer's status, including turnover by month and by year, and summary details of their performance in the past few years. There are also notes on the people with whom she deals, including personal matters such as the names and ages of children, so that she can give the impression of personal caring. Armed with that refreshed information, June enters the building.

Over coffee in the chief buyer's office, she is able to chat in a friendly way, using as triggers the information she has just recalled from her computer's database. She is interested to hear about the company's plans for going into mail order selling, and makes a mental note to add that to the database when she leaves.

Sligo are not computerised, and while June dutifully makes a wry comment about that, she is happy to walk through the warehouse with the chief buyer to examine in person the stock levels on the shelves.

Her computer has given her details of reorder stock levels for this company and of orders placed in the last few months. As they walk around the warehouse, therefore, she is able to ask in detail how the company has found their recent supplies, as well as to recommend what quantities of the different lines should be ordered now.

Back in the chief buyer's office, June confirms with him the orders that they will now place, and enters them into the terminal straightaway. The machine's tiny printer produces a couple of copies of the list (automatically inserting such details as the company's name and the date). The chief buyer signs June's copy of the list and keeps one for himself, thus saving his own company a fair amount of paperwork and time.

After another cup of coffee and the usual farewells, June returns to her car, and enters the additional information about the company and the personnel which she has gleaned during the visit.

That night in her hotel room, June will connect her terminal to a modem, and dial through on a special number to Charley's Cocoa Factory network. The modem she uses is an acoustic coupler, into which the hotel bedroom telephone handset fits snugly. (This is necessary because June cannot rely on there being a suitable phone socket for a standard modem in every hotel room in which she stays.)

By this means, the system automatically sends back to headquarters the orders and information accumulated during the day. Angela, the company's communications officer, will check in the morning that June and the others have logged in successfully and transferred the data expected.

At the end of the data transfer, the headquarters computer sends back to the terminal such information as details of items currently out of stock, and the latest information on customers and their credit standing. There may also be some messages for June or for other people whom she intends to visit, and she prints these out before disconnecting from the line.

Her last action, before wandering down to the hotel bar, is to connect the terminal to the mains, so that she can recharge its batteries overnight.

The system just described has a number of benefits to Charley's Cocoa Factory. Efficient selling is the key to progress in most industries, and this one is no exception. The use by the sales force of hand-held terminals which log into the main system daily is a great aid to sales efficiency, and the benefits have become clear already in the year since the new system was introduced. It is also important for the company to keep its sales force happy, and while others may be going for car phones, these little computers are far more value to a sales force's resources.

The customers of Charley's Cocoa Factory benefit greatly too. Not only is their own paperwork reduced but they find they have faster and more efficient ordering and delivery, and a resulting improvement in their own stock control. They can be sure now that if they order some goods from Charley's Cocoa Factory they will not have a vague message a few weeks later saying that what they want is not in stock.

From June's point of view, it is an interesting move towards telecommuting. June currently lives in Cheshire, so that she is rarely able to be with her family during the week, and has heavy travelling to do at weekends. Her husband is a teacher and has much enjoyed the holidays that the family have spent in Eire, so he has agreed to consider a move across the Irish Sea. As June travels around visiting her customers, she is now looking out for somewhere to which the family could move, and doing so with a great deal of excitement.

To work from a home somewhere in the centre of the island would have a great deal of benefit for herself and her family, and she knows that information technology will make this more and more possible.

She has discussed various ideas with her sales director, who would be quite content to allow her to visit the office in person only a few times a year. That will save the company a fair amount of money, and in exchange they would be happy to consider supplying a remote terminal for June's new home.

The sales director himself is currently exploring a new integrated hardware package, one designed to produce full colour 35 mm slides automatically from data on screen.

The graphics software on the network that was used by Alan to prepare material for the annual report (Section 3.7) has a facility that the company has only just started to use. This is to 'dump' the contents on the screen not to a printer, but to an instant camera. Pie charts and other such graphics, with high quality text superimposed, are very time-consuming to put on to slides in the traditional manner. Even photographing a computer screen presents many problems.

Now, however, this new hardware package looks as if it will be the answer to the sales director's prayers. During the year there are a number of occasions at which high quality slides are of great value, and now he thinks he will be able to obtain them from screen very quickly and efficiently. The situations where such material will be used include presentations to the sales staff and to other colleagues, national and international conferences of cocoa manufacturers, and the many relevant exhibitions at which the company takes a stand.

4.7 A summary of the system

Figure 4.8 summarises the hardware and software systems on which the work of Charley's Cocoa Factory is so much based. It is only a summary, and by showing separate activities in separate areas it does not easily communicate the high level of software integration that in fact obtains. All the same, it will help to view this picture with a number of other illustrations found earlier in this book, as well as with the text of Chapters 3 and 4 in particular.

Figure 4.8 includes a number of uses of computers which are not really relevant to the main thrust of this book. This is a suitable place to mention a few points about them.

The company's *energy management system* is designed to provide heating and air conditioning facilities for every space in the site. Throughout the building, sensors check the temperature and humidity of their environment all the time. These sensors are connected through the mains (rather than needing a separate wiring system) to the heating and air conditioning control unit, which is itself a computer. The control unit runs a program 24 hours a day whose aim is to produce an optimum environment everywhere in the company's building. Not only is the central heating switched on and off by this means, but the individual radiator valves and fans are varied too, in the same way. The control unit sends signals out, again through the mains rather than a separate wiring system, to all those separate controls.

Each of the devices in the system, whether it be a sensor (including a manual thermostat) or a control unit, has a chip in it which, among other functions, gives it a unique identity. Every second the central control unit sends out through the mains a request to each sensor to report its status. This is done by letting the mains voltage, which exists at all times through the electricity wiring, carry a high frequency signal. Each such signal includes the identity code of the sensor addressed, followed by an instruction code which tells it to report its status.

So, as the temperature fluctuates in the reception area, the chip in each of the temperature sensors there has a changing value in a certain memory location. On receipt of the sensor's unique polling code, the chip responds by sending out into the mains wiring its identity code

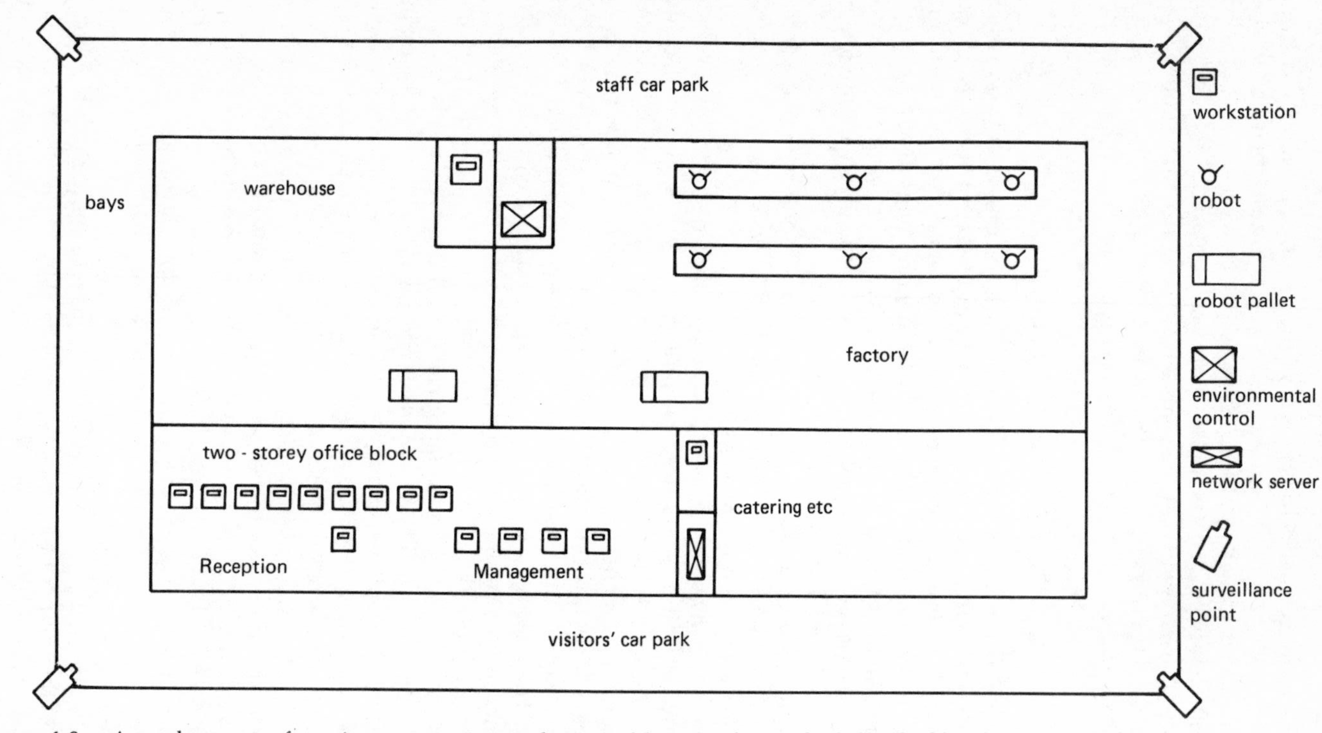

Figure 4.8. A modern manufacturing company can obtain real benefits from a high level of hardware and software integration

followed by the value in that particular memory location. Thus every second each sensor reports its status to the control unit.

In much the same sort of way, the individual control devices round the building have their own unique codes and await instructions for the action to take preceded by the correct codes. If someone leaves the reception door open and the temperature falls too much, for instance, this information would rapidly be reported to the centre by the sensors. The radiator valves would then be opened automatically to the right extent. (Mind you, the reception staff would much prefer the controller to close the door automatically.)

Fire and intruder surveillance is carried out in much the same way. Here, the sensors are smoke and flicker detectors and movement sensors based on infra-red beam, respectively. The energy management system also controls surveillance, but this time there are different outputs. The outputs include the flashing of alarms in the security office, where automated and remote control television cameras round the site display their fields of view on screen and feed continuously looping video cassette recorders.

Should the central control unit receive no acknowledgement to its flashing alarm in the security room within 10 seconds, its next step is to activate the bleeper of the security officer on duty. Should the officer not respond by pressing a special button on the bleeper, the controller would send a taped alarm call automatically to the local police or fire station as appropriate.

In the factory building itself, simple *robot systems* are playing a greater and greater part. The production of many of the goods produced by Charley's Cocoa Factory is automated to a significant extent, so that the system looks after quality control and packaging almost totally.

The principles of production control are much the same as those of energy management. Sensors monitor such factors as product temperature and chemical constitution, and automatically adjust the rate of feed of raw materials into the line and the temperature of the ovens.

The robot vehicles (automatic pallets) which cruise around the building carrying raw materials and finished products from place to place, are programmed to follow broad white lines painted on the floor. Each one has an infra-red detector scanning the area in front of it as it moves, so that if there is someone in the way it will stop automatically. Touch sensors round the bottom of each pallet also report to the vehicle's control unit so that it can stop at once if there has been an impact.

The use of robots in factories is a fascinating field, one in which many aspects of information technology produce high efficiency and pleasant working surroundings. The management of Charley's Cocoa

Factory do not envisage that they will automate much more in the foreseeable future, but the picture in many larger factories is very different.

All the same, every one of the systems discussed in this section involves the basis of robotics, the principle of feedback. By this, information input to a system causes a change in its output so as to have the input control the output actions. In this field of automatic data capture and device control, some kind of sensor feeds data to a processor; the program in the processor's memory takes account of the input(s) and sends out control signals to the switches and such under its wing. The point is made in Figure 4.9; see how it applies to some of the examples above.

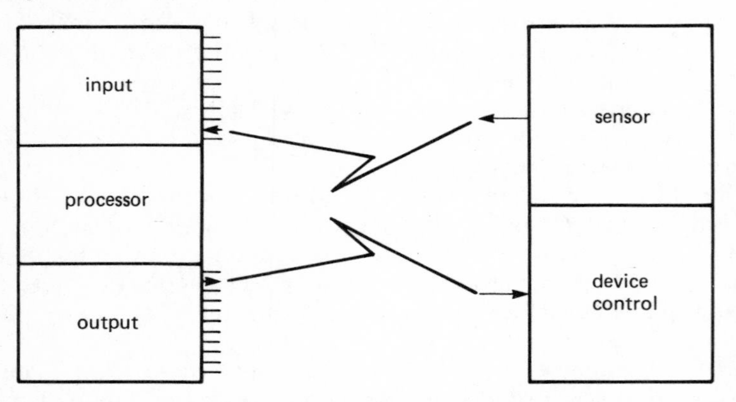

Figure 4.9. Data input from a sensor leads to output action signals under program control

There is also a feedback loop whenever a person works with a computer system. The user enters data into the system, through the keyboard perhaps; the system responds with an output (in most cases on screen) and the user in turn reacts to that. Where there is a human user we call this process interaction; the same kind of thing happens automatically in robotics and in the cases discussed above.

5
Distance No Object

The network concept has already been mentioned a number of times in this book. A network allows computer users to communicate with each other in various ways, or at least to share data and such scarce resources as costly output units. Networks are clearly important; they form the subject of this whole chapter.

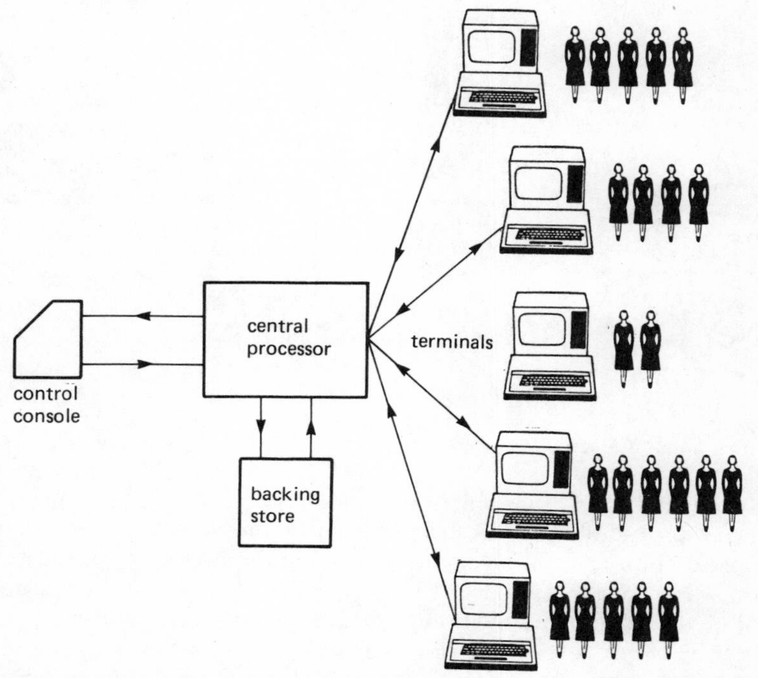

Figure 5.1 The terminal was the first step towards a computer system able to work with several users at a distance

5.1 Spreading the net

Figure 5.1 shows what we can call a shared logic (or shared processing) computer system. The mainframe or mini with its terminals has a single processing unit, at the 'centre'. The terminals are dumb: they have no processing power of their own, so are just a means to allow the individual human users to interact at the same time with the computer itself. The central processor shares its work between the terminals that are online at any given moment and looks after all their needs as well as it can.

The best modern mainframe system can handle hundreds or even thousands of terminals at once, and those terminals are now intelligent (their own processors can share the load to an extent). All the same, during busy times at least, there can well be several seconds of delay between a terminal's input of data to the system and the output of the desired response. As a microcomputer system does not have this problem – for there is only one user's needs to cater for – the movement away from shared logic to stand-alone units is easy to understand. Figure 5.2 shows the typical computer usage of the first half of the 1980s.

Figure 5.2 The advent of the cheap micro sometimes led to the appearance of a stand-alone personal computer on nearly every desk

Having a stand-alone micro to yourself is great. You have full and sole responsibility for all aspects of its use: maintenance, operations, housekeeping, as well as actually running the applications software you want. All the system's data is *your* data; all the peripherals are yours too. Rolled into one body, you are operations staff, data preparation manager, technician, librarian and user. Your system's output depends on the software *you* put in, and the peripherals you can afford to invest in. Your system's efficiency depends on *your* knowledge and on your attitudes.

Hm. Maybe your own personal stand-alone micro is not the right culmination of 50 years of computer progress. Information technology is meant to release people from irrelevant problems and cares, and to let them get on with what they can best do. Should a personnel manager have to learn data processing skills, or a factory supervisor learn to program? Should the boss have to become word processor expert and filing clerk too?

Those second thoughts spread fast after the rise of cheap stand-alone micros in the early 1980s. Certainly they offered much of value in comparison with the use of a terminal to a remote mainframe or mini. Yet the terminal user still had access to huge volumes of data, great processing power, and speed that left micros standing, as well as to high quality peripherals.

The network concept shows that shared processing does not have to mean the delays of time-sharing and cumbersome logging-on procedures. With a network, shared processing can be for the benefit of all users, and shared data and shared high cost peripherals lead to great savings of time, money and effort.

In Chapters 3 and 4 we looked at many uses of a modern microcomputer network as the staff of Charley's Cocoa Factory went about their daily business. The networks of the late 1980s are, admittedly, far from perfect, but they do promise a real move towards the cost-effective and enjoyable liberation of the individual user's particular skills.

To recap, a network is a group of micros, linked by cable to central hardware and software. The workstations now consist of intelligent machines – full feature computers with their own powerful processors and memory and (often) backing store – rather than dumb communications terminals with no more than an input and an output device. Thus the individual user at the workstation has on the desk top a system that can be as autonomous as desired.

On the other hand, there are those network links. As required, the system can copy software and data from the central assembly to any workstation. As required, any user can call on a more powerful, information-crunching central processor or a superb quality printer. As required, data as well as messages can shuffle between the units.

So, in principle, the network offers the best of the two worlds of individual freedom and shared costly resources (including information). The integration of software explored in Section 4.3 is matched by hardware integration.

Figure 1.4 showed the three main network structures that exist: the star (or cluster) that looks much like hanging terminals on to a mainframe or mini (Figure 5.1); the bus, in which there is a great saving in cable costs; and the ring, which is in effect a bus with the ends joined. Each style has its advantages and disadvantages and its different approach to handling data transfers between the individual units. The ability to survive hardware faults is relevant too, with the bus being the most vulnerable.

Perhaps the biggest question concerns the ease of expansion to bring new micros into the net. Rings and buses are not as easy as stars to add new workstations to, and it is therefore common to install these with spare connectors to allow later expansion without a lot of work. In the same way as one plans a modern office from the start to allow a truly flexible telephone system, so too should one build in network cabling that will provide for a great variety of possible uses.

In practice, though, many networks do not fall neatly into the categories of star, bus and ring. Figure 5.3 shows a typical hybrid layout, with special switching units called nodes and nexuses to keep the whole thing working properly. This kind of pattern is most likely to appear when one decides to link two separate networks.

5.2 Multi-usage

At first sight there may seem to be no problem in sharing access to common software and data through a network. Each user could load

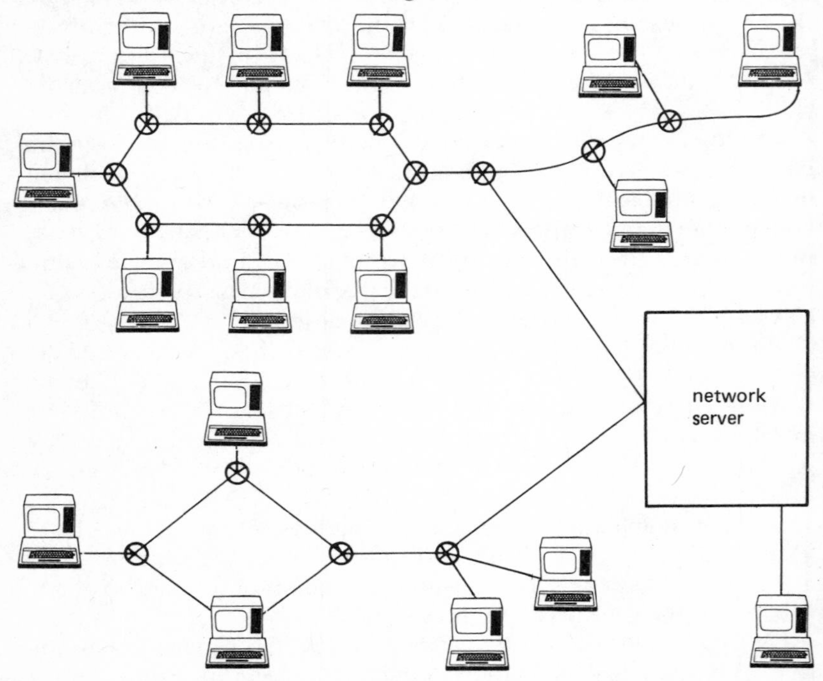

Figure 5.3 It is in practice not often that one can describe a network as a simple star, bus or ring

the program desired and work on it, calling up, adding and changing data as required. However, things are not necessarily quite so simple. Perhaps two people may decide to edit the same draft report at the same time, using word processor software. The system would not be able to stop that from happening, nor is there any way it could merge the two edited versions. As a result, there will at the end be either two differently edited copies of the report, or a single one which includes only one person's work.

The same sort of problem could arise with the sharing of accounts information. One accounts clerk could access the figures for September and start sorting them, while another could be just about to change some aspect of them. Sharing data by linked independent micros is a recipe for disaster.

Because of this, network operating software cannot be the same as single user systems software, and the applications programs need to be supplied in new versions too. A common business microcomputer operating system is cp/m (control program for microcomputers), and there is a vast world-wide pool of cp/m applications software. A network of cp/m micros needs the multi-user version of the systems software to run it, that being called mp/m. However, mp/m alone cannot detect and avoid the problems mentioned above if the users still run cp/m applications programs on the network; to be safe they must obtain multi-user versions of all their software.

Typical network applications programs come in two levels. The main accounts package, for instance, stays with the main network processor, while each workstation involved with accounting has a local 'front end' version. The front end displays a menu of allowed actions and can check entered data for validity and so on. Only when the user approves entered data does it pass to the main network program for incorporation into the correct files. As the main program can do only one task at a time, there is now no chance of clashes.

As well as handling joint access to shared data and shared resources, the network operating system will need to offer a level of security. Some kind of password system – a logging-on procedure – is needed to prevent unauthorised access to network data. This may have to be on several levels, with some people allowed only to scan certain files and others able to change almost anything.

In the same way as there is in practice a great range of network configurations between the simple star, bus or ring and something like the system of Figure 5.3, there is a range of power and style in the operating software. This is because a network can be, at the one hand, a set of powerful micros with little central processing and at the other, a sophisticated central unit with workstations of fairly low intelligence (autonomy). While the principles just set out are generally valid, the details vary greatly. The choice in practice depends a lot on how one expects one's future usage will develop. Thus a very small firm or department could purchase a network with just one micro station and only later add other user units.

Network operation is as yet far from perfect. Because it involves sharing, it is very likely to introduce some element of delay at times. The central backing store is probably always a hard disc (Winchester) unit nowadays, and that is very fast in action as well as being able to store huge quantities of data. All the same, if one user runs a program that involves many data transfers to and from the Winchester, the others are bound to find their work slowing down when they too need to access that disc. High volumes of data transfer can also cause problems in the bus and ring configurations of network. Although the cable can carry a lot of data (perhaps millions of bits per second), transfer is serial, with only one packet able to pass each point at a time. As Figure 5.4 shows, the cable can clog up, so that packets of data due to pass one node may have to wait a few seconds for a gap.

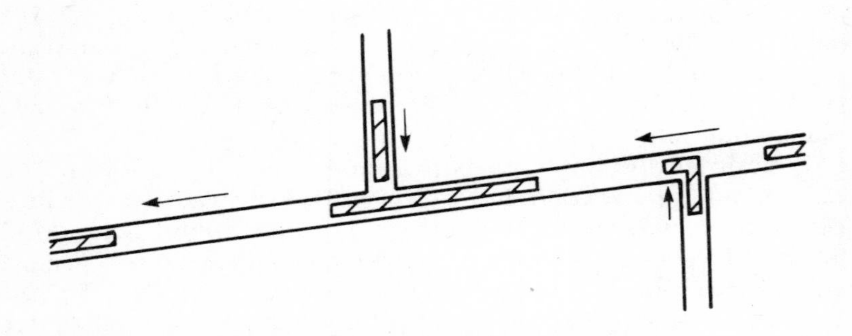

Figure 5.4 The main problem with a heavily used bus or ring is that items of data may have to wait before they can get into the cable

The network concept is fairly new. No doubt future development will be as rapid as in the past. At the moment, however, it is not possible to recommend any particular approach, and experts differ greatly as to when a mini or a small mainframe system is to be preferred to a network. If you are thinking of going along the network route, you will need to do a lot of research, in particular making visits to existing installations and talking to the users.

There is a hierarchy of microcomputer links, however, a summary of which will serve to close this section. At the lowest level, one can join several micros so that they share a printer. Some of the micros may have their own individual low cost printers as well, but that is at a higher level; Figure 5.5 shows this level – it is a typical star (or cluster) and has a manual switching unit to drive the central printer.

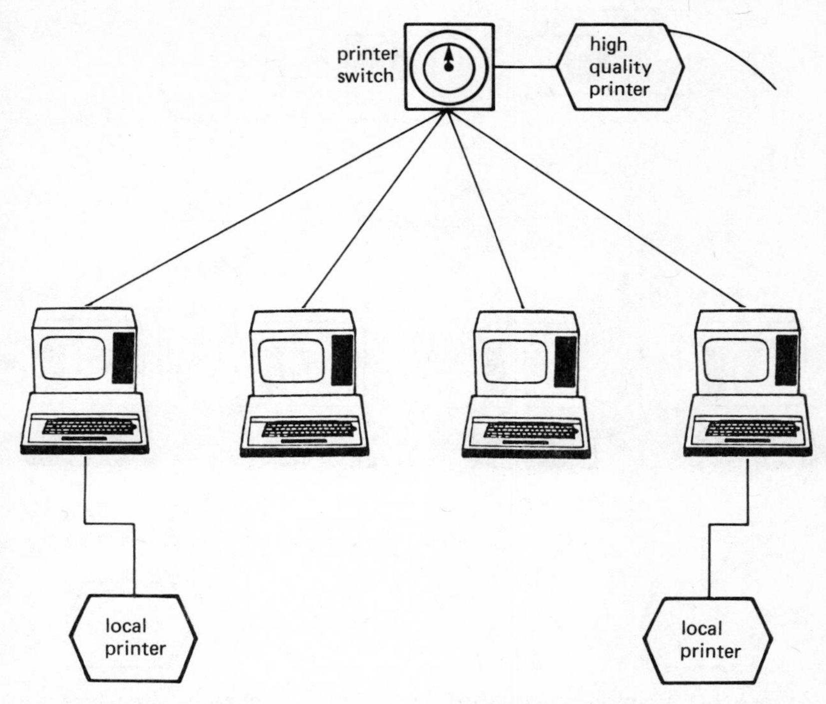

Figure 5.5 Sharing a printer between several micros is a simple way into simple networking

The big advantage of this simple cluster follows from the fact that a good printer is still not cheap and, as few users will need to print out often, to have a printer for each micro is wasteful.

The next step up is to share software and data by using a common disc drive, almost always a hard (Winchester) disc now. Again, each micro can have its own drive (for floppies or even for a hard disc); rather than a manual control, software in the central file server handles the individual accesses to the central disc. (This is because, unlike the case of the shared printer, disc data transfers are very short, rarely lasting more than a few seconds.)

There are, you recall, two inherently different approaches to the sharing of data on a central backing store. On the one hand is the dumb terminal approach (the one that is truly called multi-user) and on the other is proper networking (where each user has access to local processing power). Figure 5.6 shows the latter, again with a star (cluster) approach.

All the same, if one is buying an office system from scratch, there is sense in taking a look at the strict multi-user micro (the arrangement with dumb terminals linked to a central processor). At the time of writ-

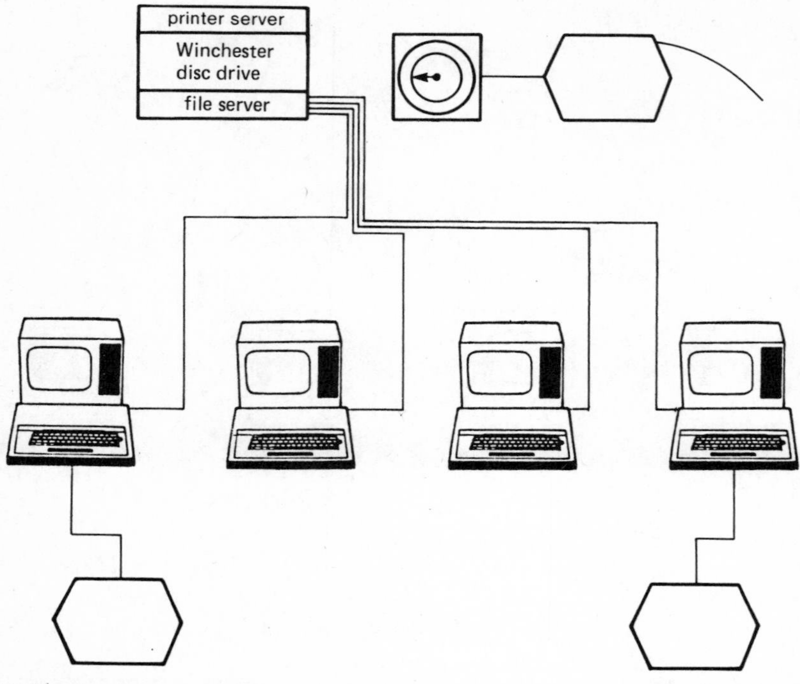

Figure 5.6 In a typical true network, several microcomputers share data on a central disc through a file server

ing, this approach still has a cost advantage to make up for the slow processing and data access rates forced by sharing processor, main memory and backing store at all times. The cost advantage is all this type of system has going for it, but it is not likely to be so much longer, as the price of microelectronics devices continues to tumble. For systems with more than about four or five stations, a network, even if it is only a simple one, is already the better answer.

A simple cluster like that of Figure 5.6 can support one or two dozen stations with little problem of delays. The top limit is typically 32, although this depends on the file server software. The stations do not all need to be of the same type; you can (if your needs dictate) mix eight-bit with 16-bit processors or even include a sprinkling of dumb terminals.

At the next level up we enter the realm of the true network (but don't forget that the word's usage is very loose and changing all the time). Now we expect a basic bus or ring structure rather than a star, a much greater upper limit on the number of users at a time, and significantly increased speed. Various standards apply in this industry, such as the Cambridge Ring (popular in Europe) and Ethernet (which can support over a thousand users). Various scrambled approaches exist too, such as the 'daisy chain' network with several clusters on a bus or ring and a similar approach linking several processors each with a set of dumb terminals.

5.3 Spreading the net wider

The upper level system described at the end of the last section often goes under the name of local area network (lan). However the individual workstations and shared central resources work together logically in the area in question, the links consist of cable whose routeing is at least semi-permanent. This is the criterion of a lan: even if the cabling is of such high quality that it can carry data at a rate as high as 100 million bits a second; even if the system includes several mainframe 'host' computers; even if the number of simultaneous users is well into four figures; and even if the distance between two extreme workstations is several kilometres. It is a rare office that reaches those upper limits of the definition, though such great lans are becoming common on campus.

In the case of such a large lan, making the data transfer links to the central 'host' processors and the shared peripherals can be a problem. One solution is to bundle the data into uniform packets at various packet assembly and disassembly points (pads). Figure 7.9 in the section dealing with packet switching in a public telephone network shows what happens here, as the concepts are much the same. Telephone systems also give a clue to the second method of cutting down the problems of handling the traffic on a large network – management can set up a private branch exchange (pbx) and look on the various workstations and shared resources as telephone extensions.

Whatever the system in question, clearly a network involves information transfer, and that is what communication is all about. The sharing of information and the sharing of scarce hardware resources are the reasons people are moving towards networks rather than staying with independent micros. However, as we saw earlier in the book, there is a great need to share information (and even resources) with computer users on other, distant sites.

It is too costly to set up a cable to extend a lan over more than a few kilometres (and anyway, for technical reasons, that wouldn't work well at the moment). To allow the sharing of information between distant users, therefore, we must call on telecommunications. This is the use of radio, microwave, light or electric current links, through space, metal cables or optical fibres. Such channels of communication exist already, in particular in the public telephone system.

Allowing data transfers between computer users in this kind of way is not hard; we explored it in Sections 3.4 and 4.6 in particular. The term wide area network (wan) covers the approach and, as its use grows rapidly, the name is coming into common usage.

It is essential that all the hardware to be used on a lan is compatible, ie it can share data without expense, delay, distortion or other problems. That is just as true of wan working, although extra difficulties are in the way of rapid standardisation. Two sets of standards (protocols) have met with some degree of acceptance: osi (open systems interconnection) from ISO (the International Standards Organisation); and X25 from CCITT (the International Consultative Committee for Telephones and Telegraphy).

A wan that consists of users at microcomputer workstations and shared resources linked over large distances using telecommunication lines can still behave as a lan in most contexts. The major difference is caused by the delays in setting up a channel through the public telephone network and the far slower rates of data transfer.

Technically, one of two types of hardware unit must form the link (or interface) between the remote parts of the wan. (This is separate from those, such as pads, exchanges and regenerators which are part of the existing telephone network.) The first is the bridge. Strictly, a bridge includes all the hardware between the two sections (Figure 5.7(a)) but in practice the term refers to the 'bridgehead' that links each to the telecommunications system (Figure 5.7(b)).

As far as each section of the wan is concerned, the bridge seems to be, and acts like, just another workstation. Each bridgehead is a processor with access to plenty of storage. However, its function is to 'know' the address of each station in the remote sections of the network, so that it can first capture the data from its own side that need to pass over the bridge. There are also likely to be security aspects to handle. It may be, for instance, that the network management does not want certain types of data to leave the local area, so perhaps only users with certain grades of password will be allowed to access data through a bridge.

The gateway is the second type of wan interconnection. Its functions are just the same as those of a bridge. However, a bridge can work between sub-networks only if they use the same protocols (data handling systems and structures); a gateway can, in theory at least, link any two types of system. A gateway's task is much harder, therefore. It has to be able to deal with different data transfer rates, different packet make-ups and sizes, different security systems, different addressing methods, different ways of handling errors, and so on. All the same, Figure 5.7 will do as well to describe a gateway as a bridge.

As with all fast-growing industries in which huge sums of money are involved, the computer world is bedevilled by lack of standardisation. We have started on the long road towards full compatibility between systems. At the end of the road is the vision of the global village in which all information activities for all groups and individuals will be linked into one huge wide area network. That wired society is far off yet, for the road to it *is* a long one. The needs of the office are bound to lead the way, for the office is where information handling is paramount.

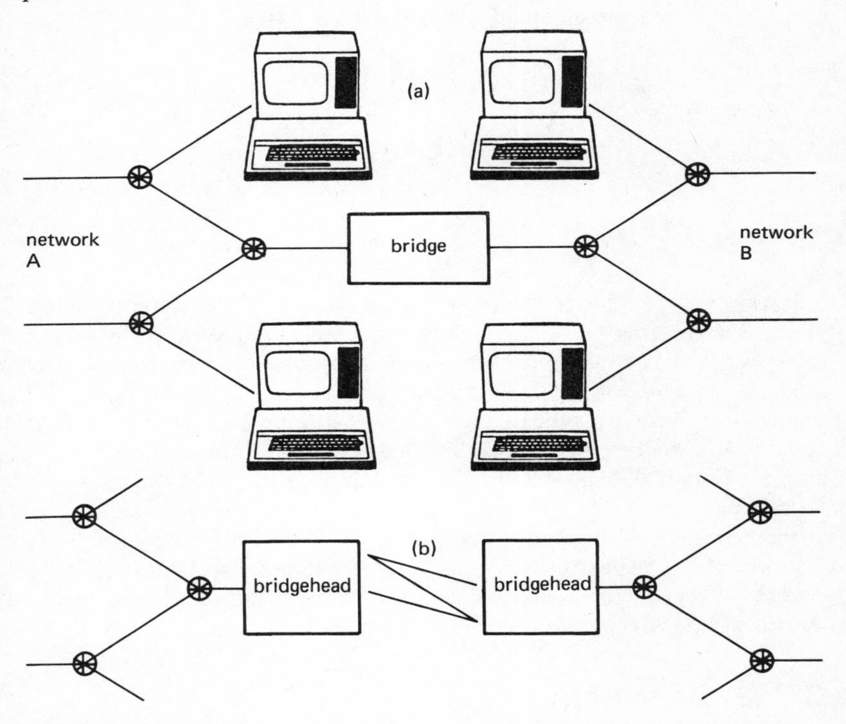

Figure 5.7 The bridge between two parts of a wide area network is likely to include a channel through the public telephone system

6 Choosing Software and Hardware

It is now time to tie together the material in the previous chapters, and to explore the criteria of choice between the various computer systems now available. We shall look at systems analysis, the study of information systems, with a view to making them more efficient. Note that this definition says nothing of computers: although it is likely that new information technology would make almost any information system more efficient, it isn't *always* the case that extra hardware saves a firm's life.

Computerisation is only, in fact, a facet of improving business efficiency, and it is not even an essential one. The right attitude of mind and the right approach are just as important; first, the current system needs to be looked at with care and realism.

6.1 Systems analysis

To move towards a better workplace, you need to consider carefully four questions:

- Just what is your business?
- How can you carry it out most efficiently and effectively?
- Can new information technology help in any way?
- What IT hardware and software system would do most good?

Even to answer fully just the first of those questions may lead to real progress. Do you *truly* know your business inside out? Do you know exactly how to describe your product? Do you know who buys it? Why? And why other people don't? How does your product compare to those of your competitors? How well do you budget? Can you predict accurately the inputs and outputs for the next year, or even the next month? Is the business truly profitable? And what of your colleagues and staff? Are they content and do they enjoy their work? Do you even know what each one does, how, and why? Why do people leave?

This book can't tell you the answers to these questions. You are the only person who can say what your business is, and only you can decide how (if) you can improve it. If you are a very busy person, you may pass the workload of this new study over to someone else. You may even invite a consultant in to carry out the lengthy process for you. Passing the buck in either of these ways could, however, mean that you do *not* know your business.

Figure 6.1 outlines in flow chart form how systems analysis applies in general to any situation. Run through it quickly to gain a broad view, and then study it with more care to see how it could apply to your own case.

There are many loops in the flow chart that lead back to an earlier stage. They exist not because systems analysis is a woolly way of working, but because any real business system is so complex that to describe and analyse it perfectly is well nigh impossible. Changing circumstances inside and outside the company can have big effects too.

6.2 Why computerise?

A surprisingly large range of answers exists to this question. The obvious one – that it makes the business cost-effective – is rather superficial and needs further analysis. Perhaps the least often cited answer is prestige; while it may not be an obvious reason, it is in truth probably a very common one for going along the IT road. It is also true that many new computer systems are never properly used and may end up in a cupboard gathering dust – perhaps because their buyers had no better reason than prestige for rushing to purchase.

Let's look at some more definitive answers.

The existing manual system can't cope. An office deals with information. The manual handling of information (mail in and out, processing, storage and access, and so on) is slow, costly and prone to error. Delays in getting statistics and reports to management can be catastrophic, and taking on extra staff to share the load is not going to work for ever, if at all.

We can't give the government (or the bank, or our accountants) the information asked for without computers. This is really a variation on the last point. It is true, however, that demands from outside for detailed accounts, statistics and reports can put great pressures on the information handling areas of a firm. Pressures from accountants and auditors can be just as bad, although these people are supposed to be working for you.

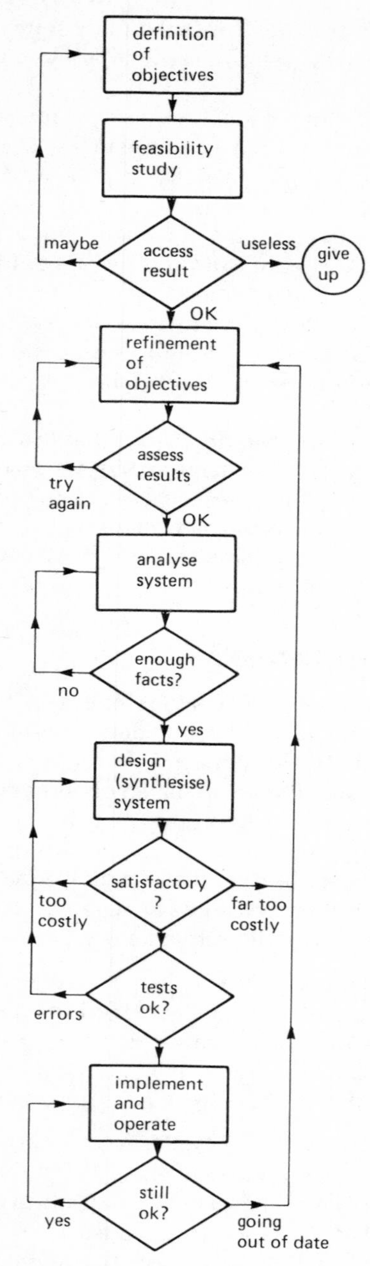

Figure 6.1 Systems analysis involves many steps and loops between the initial definition of a business and its objectives and the final trouble-free operation of a new method of working

All the demands are legitimate; computer-based information may be the only answer.

IT can increase the productivity of scarce staff. Again a variation on the first theme, but applied to higher level personnel instead of (or as well as) clerical grades. Qualified professionals such as statisticians, accountants, designers, market researchers, technical writers, stock controllers, artists, and trainers can gain a great deal from access to a suitably designed computer system suitably set up for them. Note the word 'suitably', though.

Computers can help to control the organisation. Some firms suffer from poor communication between staff, and a fall-off in procedures and efficiency results. The need for agreed systems and information structures that follows the use of computers can bring the degree of discipline needed.

Computers help competitiveness. The thought here is that suitable software can very quickly bring to your attention any undue size – or growth – of such costs as staff, handling, services, and general overheads. Once you are aware of a problem, action – an economy drive at least – is likely to follow. Computers aren't needed for that, of course.

Computers help customers. In many firms a rapid response to consumer demand is essential for progress. With computer software online to help handle queries and orders, one can reduce the delays that customers (rightly) so much dislike. On the other hand, systems can too easily become an excuse for inefficiency; there's little that annoys a client more than a glib apology blaming a computer.

Computers help the staff. Again we come to another version of the first reason on the list for computerisation. Here we think of cutting chores and raising morale, providing for diversity of jobs, and raising wages. Some surveys have shown that staff at all levels prefer to work in a proper IT-based firm than in one with a more traditional style. Others have shown the reverse, though – staff may care more about atmosphere than about flashing screens and whirring disc drives.

All those, and their many variations, are valid points of view in the context of whether to go for IT or not. However, for each case study that could prove that one or other of the above reasons for computerisation is valid, one could find a second in which a firm went wrong. IT is *not* an automatic ticket to huge profits and a happy staff. Much of the work of the later stages of systems analysis (Figure 6.1) involves tailoring a vague IT vision to the actual needs of the actual user. The four major questions that opened Section 6.1 *must* receive full and careful answers if computer-aided bankruptcy is to be avoided.

6.3 Finding the software

'Software matters more than hardware' was the title of Chapter 2. Its importance is demonstrated by the widespread belief that you should choose your programs before seeking a computer that can run them.

That may sound all very well, but in practice it is not so simple. It *is* true that the biggest mistake anyone can make is to rush out and buy a micro without knowing what it can do – and how – and what it can't do. With hundreds of micros on the market, and floods of conflicting adverts, reviews and advice, even a fair amount of research may not lead to success. It *is* true that it is better to start with your needs rather than with a blank cheque book and a desire for a nameless machine with a keyboard, disc drive and screen.

There are also tens of thousands of applications software packages on the market. Their aims, features and prices range enormously. Because of that, even a fair amount of research into software may not lead to success.

Consider taking on a computer in the same way as you recruit a new member of staff. Recruitment involves internal reorganisation; drafting profiles and job descriptions; budgetary aspects; a campaign that consists of research, long lists, short lists and references; face-to-face interviews and aptitude tests; discussion – and only then (perhaps) decision. Once a new colleague is in post, there is a period of induction, training, and mutual adjustment before he or she can be relied on to get on with the job without problems.

Taking on a computer should be no different, even if the running cost seems a lot lower than a salary.

By having read this far, you will have gained a useful grounding in the sorts of work a computer system (software as well as hardware) can do. However, no single person can know the practical details of every system in existence, so you cannot expect to gain that knowledge yourself. It can take weeks of training and months of practice to become a fair expert in the use of just one computer with just one business program.

What can you do at this stage, then?

First, you need to decide the types of program you require in order to make your business more effective: back to systems analysis, but the material in Chapters 3 and 4 should give you a good start.

Second, you need to think about the matter of software integration. Using an integrated package offers tremendous potential benefits, but the early days with it can cause hair-raising problems. It is possible to integrate the software over a period by taking the modular approach mentioned at the end of Section 4.3 – that at least spreads the problems out.

Third is the question of hardware integration; whether you can get by with a single stand-alone computer or rather need to think about the various kinds of network. Chapter 5 looked at this in some detail.

The fourth stage of computerisation is to make a checklist of the features you need for each program specified. This should not be too detailed, though – some programs could have hundreds of features.

All that, to pursue the staff recruitment comparison for a moment, corresponds to the stages leading to job descriptions and profiles.

Next one goes to the market-place, to reduce the choice to a long list, and then to a short list. This is where you need specific advice about the packages available; armed with your checklists and other criteria, look for that advice now. Be wary, however, of consultants who are not truly independent of suppliers. As consultants include sales people, magazine writers and authors of books that survey computers and software, that statement means you can hardly trust anybody. You may need to spend several weeks as you narrow your search down to half a dozen packages – the fifth stage.

Sixth, interview the candidates, which in this case means you should arrange full demonstrations. These should be in your office, and not in a series of software shops. In your office you will be able to remember your needs better and involve other colleagues. As it's your home ground, you will also feel more able to stretch the demonstration your way rather than putting up with standard patter.

It is important to become involved in this kind of software demonstration. You have your checklist of features, but it isn't enough to see that what you want to be able to do can be done. How easy is each program to learn and to use? What is the standard of reference material and on-screen help routines? Are the displays clear and easy to read? Are the features accessed by menus, icons or strange combinations of key presses? Is it possible for *any* member of your staff to work the system to an adequate level without lengthy and detailed training?

At the end of this stage, you will have narrowed your short list of packages down to just two or three. Only now is it time to investigate the actual hardware that can deliver them adequately and to start thinking really hard about costs. Here again you'll need to work through a planned process of finding out what's on the market, checking reports in magazines and books, looking at existing installations in other places, and so on.

It is very likely that you'll end up wanting a big-name computer system, with a big-name suite of operating system, and a big-name integrated software package or combination of standard programs. There's nothing wrong with buying popular hardware and software;

the only criterion should be whether it does what you want in a way you and your colleagues will like and your firm can afford. You may succeed with a second-hand home computer sold through a notice in the corner shop and running business software written by a fifth former at the local school – but you may not. Computerisation is not like buying paper clips; it's a big investment that needs research before spending.

6.4 A case in point

Let's detail the example of word processor software to illustrate how consideration of any software package should be approached. What possible features are there to look for?

Word processing is one of computing's main success stories. A couple of decades ago the concept didn't exist, but now it is a major use of computers in most offices and educational establishments as well as very many homes. For some popular computers, the number of competing word processor software packages runs well into three figures, and making useful comparisons is very hard indeed. As a result, buyers tend to go for leading edge products, as they assume that the newer something is, the better it will be. That attitude shows a lot of sense, but actual features are important. Let's check them through.

As we saw in Section 3.3, word processing involves typing text into a computer running the right kind of software. The text appears on screen, where it should be easy to edit (change in minor and major ways), lay out, preview, print, and save to disc for the future. No doubt any word processor package can let you do these things, but the questions lie in the ease and versatility of doing them, and in the other tasks it can carry out for you.

There should be no problem in typing in the text. A standard (Qwerty) keyboard is the norm, though there are others. These include the Quinkey, with which you enter characters with one hand in a coded form, claimed to take about an hour to learn; purpose-designed layouts like the Maltron which give far faster typing speeds under the fingers of an expert; and devices for blind and otherwise disabled users.

The text you enter goes into the computer's memory and also appears on screen, normally with white characters on a black background. Again there are variations. Some word processors let you select the colours you find most clear and restful (maybe blue on yellow); others use colour coding on screen for different effects. On the whole, though, a monochrome (light and black, green or amber) screen is all you need, with enough quality to provide a rock-steady flicker-free image of sharp, well formed characters. Most screens still have the traditional landscape format of a tv set, with an aspect ratio of three units up to four across. However, there is a move towards upright displays than can show an A4 sheet's worth of text at a go – ten units up to seven across. Some even have dark characters on a light background to make the screen look even more like a sheet of paper.

To edit text that is in memory already means you want to be able to move fast to any point in the document and there carry out any of the following:

- Delete material – a character, word, line, sentence or longer section.
- Type in fresh material – insert it, in other words.
- Move a chunk of the text in from elsewhere in the document, either by copying or by changing its position.
- Move in a chunk of text from disc or from another document – a standard paragraph perhaps.
- Replace what is already there by fresh material – overwriting the old with the new.
- Highlight parts of the current text in some way – making it bold (heavy), underlined, or italic, perhaps.

All this means you need to know where you are in the text at all times. Unless the document is very short, it won't fit on to the display; the software will have to make the material scroll up and down so that your current position is always in view. In some cases, where the length of the text lines is more than the system can display, you may have to scroll left and right too.

A cursor marks your position on screen. This may be a square blob or box or an underline symbol; often it flashes so you can see it more clearly. How easy is it to move the cursor through the text? Movement involves using special keys on the keyboard – the cursor control keys, in most cases marked with arrows – or a mouse, tracker ball, or joystick. Other keys pressed at the same time may allow faster cursor control, to top or bottom of text, left or right of the line, or in units of a word, line, sentence, paragraph, screen, or page. When you test cursor control, check how easy these larger jumps are to make; slow cursor motion takes time and can make you giddy. Check too what happens to the cursor; some programs switch it off during fast movement and it then becomes hard to know just where you are.

The display itself is likely to be called wysiwyg – what you see is what you get. This is an overworked phrase; strictly, it means that the screen shows the text at all times in the exact form it will appear in printout. That must include the right layout of line and page length, indents and outdents, justification, highlights, page numbers, headings and footings. Wysiwyg software is, however, sometimes far from that, so there's something else to check. Printer technology is generally in advance of screen displays, and this makes things harder. Printers can output text that contains foreign characters, accents, subscripts and superscripts (as in H_2O and 5×10^4 kg m^{-3}), and in a large range of character sizes and line spacings. No wysiwyg software yet on the market can match all that – decide what you need before you go too far towards purchase.

Figure 6.2 explains the main technical terms in this section.

You achieve text layout effects by various means in different word processing systems. A switch-on code has to go into the text where an effect is to start; a switch-off code goes at the end. These codes tell display and printer what to show, but in some programs they actually appear on screen, in the text or in the margin. This can be intrusive, although can make things simpler to check.

The usual way to obtain these control codes is to press the right combinations of keys. For this purpose, most packages expect your keyboard to have a number of extra 'function' keys. There can be anything from four or five to a couple of dozen or more of these. Perhaps the key tops are permanently marked with their functions (if you buy special hardware); or special covers can be slipped on them. Alternatively, a printed card template can be laid over the keyboard to show what each such key's effect is; or perhaps a 'help' screen or a pull-down menu can be displayed. All these methods have advantages and disadvantages, and these differ between learner and expert user.

Search and replace is a powerful editing feature that most modern word processors offer as a standard (even if only in a crude form). You enter a string (a character, word or phrase), and then a second one. The program now searches through the text for the first string and, each time it finds it, swaps it for the second. Thus you can replace each occurrence of 'I am' with 'we are', for instance. However, does the system just replace automatically, or does it also let you select whether to make the change on each occurrence? Does the system take account of lower and upper case letters in a logical way? Can it handle control codes, letting you, for instance, change italic to underlined?

Getting a preview (if needed) or printout and saving the current text to disc should be – but aren't always – each to achieve. In particular, do you need to mess about with disc drive and printer before you can get the information transfer you want? Disc transfers are as important as getting hard copy. While the purpose of word processing may be to put something on paper, many of its advantages follow the use of backing store.

Text stored on a disc is called a file; what flexibility do you have for naming files? Long names are likely to be more meaningful, while short ones are simpler to read and to type. Or does your system save automatically to disc and suggest file names? Does it 'date stamp' each file, letting you see when each document was created each time you catalogue the disc? Does storage even include amendment dates and

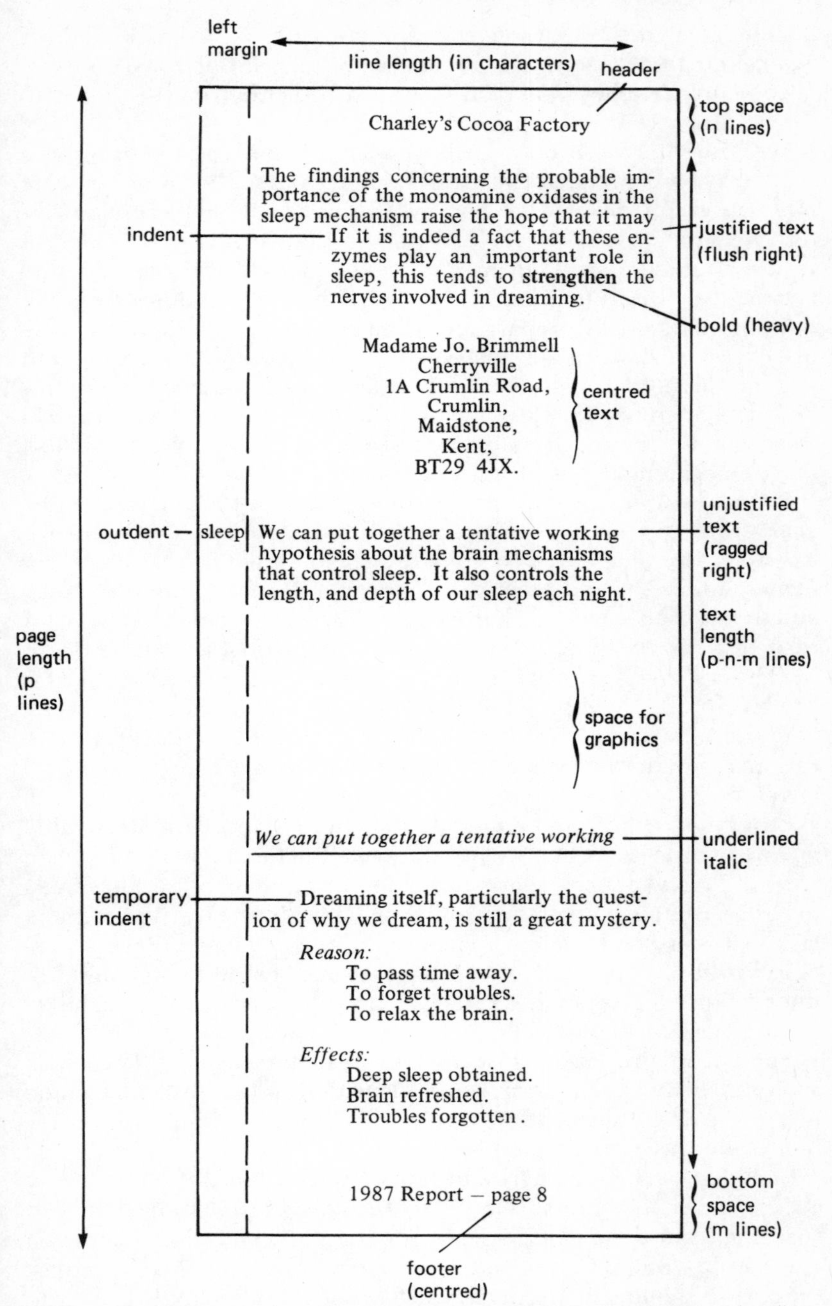

Figure 6.2 Here are some of the special terms used with word processed text

document lengths? With some systems you can use directories and/or extensions to help you with filing clarification. If these are on offer, how flexible are they? Can you save a marked chunk of a file, ready to insert it into a second document later?

Working on two or more texts at once is beginning to appear as a standard word processor feature. It is, in effect, a form of software integration and, if you have windows (Section 4.4), can be very powerful. The ultimate is to be able to display several documents in different windows, moving through each as you need and cutting and pasting between them. Cutting and pasting is a phrase that comes from the days of manual text preparation; it means lifting a chunk from one place and sticking it elsewhere. Now that computers come with enough memory to hold tens of thousands of words at a time, all this becomes open to suitable software. It was much more fiddly the old way, which required frequent access to disc as the system loaded, saved and merged bits of text and whole documents.

By the features of a word processor we mean the tasks it can handle apart from the standard ones listed above. Mail merge is one such example. This allows you to prepare a standard letter with spaces for names, addresses and greetings – personal details, in other words – and then to run it with a database to produce a personalised copy for each of a dozen, hundred or thousand recipients (see Figure 3.15). Mail merge varies greatly in ease of use and versatility but not all word processors offer it. Should the database be word processed too, or can you just call up your file of customers? Can the system quickly turn to running off sticky labels as well, or will you have to use window envelopes?

Programmability can be the key to mail merging. The remarkably few word processors that are programmable at the moment can offer a splendid range of user-defined facilities. Programmability allows you to write a routine that can carry out automatically any word processing task that is normally manual. Such routines may allow the word processor to absorb the features of a database and sort addresses and produce reports, for instance. A program can analyse a text for readability, carry out calculations, or provide dictionary features.

Some word processors do include some of these aspects. Thus, with a number of them you can type in a calculation and the text will include just the answer. Related to this is the ability to add columns or rows of figures in a word processed table.

Spelling checkers are becoming common and effective too. You buy a chip or disc that contains anything up to 150,000 common English (or American) words and, as you type (or at the end) the system will check each word in the text to see if it is in the list. If not, it may suggest the correct spelling or just invite you to try again. You should be able to add your own special vocabulary to the list – chemicals, product names, and so on – so that the dictionary grows to suit you.

Another useful feature is the ability to have the text output in columns; it is often easier to read or lay out that way. If the system offers columns, does it do so on screen as well as on paper, and how many columns can you have? In this kind of way, word processing programs are coming closer to desktop publishing. This is such an important new field that Chapter 9 is devoted to it; a quick scan through that now will give you other ideas.

The point of this section is to show the basis on which to build up a list of features and points to check on *any* class of software that interests you. Research each software type in the same way, produce a checklist, and then complete it as shown in Figure 6.3. Here, a cross shows that a particular program doesn't offer the feature, while the more blobs the better the product (the more powerful *and* easy to use).

If you and your colleagues can spend the time on this research, you are likely to obtain exactly the software you need and the right hardware to run it. If not, you may well find frustration and loss of morale, and see your pretty new toy end up on a shelf.

DATA BASES	Easy data	The Base	X data	Data One	Top base	
1. Cost	£99.99	£195	£225	£145	£200	+ VAT
2. Setting up	••••	•••	•••	••••	••	
3. Forms, std	X	5	10	15	9	Extra £30
4. Layout	••••	••••	••	•••	•••	
5. Searching	•• (4)	••• (6)	•• (3)	••••		
6. Sorting	X	••	X			
7. Saving	•••					
8. Hol						

Figure 6.3. If you devise your own checklist of software features, you'll find choice a great deal easier

6.5 Hardware checks

Much the same level of research should be applied to hardware choice, but as software matters more, by choosing software that will meet your needs, you automatically reduce the number of hardware systems to a level that is easy to handle.

This is not the place to work towards a checklist for computers. Price, comfort and support are now the main criteria anyway.

As far as comfort is concerned, you should apply ergonomic criteria with care throughout your search for a system. That doesn't just mean noting what the machines look like (although that is important). It implies that you need to think about layout on the worksurface; reflections from the screen; angles and the ease of changing them; key and keyboard design and layout; the resolution of screens; noise levels; speed of action. Some of your staff, if not you yourself, may often have to sit at a computer keyboard for half a dozen or more hours a day (even if you insist, as you should, on frequent breaks).

Support concerns the details of how the suppliers (or their agents) will be able to handle breakdowns, repairs and maintenance. How quickly do they expect to be able to answer your screams for help? How large is their stock of spare parts? Do they offer a standby system if they have to take yours away? Support also includes their being prepared to answer your technical queries: if a study of the manual fails to resolve a problem, are they happy for you to give them a ring?

Apart from that, I cannot here offer details of how you can assess central hardware. Peripherals are a different matter, though. We'll take a quick look at printers, so you formulate the types of question to ask for yourself. You can use the same kind to approach for the other main peripherals – hard and floppy disc drives, modems and monitors, as well as for networks and any special input or output units your business may need.

The function of a printer is to transfer a copy of material from computer storage to paper. There are many types and many features, and this is as fast growing a field as any other in information technology. The main types are detailed below.

The first has grown from the electric typewriter. The characters are raised outlines that press against a ribbon to make the image. In a daisy wheel printer the characters are at the ends of the 'petals' of a rotating wheel; a thimble machine works more like the golf ball system. To print each character, the wheel or thimble must turn to the correct position before hitting the ribbon, which means that printing is slow and noisy and also prone to mechanical problems. In addition, to change a typeface, you have to change the print head, and this is partly why such machines are costly in use.

Dot matrix machines, on the other hand, build up the pattern for each character from a series of vertical lines of dots. Each dot is made by a tiny needle punching through the ribbon on to the paper. This system is at once quicker, quieter and more reliable, and allows a huge range of character shapes. The traditional dot matrix printer has only nine needles in its print head; this means that the dots don't overlap, so print quality is poor. More modern ones achieve 'near letter quality' (ie quality almost good enough for office correspondence) by printing each column of dots twice, slightly offset from each other. The latest approach, however, gives true letter quality by having, say, 24 needles in the print head. These machines can produce versatile output that is perfectly good for all purposes, doing so several times faster than the others and at half the cost. It is likely, therefore, that dot matrix printers will soon replace all others at the low cost (below £1000) end of the market.

In exchange for higher purchase and running costs, you can obtain printers that do not involve any impact between a mechanical unit and a ribbon; these can work even more quickly and quietly, yet give high versatility and high quality. The various page printers, including those based on lasers, are in effect like photocopiers that make the image from what is in computer memory rather than from a sheet on top. The main alternative is the ink jet; as the name implies, this fires tiny drops of ink at the paper to form the patterns required. These are all quiet and very effective machines, but they are at the moment costly to buy and to run.

There are two main ways to feed paper through a computer printer. Continuous paper comes in roll form (rare) or as fanfold packs. The individual pages in the packs can be printed with your letterhead, say, or as invoices. On the other hand, you can pass cut paper through, a sheet at a time, though the amount of paper that can fit into a typical automatic sheet feeder is often sadly small. If you decide to use your existing printed paper in a sheet feeder, check that it works well; some paper can slip or jam in some feeders. Check too that the machines can print on to card or plastics film if you need that.

Another question of compatibility that too many people overlook is that between computer and printer. It is frustrating to buy the hardware and then find you have to spend a lot extra to link the units together. Explore the costs of the relevant interfaces and leads, and get a demonstration of your proposed system before turning to your cheque book. In the last decade, problems of incompatibility have grown hugely rather than falling, because the number of micros and printer firms has grown to astronomical levels. At the beginning of the 1980s there were only two major makers of computer printers (and one of those has all but vanished); now there are hundreds.

There are only three special printer features you may need to think about before setting up your final checklist. The first is colour output–

if you want it, you can have it. Colour printers range from those with the old black/red ribbon (and the ability to switch between the two on receipt of a suitable software code) to sophisticated devices whose output quality is not far short of that of a colour photograph.

The second feature is the ability to handle graphics with adequate quality. As we have seen (Section 3.7), there is good graphics software around now, for drawing, plotting and 'painting'. If you use that, you will very likely want hard copy of the lovely screen displays produced. Not all printers can handle graphics well.

Third is the printer buffer. If the printer contains a large memory of its own to hold text and graphics data for transfer to hard copy, you can dump to it what you want printed and then get on with a new task. This is particularly relevant if you are using stand-alone computers; most networks will use the hard disc for the same purpose.

Printer manuals have improved as fast as printers. However, they still need a lot of study in the early days after purchase, so that you can link the machine fully to the rest of your system. If you can easily follow the first few pages, the rest should not be too hard.

6.6 Questions of cost

In a field which has recently seen radical new features, yet a general halving of prices, a book is not the place to go into costs in detail. The last chapter closes with a glimpse of a future in which each person has access to a sophisticated world-wide computer system. Costs have to fall a great deal further before this picture can become real, but there is no reason to suppose they will not come down to the right level by the end of the century.

However, it is possible to make a few sweeping statements. The first concerns purchase and the message is to shop around. As with most other items of office hardware, it is not hard to unearth discounts of 30 per cent, or even more. Look for discounts on computer hardware and software, but always keep your checklists in view, and make sure you don't lose out on support.

The second message is that costs continue after purchase. The use of electricity is, admittedly, something you can almost ignore as computer systems do not use much power, but there's a formidable list of other consumables. Special cleaning materials, floppy discs, paper and ribbons for printers, toner and drums for page printers, storage units – all those things add up. Maintenance and insurance are the big current spenders, though, and you can't do without them. Be prepared to spend 10 to 20 per cent of the system's capital cost each year on these recurrent expenses.

Third, there are transition costs to think about. As you unpack the boxes, you'll need to think of changing things round – furniture and services of course, but also staff roles. Even if your staff don't feel threatened by the entry of IT into their living space, they will need time and care as they move into new systems, and they must have training in using their new tools. It can take anything from a couple of weeks to six months or more to integrate your business with the new recruits of IT; all the associated transition costs can match the money spent on buying the software and hardware.

7
The Reinvention of the Telephone

With a history spanning over a century, the telephone is one of the longest established methods of electronic information transfer. During most of that time, however, apart from the invention of the concept itself, there was only one truly significant advance: the development of telephone networks based on exchanges (switching centres).

Previously telephone communication between two people could take place only through a special ('dedicated') cable link from instrument to instrument. It was several years before the step away from that was made, despite existing experience with the somewhat similar telegraph system.

Figure 7.1 shows the principles of making a connection between two instruments (handsets) in two countries.

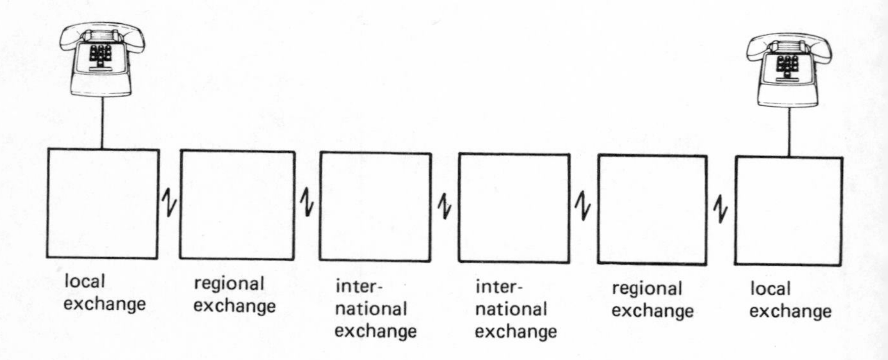

Figure 7.1. To allow communication between two individual handsets, a number of switched connections are needed to produce a continuous electrical link from one to the other

The exchanges (switching centres) have functions other than making connections. Each exchange line carries a meter for billing purposes, and also electronics to ensure roughly equal signal strength in the two directions for a given call.

One other factor to do with signal strength cannot be shown in Figure 7.1. It is the need for repeaters every few tens of kilometres along a trunk line. The resistance of a wire to the passage of electrical signals is not insignificant; this means that if a line is longer than a certain distance, an input signal is so weakened that it cannot adequately be detected at the output. In essence, a repeater is an amplifier in the line, able to boost a weak input signal back up to a strength adequate for the next stage in the journey. A repeater needs its own power supply, and the current for this must travel along the cable as well as the information signals.

The repeating amplifiers of the analog channel are replaced by regenerators; these pick up the pulses and re-transmit them afresh. Not only is interference much reduced as a result, but also the efficiency of the system means that it needs fewer regnerators than repeaters. Figure 7.3 shows how effective digital transfer can be.

A major advance in telephony is the concept of multiplexing. This allows a number of different signals to pass through the same link at the same time. In analogue systems the technique is much the same as that used for radio broadcasting – each signal has its own range of

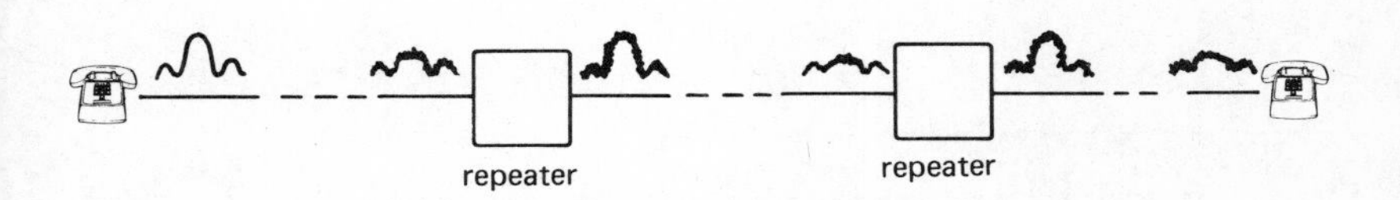

Figure 7.2. Analog voice transfer over a long telephone link causes severe loss of quality

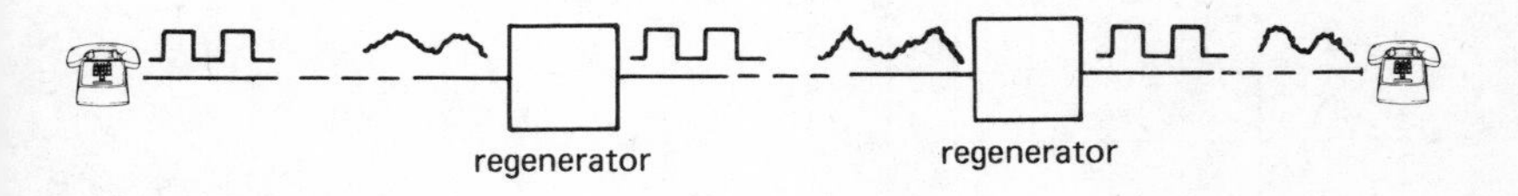

Figure 7.3. In a digital link, the signals are cleaned up by regenerators so that quality is maintained

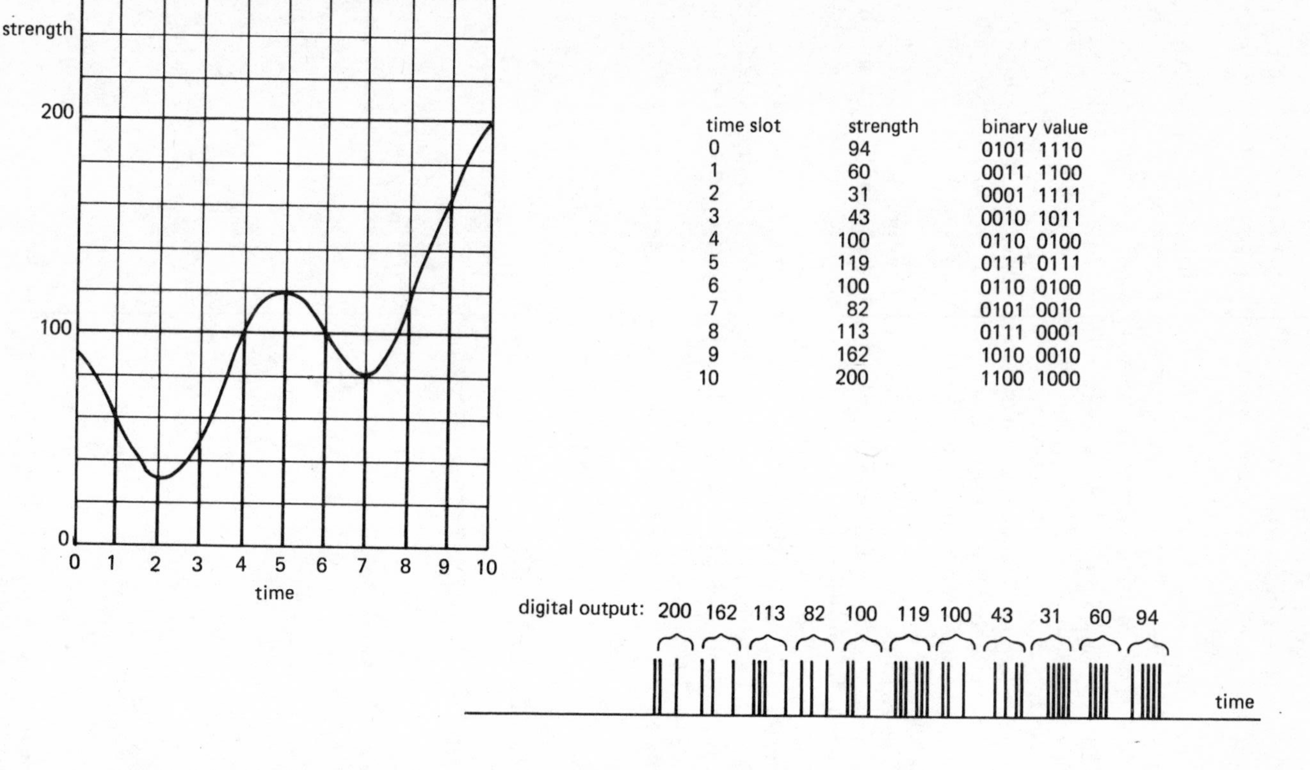

time slot	strength	binary value
0	94	0101 1110
1	60	0011 1100
2	31	0001 1111
3	43	0010 1011
4	100	0110 0100
5	119	0111 0111
6	100	0110 0100
7	82	0101 0010
8	113	0111 0001
9	162	1010 0010
10	200	1100 1000

Figure 7.4. Analog to digital conversion involves sampling the input wave 8000 times a second, and coding each measured value as a binary digital value

frequencies so they don't become mixed up. A single wire can therefore carry anything up to several thousand conversations at once by this frequency division multiplexing (fdm) method. As figure 7.5 shows, each speech signal that enters the trunk line has a spare base (carrier) frequency added to it. At the other end the system removes the carrier to leave the original wave form.

In the early days, local telephone systems were set up by private enterprise; only later did links to others appear. There is a vestige of this in Britain still, where the Kingston-upon-Hull exchanges, though no longer privately owned, are independent of British Telecom. Two benefits to the people there are that Hull's call rates are cheaper and the lengths of local calls are not metered.

In Britain as in most countries, private enterprise in telephony gave way to monopolistic nationalisation, with a single telecommunications organisation. In most cases that organisation is also the one that handles mail, although in the UK British Telecom separated from the Post Office a while ago, before being privatised in 1986.

Competition has been reintroduced here with the development of the separate Mercury telephone network. Generally Mercury competes with British Telecom only on trunk routes (with its cables laid

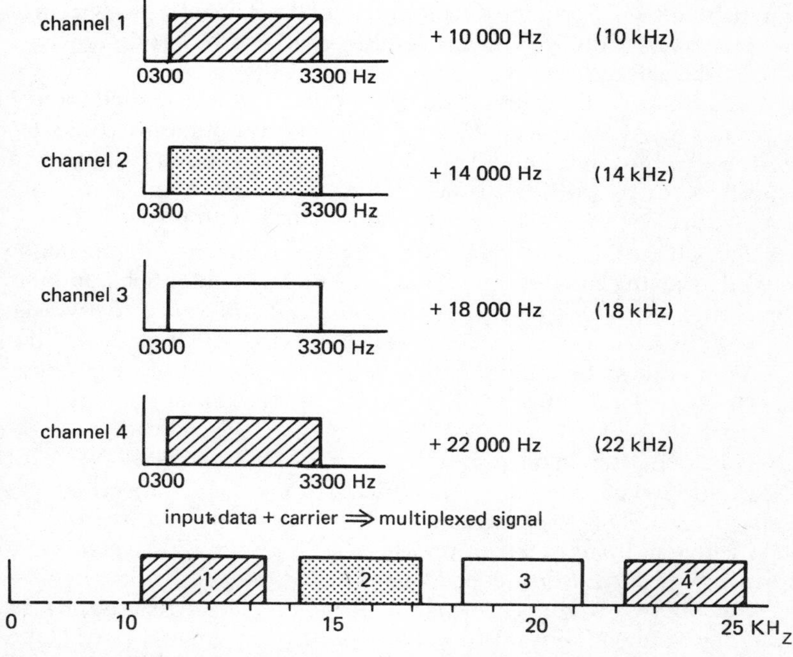

Figure 7.5 Frequency division multiplexing allows a single channel to carry a number of analog signals without interference

along the railways). Only for very large organisations is it normally worth considering Mercury rather than British Telecom unless, again, you're in Hull where, for each call any subscriber makes, the choice of network is on offer.

There are other electronic information transfer systems organised similarly to the telephone network, with some using it directly. Three of those – telex, fax and electronic mail – have been mentioned already. We'll look at all those other systems in detail in this chapter before going on to modern telephone systems.

7.1 Telex

Telex grew out of the telegraph system and the original telegraph owed its importance to the need for sending messages associated with the growing network of railways in the 19th century. It was a laborious and slow method of information transfer and was rather open to error. This was because it involved the manual keying of messages character by character using Morse code or similar. This code is built up of short and long pulses of current in the telegraph wire, with the transmitter's Morse key (a sort of simple switch) held closed for short or long periods.

A major advance was the development of the Baudot code system at the start of this century. Now the sender could use a sort of typewriter keyboard; each different key press automatically generated a five-bit combination (word) of current pulses or pulse absences, called 1 and 0 respectively. At the receiving end a special output unit could reproduce the message, either by punching holes in coded patterns in a paper tape or by putting readable characters directly on to a paper tape. Figure 7.6 shows these two methods of telegraphy.

Although the Baudot code system was a great advance, in one major way it caused the later telex network to lose a lot of potential: Baudot is a five-bit code, which allows no more than 64 different code words. Many of these are reserved for special effects like ringing a bell at the receiving end, so telegraphic messages could consist of only upper case (capital) letters, the 10 digits and a few common symbols and punctuation marks.

The next big step in telegraphy came in the 1930s when the concept of a public switched network, to which anyone could subscribe, was realised. Now, instead of there needing to be dedicated lines (one each way) between a pair of telegraph users (as in Figure 7.5), systems like those in Figure 7.1 were set up. This is telex ('telegraph exchange'), a switched network entirely separate from that used for telephony. Automatic transmission of messages using pre-punched paper tape appeared, as did the teletypewriter, with its output on sheet paper rather than tape.

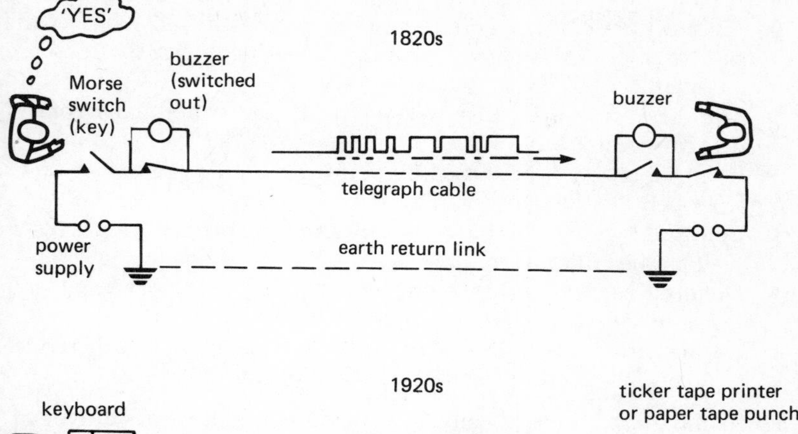

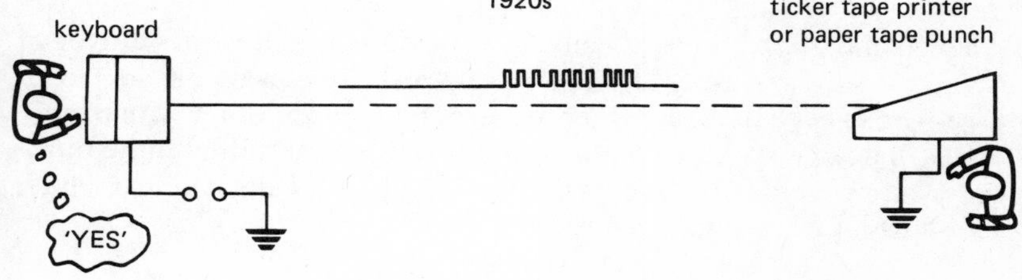

Figure 7.6 It took almost a century for the telegraph be become a user-friendly system

Until very recently telex has hardly changed since then, except that the number of users has grown to a current world figure approaching a couple of million. It works as follows:

Using a special telex terminal, a user with a keyboard prepares messages for transfer. Perhaps they are stored on punched paper tape. The sender dials the number of the receiver and switches the terminal to transmit. At the other end the terminal will acknowledge that it's ready, then take the call and print out the message. It may also prepare a punched tape at the same time. Telex reception is automatic, therefore, as long as the second terminal is connected to the line; there is a much lower degree of automation at the sending end.

In recent years a number of improvements have begun to appear, particularly with the very slow introduction of British Telecom's single channel voice frequency (scvf) standard. This involves new exchanges, new lines and new terminal equipment, which is why it is taking so long to become widespread.

If scvf brings all that people hope, the telex network of the 1990s may offer such features as these:

- A closer approach to automation at the sending end.
- A kind of exchange-based answering machine, in which you send a message to the exchange and that message goes to any caller.
- The ability to use the terminal keyboard keys rather than a rotary dial for calling out.
- Itemised billing, where the bills show the details and cost of each telex sent.
- Itemised logging, showing the date and time of each telex sent as well as the called terminal's code.
- Detailed reports on problems on the line if a telex can't get through.
- A full character set rather than the limited, upper case only range that follows from the use of the five-bit Baudot code.

All well and good, but in Britain the slow transition towards universal scvf is causing a number of problems. If you have new equipment in an area whose exchange and lines are old style, or the other way round, you will need a special adaptor. Another difficulty is due to the number of equipment suppliers on the market– it is not always clear which standard a given device meets.

7.2 On to teletex?

Meanwhile telex faces more and more competition from alternative systems of electronic information transfer. That competition is not just a threat; it is also a spur to telex to come up to date more quickly. Whether telex can (or should) survive in a world with so many more friendly alternatives is a question which cannot be addressed at this stage; however, the situation will become clearer within a few years.

The main strength of telex is those two million users. They are prepared to pay a lot of money to stay with a system they know and rely on.

Already modern telex terminals look to the user much like word processors connected to a special communications link. You can now prepare material offline (ie without being connected to the link), editing as much as desired, and recording the messages in a backing store for later despatch. You can give each message a priority rating, to determine its place in the queue when transmission starts; it is even possible to record the time it should be sent (though there's not a great deal of use for that feature).

Some terminals also allow multi-addressing: you can code a given message with several recipients' numbers and then have it sent to each without saving it more than once. The opposite of this is batching, where the system collects together all messages coded with the same address and sends them in one go.

During the offline message entry process it is possible that an incoming message will arrive. This should not interrupt the current task (or even abort it as was once possible); rather, the modern terminal will let the telex received be printed out and/or stored on the disc while the user gets on with the typing.

As far as telex despatch is concerned, the modern terminal may offer two new features as well as those just mentioned. The user may be able to address each message with a short code rather than in full, with the system keeping a list of the short codes and the full telex addresses. The second option is automated repeat of the calling and despatch process if the message doesn't get through first time. (As telex is slow, engaged lines are common, and having to keep on trying can be very time-consuming if done manually.)

Telex can nowadays even be used in 'chat mode', when the line between the two terminals stays open, so that messages can pass to and fro in turn. The advantage of this is the paper record of the whole 'conversation' that both parties end up with – telex machines print out both outgoing and incoming text.

All that may well water the mouths of managers used to working with traditional telex. Yet these modern telex terminals are far from cheap, and, although they are like computers superficially, they are *not* general purpose machines. For as little as half the price one can purchase a good stand-alone, general purpose micro with communications software quite adequate to let the user link with telex. And using telex remains a costly business itself, even if the number of messages in and out each day is high. Indeed, its only advantage over post is speed.

If you *are* in the high volume telex market (as a stockbroker or dealer, maybe), you may well find you have to explore the telex equivalent of the telephone switchboard (pbx, Section 7.5). This gives you the ability to link several telex terminals to several telex lines. Commonly the switching unit will contain the communications software and the backing storage disc drive; it is likely also to offer many of the features noted in the last few paragraphs.

However, for almost a decade now, teletex has been in the offing as a viable and much better alternative to telex. Teletex has undoubted advantages, yet it still remains only in the offing in most countries. (Just Canada, Sweden and West Germany have proper systems running at the time of writing in early 1987.)

Teletex is an international standard for information transfer between electronic equipment using the telephone network. Both aspects at once make teletex far cheaper than telex. There's no more need for special terminals, as any computer or word processor (or even electronic typewriter) can use the system if its communications software is teletex compatible.

Teletex has two other important features in its favour. The first is that data transfer is in units of eight rather than five bits; this allows a message to include a large range of characters. Second, data transfer can reach 50 words a second, whereas telex can't do much more than one. In addition, the use of the telephone network rather than the dedicated telex system makes things simpler and cheaper in many ways.

Maybe telex is definitely on the way out, then, despite those millions of users? It is important to mention an interesting development that could slow any decline. This is Interstream, a system linking the telephone and telex networks so that teletex users can transfer information to telex terminals and vice versa. The speed of information transfer has to be that of telex, though – one word a second. Again, the costs of using Interstream would seem high to a teletex user, not just as a result of the slow message speed, but because telex access and line charges would be added to what may well be long distance phone charges.

The crucial thing about teletex is that it *is* standard. Many features that are options in a modern telex terminal are the norm for teletex equipment, such as the various forms of detailed message logging, automatic re-try, and the ability to receive teletex messages while working offline on the preparation of outgoing ones.

7.3 Getting the fax

Facsimile transfer – called fax for short – is another fairly ancient technology that is now expanding fast in the general office market. Like telex and teletex, this kind of information transfer requires special equipment connected permanently to a switched communications line. Unlike telex, however, the standard telephone circuits are used, thus adding flexibility, increasing the potential user base, and cutting running costs.

Using fax is much like photocopying, except that the copy comes out from a different machine somewhere else in the world. There has been great growth in this market in recent years; standardisation, reduced costs, increased effectiveness, and improved features all combine to increase the number of users and the number of hardware suppliers. As the major competition is provided by courier services, it is easy to see the advantages of fax.

Figure 7.7 outlines the concept. At the sending end is a document reader; a light beam scans the original, in effect treating it as hundreds of rows of tiny cells which may be either light or dark. The light reflected from each cell becomes part of a digital electric signal (Figure 3.9). This

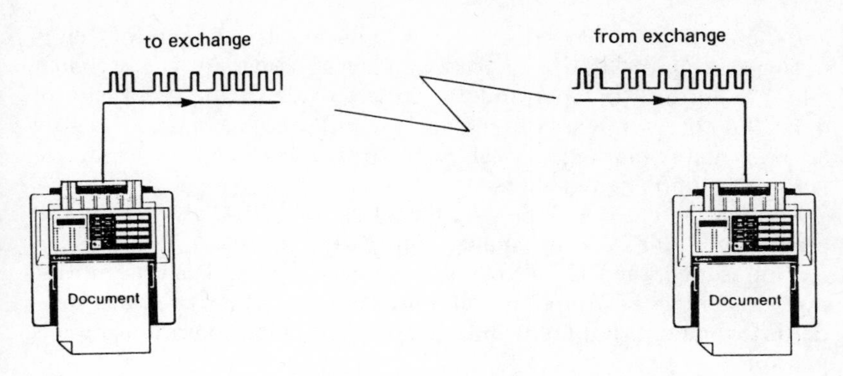

Figure 7.7 Facsimile transmission requires an open line between the sending and the receiving machines

passes through the switched telephone network to the receiver, which in turn reconstructs the original dot pattern on to a sheet of heat sensitive ('thermal') paper.

As with telex, the two special machines must be online at the same time. This means that the sender has to make the connection as required; in turn that implies that a fax machine ought to have its own telephone exchange line.

The strength of fax over telex and over the much more recent electronic mail (Section 7.7) is that copies of almost any kind of document can be transferred. The system can handle anything you can photocopy (though the output quality is not yet as good) – diagrams, graphs, signatures and other handwritten material, newspaper cuttings, computer printout, and so on. Historically, the major uses have been for the transfer of newspaper pictures (and more recently whole newspapers) and weather charts.

As far as costs are concerned, fax beats telex hands down too. With telex it is almost certain that the document will need to be retyped before transfer, and transmission is far slower. Modern fax links can transfer an A4 copy in much less than a minute – as little as 20 seconds or less; telex transfer would take several minutes, at higher call rates, to pass that much text.

All the same, the number of fax systems installed round the world is far below that of telex. Why is this, when fax has been around for over half a century?

Despite its long history, fax has been bedevilled by incompatibility problems. It took telex a century to reach the form in which we now recognise it; similarly, international fax standards are only a few years old. Since the breakthrough of standard setting, the growth rate of fax has accelerated significantly. The biggest increase is in Japan, which has something like 50 per cent of world users. (The reason for that is not hard to find – the Japanese character set does not easily match telex.) While only in Japan and the United States are there more users of fax than of telex, Britain is high on the international list, and is now facing a major marketing push from British Telecom and from the various equipment suppliers.

The equipment now being sold is all digital, although there is still plenty of older, slower analog equipment in use. The modern machines meet the CCITT Group 3 standard. Group 1 is now almost non-existent, but Group 2 is still quite common; these are both standards for analog equipment, but a fair degree of intercommunication is possible.

Computers are also digital in the signals that they use to transfer information. To connect a computer to the analog telephone network requires a modem, and it is just the same with a fax machine.

A modem, short for modulator/demodulator, is a type of equipment interface which converts input digital signals to analog and input signals to digital. Figure 3.8 shows the place of a modem in information transfer between computers using telephone links, while Figure 3.9 illustrates how analog and digital signals differ. In Figure 7.8 the function of a modem is shown in more detail.

As with an increasing number of computers, the modem needed for use with a fax terminal is built into the machine. The design fixes the maximum rate at which it can transfer information. This is often up to 9600 baud – 9600 bits (pulses and pulse absences, 1s and 0s) per second. In practice, however, the quality of the line joining two fax machines is relevant to the transfer rate, and transfer cannot be faster than what the slower of the two modems can handle.

On the other hand, if the line is high quality and the two fax machines are suitable, high transfer rates are possible. The time to pass through a copy of an A4 sheet can be brought down to as little as 12 seconds or so, and is quite likely to fall to a couple of seconds within a

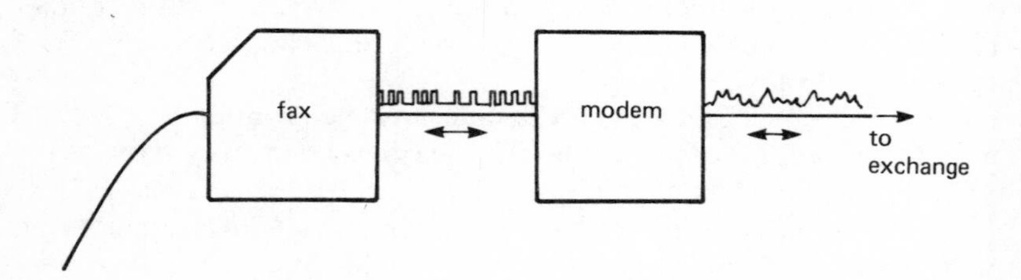

Figure 7.8. To convert electronic signals from digital to analog or vice versa requires a modem

few years. The real limit on fax copy speed is the quality of the line linking the two systems. As you will appreciate from your knowledge of modern photocopiers, it takes far less than a second to scan and code an A4 sheet. When line quality reaches a similar data handling rate, fast fax machines with automatic feeding of originals will become the standard; at the moment they are rare.

The norm for transfer of an A4 copy is still a minute, but this should rarely cause problems; it's still rather quicker than the mail, and far cheaper once the system has been set up. British Telecom publishes a directory of fax users (few offices with the facility yet put the details on their letterhead); you can, however, send faxed documents to non-users by way of the Bureaufax or Intelpost service.

Now we have looked at the main concepts of fax, it is worth noting some of the features that individual machines may offer. Again there is much in common with photocopiers.

Sending a copy in A4 size (or very occasionally the slightly larger B4) is the maximum at the moment. However, the ability to reduce an original from A3, say, to A4 is a common feature that costs little extra and is of value in many contexts, such as computer printouts and architectural drawings.

The opposite feature, to enlarge all or part of an original before transfer, is less common. For many users, however, it may be of even more value than reduction. If the line is poor, output quality may be poor. To enlarge material, it would help if one had a photocopier with these features; then they might not be quite so crucial in the choice of a fax machine.

Using enlargement is also a good way to send material with a lot of fine detail. (Remember that fax printout in the general market is nowhere near such high quality as photocopier output.)

Another method, offered by a number of machines, is to increase the resolution of scanning. The tiny cells are small enough to allow the system to resolve about eight dots per millimetre across the sheet and four downwards (see Figure 7.9(a)). If this is not enough to show fine detail, the machine may be able to switch to an 8 × 8 scan mode Figure 7.9(b)) or even better, but the line needs to be high quality for this.

To transfer material at even higher resolution you will need a better fax machine. The sort newspaper offices use are very high quality, and very costly to buy and run. However, such machines cannot send information through the normal telephone network, for this is just not adequate. The British Telecom packet switching system (pss, of which more later) has to be used instead. While this can be accessed through the telephone lines, it is not so cheap in use.

A big drawback of fax transfers is that each cell is treated as either black or white. If the original contains photographs, diagrams with shading, or second colour material, reproduction can suffer. Some fax machines now offer scanning and printing on a three-point scale – white, grey, black – which provides significant improvement in these special cases. Full colour fax is not far off, though it will be very costly when it first appears.

Aspects of automatic dialling are becoming common with telex, and, as appropriate, with voice telephone. The same applies to fax systems where, for instance, commonly used numbers can be stored for recall at the press of a couple of buttons on the keypad. Automatic re-try is also of value here as in the other two contexts; the system will keep attempting to get through if it receives an engaged signal. Telex-like original date stamping and log production are widely available too. Last number re-call and sending the material at a specified later time are further useful features on offer.

That last feature – delayed send – makes rather a nonsense of the widely marketed polling system. A fax terminal with a polling feature can automatically access a number of different machines in turn, send the required special password, and 'collect' any waiting fax transfer. Doing this needs a lot of advance preparation, including telephone calls in most cases, so is rarely worth the effort except for routine regular transfers between branches of big firms.

Of more value in these and similar situations is the ability to save the signal from a scanned document on to disc for later transfer. This may be of use if the same document is to be copied to a number of systems elswhere in the near future, or over a period (if it is a price-list that fax users may request, for instance). However, this feature does not mean you can connect a computer or word processor to the fax machine to transfer other forms of information. Such system flexibility, however obvious its value, is some way off yet.

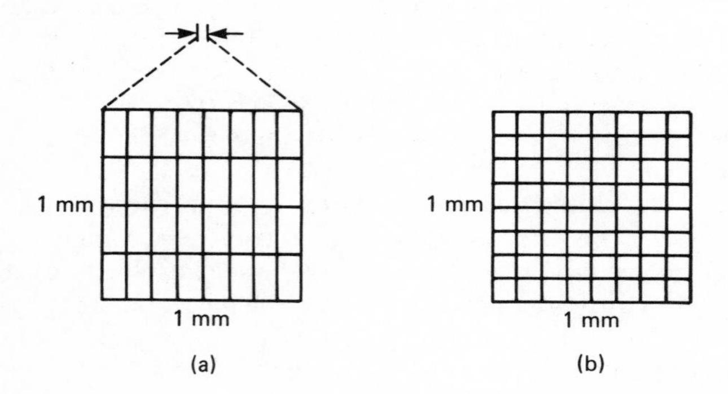

Figure 7.9. The detail of fax reproduction depends on the dot resolution of the scanner

There are, all the same, some exciting trends. In the near future we can expect, for instance, portable fax machines. Of special value to travelling staff, these could plug into a telephone socket anywhere, or even be used with the cellular radio telephone system (Section 7.9).

On the output side, the latest breakthrough is the ability to print on to plain paper rather than the special (but poor quality) thermal paper. Considering the poor quality of fax output (partly why fax documents are not yet accepted as having legal standing), it is surprising people have put up with it; after all, that poor paper costs several pence per A4 copy, swamping the equipment costs and telephone charges in all situations other than of very low usage. Again photocopier technology shows what can be done; there is absolutely no technical reason why we should have to restrict ourselves to the costly thermal system with its inherently poor output.

7.4 Getting the digits out

The question of the quality of the lines that carry information has appeared already in this chapter. It applies to the telephone system lines that carry fax signals and teletex messages and to those in the separate telex network. It applies too to voice signals transferred through the telephone network in the traditional way– and it is time to consider the subject of voice links.

All telephone users will be very much aware of the basic technology and of its main current limitations: wrong numbers, crossed lines, bad lines, delays in operator service, being cut off, and so on. Things have certainly improved greatly in recent years, and the main cause of the improvement is the change from analog signal transfer to digital. Figure 3.9 will remind you how analog signals differ from digital.

Speech is carried by sound waves, and is itself an analog signal. There's a lot of sense, therefore, in using an analog system for the electronic transfer of speech. The simple microphone in the handset converts the input sound waves (analog) to a wavy electric current (analog). This passes through the system of Figure 7.1, being amplified by repeaters every so often. At the receiving end the speaker (earpiece) in the handset converts the wavy electric current back to an analog sound wave.

The quality of the sound output by the speaker depends on various factors. Prime among these are the quality of the speaker itself and that of the microphone. Both devices are marvellously simple but of ancient design. They cannot handle signals with much fidelity, nor are they able to pass high frequencies (those of high pitched sounds) very well. Because of these limits the installed analog network does not itself need to be high quality– so it isn't. A major result of low quality in the system is line noise: the hisses, clicks and buzzes caused by interference.

Digital transfer – passing the signals in pulses rather than as wave forms – has many advantages. It is faster and can deal better with high frequencies; interference is reduced and line noise can be cut out; the lines are cheaper yet can carry far more traffic; automation can increase too.

Changing the country's system from analog to digital is a huge task, though, even at the rate of many kilometres of cable and several exchanges a week. The new cables are not made of lots of metal wires, but are bundles of hair-thin strands of very pure glass fibre. These cost much the same as copper cables, but the signals pass through them as light rather than as electric current; this feature, as much as going digital itself, is the cause of the huge potential improvements mentioned above.

Within a few years the digital networks of British Telecom and Mercury will be complete: the digital exchanges and optical fibre trunk lines will be universal. Analog elements will remain for much longer, admittedly, as it is not yet worth the cost of bringing an optical fibre line to every phone in the country.

Analog equipment, such as the standard telephone handset, will work just as well as before. However, only digital equipment will be able to give its users all the potential advantages. As digital equipment includes communicating computers, fax machines and teletex terminals, every office will be able to gain a great deal. In particular, data transfer rates will increase without problems, while data transfer costs fall.

7.5 Telephone equipment

The basic difference between a domestic telephone system and the type used in a business environment is that more than one incoming exchange line feeds the various business 'extensions'. That being so, a business system needs some form of switching arrangement, so that any given unit can access any given line. Figure 7.10 shows this difference; it applies whether the system is to carry voice signals only or is linked to data equipment.

The traditional method of filling the switching need is with a private branch exchange or pbx. The former term was pabx but the a, for automatic, is no longer needed as fully manual switchboards are now very rare indeed. A pbx is not truly automatic, however, as it still needs an operator.

The operator's main task is to accept calls that come in on the exchange lines and switch each one through to the correct extension. He or she will also need to connect the extension line for each out-

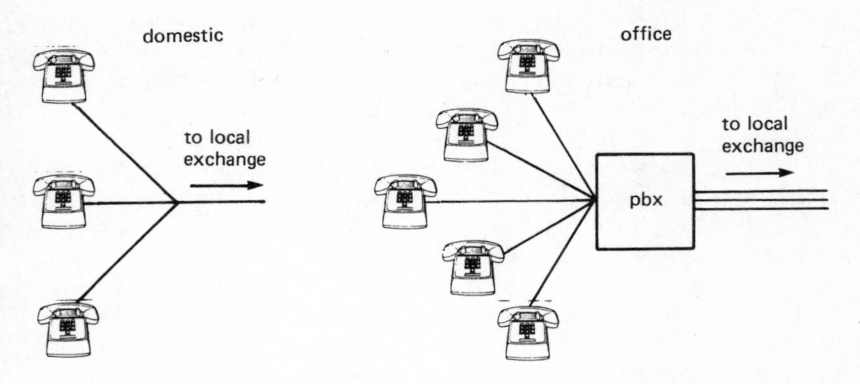

Figure 7.10. An office telephone system is more complex than a domestic one, as there is more than one line to the outside exchange network

going call to a free exchange line. In most cases this latter task is more often automated, in that dialling '9', for instance, at an extension will cause the switchboard circuit to connect a free outside line without the operator's aid.

The pbx is still the only way to handle systems with more than 50 or 100 internal lines, but for smaller units key systems are becoming common: each handset carries a key (button) for each exchange line, therefore the users in effect all become operators, with the ability to press a key to answer an incoming call or to make calls outside. The key system sounds as if it could present organisational problems, and indeed it does; it is fairly costly too. On the other hand, these new phones have a marvellous range of useful features, and this tends to make them better value for money.

That description makes things seem much more clear-cut than they are in practice. For a start, there are also systems which have a central pbx yet whose extension units offer some degree of key control. Then again, the loss of British Telecom's monopoly of equipment supply to users means that a highly competitive and rapidly changing market now exists.

Electronics, computers and telecommunications are, you recall, the three jigsaw pieces that make up information technology; they are coming together in the voice and data links of the modern telephone system. The system itself is a telecommunications network, allowing information transfer within a few seconds between any two of several hundred million units world-wide. Electronics is at the heart of all pbx boards and all modern telephone handset units (key or otherwise). Computers, with their element of general purpose programmability, are also coming in fast.

Outside the local level, the trend to a fully digital telephone network is moving to fruition at great speed. Although, as we have seen, voice signals are intrinsically analog, digital lines are of much higher quality. This means that the process of converting voice to a digital signal, passing it through the network, and changing it back to analog at the other end, still enables much better quality than the traditional fully analog method. At the same time, data from computers and fax units, for instance, is much more effectively transferred by a digital network.

It will be clear from this chapter that we are moving towards a single telephone network, able to transfer voice and data signals with equal ease and success. The 'old' system is called the public switched telephone network (pstn); to that, especially for data transfer, we currently add a partly separate packet switched system (pss) and a partly separate circuit switched public data network (cspdn). Within a decade or so there will be a single approach – the integrated services digital network (isdn) – and eventually that will span the globe. Already, a few computers come with speech telephone handsets and highly integrated software that can make the most of joint voice and data transfer. Using them, you can transfer data files and chat about them at the same time, thus the line may carry a spreadsheet table you want to hack about with a colleague elsewhere.

Partly in preparation for that integrated system, and partly as a spur to its rapid arrival, a fast increasing proportion of users' telephone equipment is now digital. This means more than push buttons to replace the dial and perhaps a liquid crystal display of the number called. It means the ability to store commonly used numbers in a chip and to recall them easily as required. It means programmability, and a whole host of other useful features.

One important point must be made: a multi-function extension telephone is a complex device to learn to use. As with any complex electronic device, one must study what to do and how to do it, and then practise. Surveys show that many people avoid using more than two or three features of their new phones, yet still demand more and more. In fact, some people even ask for features that their phone actually offers already! When you have looked through the rest of this section, you may like to sit back and build up in your mind a picture of the unit you would ideally like to have on your desk. Then you can try to find out if such a machine actually exists.

Memory features are very common, even in domestic handsets. They include the storage of numbers used often (from 10 to 100 in total), with access to any of these by way of two or three simple key presses. There is the ability to re-call the last number 'dialled' (or, in some cases, any one of the last few). Some systems even have automatic re-try, calling several engaged numbers in turn again and again until the connections have all been made.

Intercom facilities are offered in most modern pbx and key phone systems. A user can thus call another extension, again usually with only a couple of key presses, without either going through an operator or setting up the connection by a process of hand waving across the room. Conference calls are a variety of this; several people, on some combination of internal and exchange lines, can discuss a topic together without leaving their desks. (A rather similar national service is teleconferencing, considered in Section 7.9.)

Call transfer also relates to the use of extensions. This is the facility whereby you can transfer a call to a different unit without going through an operator or losing the connection. Your being able to pass the buck in this way is not, however, automatically welcomed by the caller, even if the system plays soothing (but rarely appropriate) music during the waiting periods.

Programmability can offer a lot here. Fairly simple systems allow different extensions to be able to receive calls at different times of day (or night); with others, units can be grouped so that if a call to one extension meets the engaged signal or isn't answered within a few seconds, the call transfers to another phone in the group. Then again, you may be able to program your unit to transfer all calls to another one until further notice – when you're off sick, for instance, or having a meeting at someone else's desk.

Related to all these uses are such features as lights which show which exchange lines and/or extensions are engaged; the ability to break into a conversation on another extension (and a warning signal when someone does it to you!); and a signal that another person is trying to connect to your extension when you are using it. That person may even be able to 'camp' on your phone, so that the system makes the connection as soon as you finish your current call.

Hands-free operation is welcomed by all people who have experience of it. While aircraft pilots and telephone exchange operators have long been able to use comfortable two-way communications headsets, it is strange that the far from convenient or efficient design of the telephone handset has changed little for decades. Various approaches to hands-free – and even shoulder-free – operation are at last on the way.

With hands-free dialling (a silly phrase really), the user doesn't need to pick up the handset until the call is answered. The handset remains in place while the number is called, and a small speaker lets you hear the ringing tone; when there is a response it is time to pick up the handset and start your conversation.

A development of this is to have a separate microphone and a better speaker. Then the conversation itself can take place without your raising the handset. Not only does this provide free hands for other tasks during telephone usage, but it lets other people listen, and even join in easily. The corollary is a loss of privacy, but with such systems you can still pick up the handset if you prefer to talk privately in the traditional way. There are other problems with speaker phones, especially with those (half duplex) types that allow speech in only one direction at a time.

Another feature of hands-free phones, that can cause some annoyance, is that they can be used for paging or even general announcements. Alarm call facilities may be almost as bad, with the phone ringing automatically at two o'clock each afternoon to wake you after a heavy lunch, for instance.

Logging involves giving the user details about each call made. The information supplied can range from a liquid crystal display of the number currently accessed, to a paper printout of the destination, time, duration and cost of each call. To obtain printouts of any detail, you will need an interface in the extension or pbx concerned, to which you can connect the printer or special call logger unit (Section 7.6).

If you don't want to go so far, note that a few phones have the facility for showing on their liquid crystal display the mounting cost of the current call. This feature needs programmability: you will have to tell it, often with a special punched card, the different current call rates, and to change the details when charges go up. It also needs an internal clock, for phone call rates depend on day and time of day. However, many phones with liquid crystal displays will show the time when they are not in use.

Most of the features noted above – and the list isn't complete – are available in both pbx and key systems. However, they are generally best when under individual extension control. Thus, if you want easy use of such modern features, a key system is the one to go for.

7.6 Ancillary telephone equipment

Increased competition in the British telecommunications market has opened these systems wide. Not so long ago an answering machine was a large ugly box that cost a huge sum to rent and was inflexible in use. Now you can buy such systems over many counters at not much more than the cost of a simple tape recorder; modern equipment is compact, pleasing to the eye, and versatile.

The simplest machine, when connected to an exchange or extension line in parallel to a handset, will answer the phone if you don't and play through the line an announcement previously recorded on a tape. The next step up is to allow the caller to leave a message in response, though cheaper devices will cut this off after, say, half a minute. The most sophisticated telephone answering machines now on the market allow the owner to select which of several announcements to leave ready before departing, and to have yet another message for when the recording tape is full of incoming messages. Perhaps you can call in from elsewhere, and scan through the recordings. In this case you may even be able to tell the machine to switch to a different opening announcement.

Some answering systems incorporate features of other types of equipment. Thus you may be able to record ordinary telephone conversations, and/or to use the device as a transcription (dictation) unit. That last feature will need the unit to have sockets for the audio typist's headset and foot control, but makes it easy to have hard copies made of voice messages and telephone conversations. The legal position of recording your calls is unclear, however.

Another telephone answering machine feature allows it to be linked with the British Telecom radio paging service. This means that your pocket bleeper will signal that a message awaits you; you can then (if you wish) call your answering machine and hear what's new.

The main problem with the current designs of answering machine is that they can work on only one line at a time. We need a design like that of some central ('pool') dictating machines, with several separate cassettes able to record incoming messages at once. The problem is not really that one expects to have a number of people ringing in on different lines at a given moment, but there is a general need to be able to field calls on more than one exchange line without losing contacts.

Some solutions to this problem are now available, but none is satisfactory. Many firms therefore prefer to use human answering bureaux; apart from the cost and administrative difficulties, these cannot easily offer a properly tailored service as they are of course handling the calls of a number of clients at the same time. British Telecom's standard call transfer systems may be a better solution until more suitable equipment appears.

These call transfer services are much like the programmed call transfer mentioned above as a feature available on some office telephone systems. Provided either by exchanges that have gone digital or by an extra item of hardware in your own system, the services are too costly for common use. Their value is to people running small businesses who would otherwise have to fall back on an answering bureau when they're not around, or who are prepared to have their calls transferred to, for instance, their private number out of office hours. (Incidentally, the Star service offered by digital exchanges can include a lot more than call transfer – many other key system features are also there to be explored.)

Finally, note the existence of Voicebank, of particular value to firms in London (though usable from any part of the country). This is British

Telecom's telephone answering machine service, on which up to seven incoming messages of up to half a minute each can be stored for you at a time. Each user has a remote control to allow him or her to call in and listen to the messages and/or change the announcement, while a bleeper can also be supplied for paging by radio when a call comes in.

Another type of ancillary equipment for phone lines that is fast growing in popularity is the logger. This provides a full record of all outward calls made on the line(s) to which it is linked; it thus allows management to see how their huge phone bills are actually built up. The information provided can help in campaigns for the staff to cut phone usage costs and to rationalise usage in general, as well as aiding your attempt to query phone bills if you suspect your meter at the exchange is faulty. A logger report is also useful if you wish to pass individual call charges on to various clients.

In due course, British Telecom and Mercury will provide itemised phone bills anyway, so that do-it-yourself call logging may not be so helpful. Also the cost of a logger to provide really helpful breakdowns is high, so it may be better to rent one for a short period.

7.7 Electronic mail

The term 'electronic mail' includes teletex (Section 7.2) as a way of allowing information transfer between computers. Here we shall consider the more restricted use of the phrase in the context of store and forward systems.

Sometimes working under the name of electronic mail bureaux, these systems allow a user to send a message or a longer text for a second user to a central storage computer (host) that can be viewed as having lots of pigeon holes for the purpose. When the other user next connects to the system, a notice will show that there is mail in the pigeon hole.

Electronic mail in this sense, therefore, is cheap (as it uses high speed transfer through the telephone network), but its efficiency in practice depends on how often the users check their mail boxes. While enthusiastic subscribers describe the Post Office's paper-based system as snail mail, electronic mail is not speedy and reliable if recipients don't often check if there's anything for them.

Electronic mail bureaux often provide other services as well as mail box control, partly to encourage their members to log on as often as possible, partly to encourage more people and firms to join, and partly to increase profits. Thus electronic mail is only a small part of what's on offer from Britain's main bureaux of this type, such as Telecom Gold and One to One. More of these other (database) services can be found in Chapter 10, but it is worth noting here that letting their members link to the telex system is a very powerful incentive to join bureaux, even if (as sometimes happens) telex 'mail' attracts an extra charge.

Of course, all the costs of electronic mail have to be considered with care anyway. You may already have a computer, but you also need a modem (priced from a few tens of pounds to over a thousand) as well as suitable communications software (perhaps £50–£100). Those once-off capital costs are likely to be fairly small in comparison with that of the rest of your hardware and software, however.

Running costs can be far more significant. There will be a membership subscription for using the system and (in most cases) a charge based on the time you are online to the host computer. If you use the computer to store data of your own (including keeping messages received once you've looked at them), there's likely to be a rental to pay, while additional costs may also appear.

Finally, there are the phone charges. These can build up just as fast for data communication as for speech conversations. Most systems of any value are, however, accessible by local rate phone calls from most parts of the country. This is so even if there is only one host computer; it has links to nodes in different regions, so all you need do is call the nearest node to get online.

There are drawbacks to electronic mail, then, in comparison with the far more costly telex and fax routes to rapid information transfer. However, as long as the people to whom you send messages check fairly frequently (say, twice each working day) then it does beat 'snail mail' for both speed and low cost. As the user base grows, it will become more and more effective.

7.8 Triumphs of technology

Figure 7.11 gives a picture of the various telecommunications techniques described in this chapter.

A few decades ago the public telephone network and that used for telex were quite separate. Now there are growing links between them, and the telephone network handles more and more types of traffic. The result of these trends ought to be a single network with interfaces (sometimes called gateways) between the various functions.

Britain is working towards a single telephony system, able to carry voice and data traffic without distinction. Its name is the integrated services data network (isdn). This will be the digital system already mentioned and it will be part of a world-wide common carrier (see Figure 7.12).

While being cable-based has been noted as a criterion of the telephony networks discussed here, that is not to say that all information is carried by electric currents. Much of modern digital transfer is by electromagnetic radiation in optical fibres or through microwave

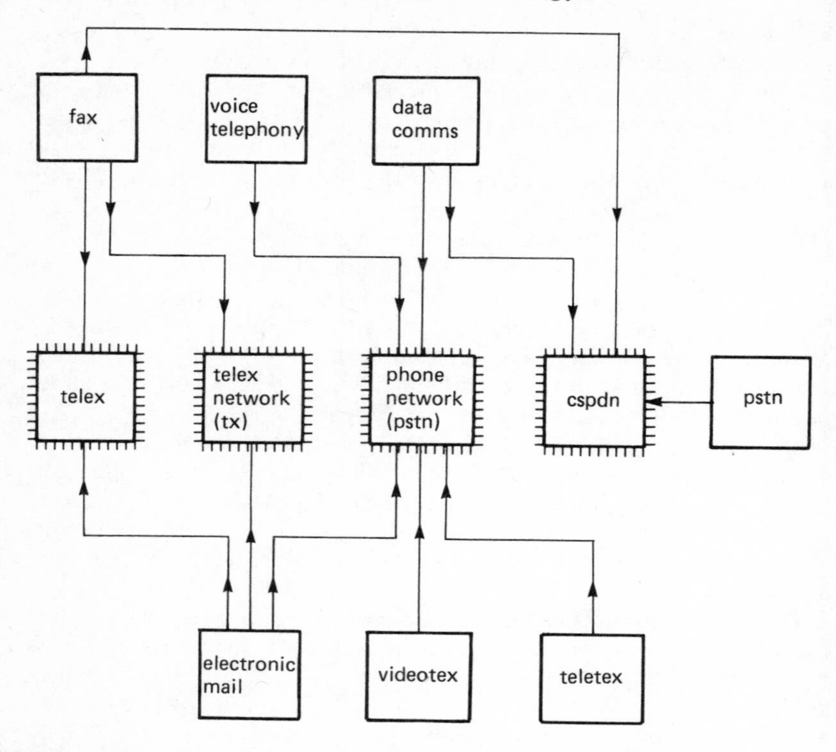

Figure 7.11. There are various public cable-based telecommunications systems

links, while radio also plays a part (particularly in the context of mobile and other wireless telephones). Indeed, it is not widely known that the amateur radio system has developed excellent techniques for digital data transfer; maybe this will also gain gateways to the public telephone network in due course.

The circuit switched public data network (cspdn) is specially designed for major users of digital information communication. For each data transfer, a circuit is set up in just the same way as for voice telephony (Figure 7.1); at each end, however, is an item of digital hardware rather than a person. There are many growth areas for cspdn: as well as teletex communication between computers, there are the rapidly expanding needs of electronic funds transfer, credit card authorisations, and computer booking traffic to handle. Here are some examples.

Automatic teller machine (atm) is the name for the electronic terminals fitted into the high street walls of many banks and building societies.

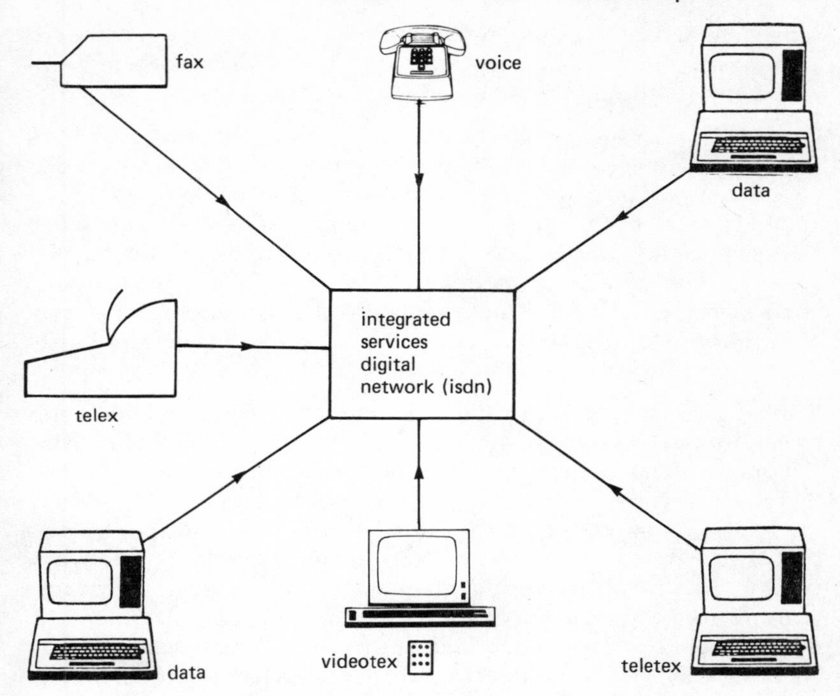

Figure 7.12. Eventually an integrated services data network will carry all voice and digital signals

These are terminals in that they can link to distant mainframe computers. While the terminal's own (local) processing power can deal with verifying the user's cash or credit card and issuing bank notes, services such as displaying the balance in the user's account or ordering a statement or cheque book need data transfer. The terminal will then call for a line to the central computer to allow the information exchange to take place.

Electronic funds transfer (eft) is also growing fast. By putting your plastic card into a terminal rather like an automatic teller, you can already obtain fuel from unstaffed petrol stations in several parts of the country. In some areas too, retail outlets are taking the same kind of system on board. Here the shopper inserts the card and keys in his or her personal identification number (pin). The terminal links to the till at the point of sale (pos) and to the bank's computer; effortlessly the till total transfers from the shopper's account to that of the trader. If the shopper's card is a 'smart card' – one with a chip inside it instead of, or as well as, a magnetic stripe on the back – the card can keep an ongoing record of transactions and balance for later printout or display on a screen. In this context, though, the important thing is the use of the circuit switched public data network to transfer the data that represents cash between the till terminal and the banks' computers.

Computerised booking (telebooking) is offered by Prestel and we'll return to it in that context in Chapter 10. At the moment, however, it is far more important in the daily work of specialist companies like travel and theatre agents. Again the cpsdn provides the crucial links. When someone visits a travel agent to book a flight, it is likely now that the agent will be able to key in the relevant information and questions and confirm the best available booking at once. To do that requires a communication link to the airline's computer, which stores and keeps up to date the current status of all flights.

Each such communications link needs to be two-way (so called duplex or half-duplex), as information transfer in both directions is involved. Keeping a circuit open for the duration of the call makes a lot of sense therefore, as is the case with a voice telephone conversation. Where the transfer is basically one-way, however, it is much cheaper to use a packet switching service (pss, or packet switched public data network, pspdn). This breaks down the stream of data that's being sent into uniform compressed chunks; each such 'packet' gains a header with the recipient's address code and the packet number, and a tail of checking data bits. Computer software in the exchanges from moment to moment decides the best route for each packet to use, and interleaves the packets with those that carry data from other sources.

Figure 7.13 compares the circuit and packet switching of data transfer, although the packet switching is much simplified, in that the sketch shows all the packets from a given source following the same route. In practice, however, there are always a good number of possible routes between two points, and as the volume of traffic along any one will vary all the time, the system computers decide the best route for each packet. At the far end there is software to join the packets together in the correct order, so reconstituting the original stream of data.

Some examples of high volume, one-way data transfers that benefit from packet switching follow. That is not to say that pss is reserved for truly high volume, one-way transfers: as the packets are fairly small and the control software is highly effective, it is sometimes even of value to interact with Prestel this way. However, pss really comes into its own with the transfer of data in bulk, as with a long report between two offices, research data from one laboratory to a second, data from a major public database, or book texts between publisher and typesetter.

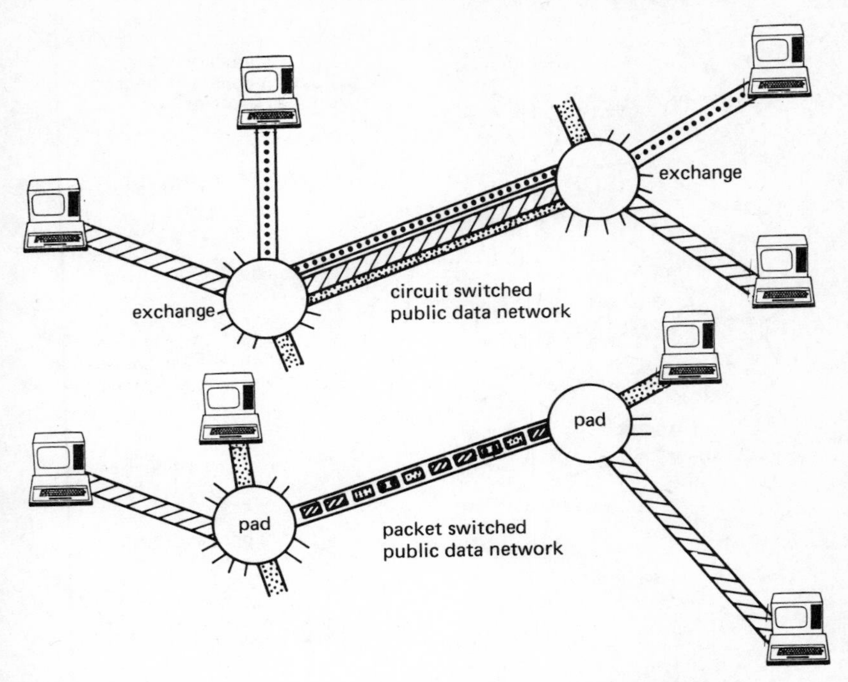

Figure 7.13. Two-way data transfer is best by a circuit switched network; packet switching allows one-way transfers to be made very efficiently

7.9 Mobile telephones

There has long been a need for communication between people who move around a lot. Traditionally, these needs have been met by radio (wireless telegraphy) in military contexts, for vehicle drivers (taxis, trains, buses) and ship-to-shore, and for the police and emergency services. Links with the conventional telephone system were difficult and costly if not almost impossible.

As far as a modern mobile telephone user is concerned, there should be no difference in practice between the instrument used and that in the office. Two-way conversations should be possible, and the actual geographical positions of the people involved should not be relevant (as long as they are within the area covered by the system). All the usual telephone services should be available to mobile users, even if they have to accept much higher costs for the convenience.

The mobile telephone system being developed in Britain has the name cellular, because the areas covered are thought of as being made up of separate small cells. As the user moves from cell to cell, the radio

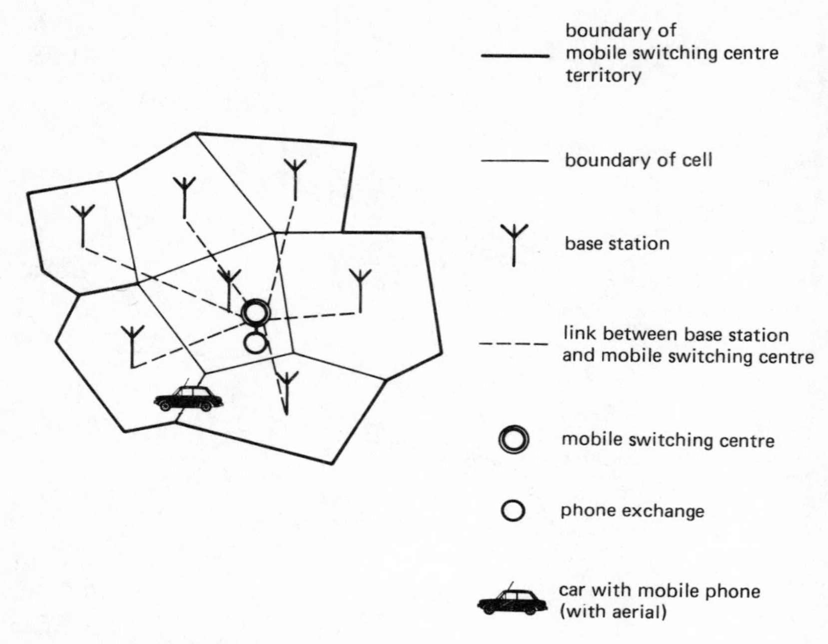

Figure 7.14. Mobile telephone users move between geographically small cells served by separate aerials

telephone link switches from one central transmitter/receiver to a second while the call continues without interruption. Figure 7.14 shows the arrangement.

The base station at the centre of each cell in a group, with its separate radio transmitter/receiver and aerial, connects to a mobile switching centre (msc). Despite its name, this is fixed. It is the equivalent of a conventional telephone exchange; indeed, it is linked to such an exchange, so that calls can pass between mobile and other subscribers, as in Figure 7.15.

The high costs of using a mobile telephone are partly due to the complex equipment in the network. However, the system has a lot of monitoring to do, in order that the position of each subscriber is always easy to find, and that task is also costly because a given mobile telephone has a unique number that doesn't depend on its position at any time. The system still works by giving each phone a 'home' exchange in the mobile network. The home exchange must at all times keep a record of which mobile switching centre's area each of its instruments is in. This is done by linking the phone to the nearest base

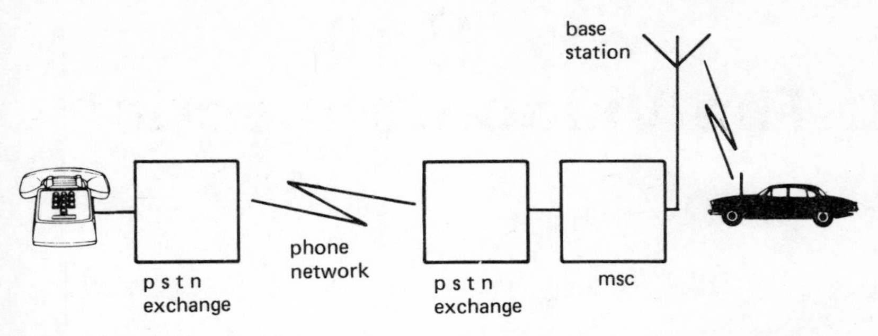

Figure 7.15. The mobile telephone service links closely to the standard network so that users can keep in touch

station by a control channel. Typically, a base station can handle no more than a few dozen control channels, so the maximum number of mobile calls in a given cell at a given time is quite low. (The limit is a result of the fairly small range of frequencies that can be used; frequency division multiplexing needs at least 4000 Hz for each signal in each direction.) This is one reason why cells are small; another is the range of the radio signals, restricted particularly in heavily built-up areas.

Still, maybe the days of the mobile executive with his or her mobile telephone are numbered. This book has already hinted how information technology could extend the home into a workplace at the centre of a web of modern communications. With telecommuting it is possible to stay indoors and use a terminal to link to whatever computer systems may be needed. Teleconferencing is the equivalent within the telephone system.

Using a teleconference link, more than two people can take part in a telephone conversation at once (see Section 7.5). True teleconferencing is similar, but all the people concerned are on outside lines.

Currently such calls are arranged manually by British Telecom; in the systems on trial at the moment, an 'operator' listens in to the conference to ensure even technical quality and to deal with any problems. Among the problems is the fact that as the callers cannot see each other, 'chairing the meeting' and keeping control are not easy. The more people taking part, the more the conference needs discipline. One way round such problems is to use videoconferencing instead, but that is less convenient and more costly (see Chapter 8.)

However, the high quality integrated digital telephone network of the near future is sure to play a major role in this move away from excessive travel. Whether telecommuting, teleconferencing, mobile telephones, or videoconferencing become prime factors in that trend remains to be seen.

8 The Video Connection

Video and video technology cover much more than broadcast television. They already play such an important part in the information revolution that some people put them in the information technology trilogy: computers, video and communications, rather than computers, electronics and communications.

Video has an obvious role in the monitors that flicker all around the electronic office, but it has other less obvious functions that will grow in importance. Local production, cable services and interactive video are the main such areas covered in this chapter; Chapter 10 has more.

8.1 Television background

With the average Briton spending, it seems, some 25 hours a week in front of the tv set, it is clear that this communications medium has by far the most influence on people's lives. This has long been known to marketing experts, as well as to the people who control the media.

In this context the tv set is the crucial part of the system. In essence, it is a simple device for taking in a certain type of electrical signal and turning the information carried into an image (or frame) on the screen. The system replaces (refreshes) that frame 25 times a second and if new information comes in fast enough, moving pictures result.

Various kinds of hardware can feed information to a tv set, as Figure 8.1 shows. All the system needs is the right kind of signal and an adequate rate of information transfer.

Around the world there are three different video broadcast standards. Each requires its own types of camera, recording and transmission systems, and tv set. The standard used in Britain is called pal, secam covers France, the Soviets and their satellites and the Middle East, while North America and Japan use ntsc. The systems are not

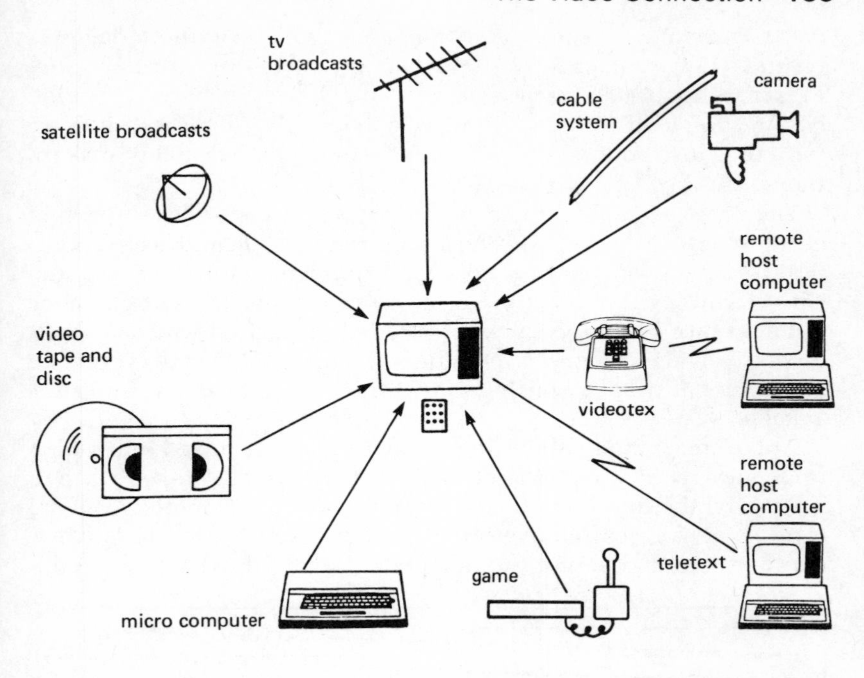

Figure 8.1. A tv set can accept information, in suitable form, from many sources

entirely incompatible; they overlap little in practice, however, and there are now moves to devise for the next century a world-wide standard that will also provide better pictures. There is a growing need for this universal standard (high definition television, hdtv); this includes the fast increasing demand for the transfer of information in video form across borders. That demand is not just for broadcast and video tape material; it is also for computer data, software and graphics, for a video channel can also carry these with ease. Transfer of Prestel pages to the USA, for instance, is complex because of the need to change between video standards on the way.

The illusion of a moving image on screen results from our persistence of vision: our eyes cannot detect flicker at rates above a few tens a second. In the same way as a cinema film is really a series of still pictures projected at a rate of 48 per second, so too is a tv picture.

Inside the tv tube a beam of high energy electrons swings to and fro and up and down at great speed. Where the beam hits the special coating inside the front of the tube (the screen) the energy produces a point of light. The brightness of the light depends on the number of electrons hitting the screen at that moment, while the colour depends on the coating. As Figure 8.2 shows, the spot covers the screen by moving across hundreds of times while moving down slowly. It reaches the bottom after a fiftieth of a second then jumps back to the top again, to start the next field (screenful of information). Two fields make a frame.

The analog signal that comes into the set to control the swinging electron beam has two parts: the luminance, which handles the brightness of the spot, on a grey scale from white to dark; and the chrominance, which adds the colour information. The chrominance signal in turn has three parts, the strength of each of which controls respectively the red, green and blue make-up of the spot. It is possible to produce any hue by mixing those three primary video colours in a suitable way.

At the transmitter, all this information has to be mixed into a high frequency radio wave (the carrier) so the system can send it out. Therefore, the first thing the tv set has to do to the amplified signal from its aerial is to remove the carrier and separate the luminance, chrominance and sound (audio) parts. Mixing these three compo-

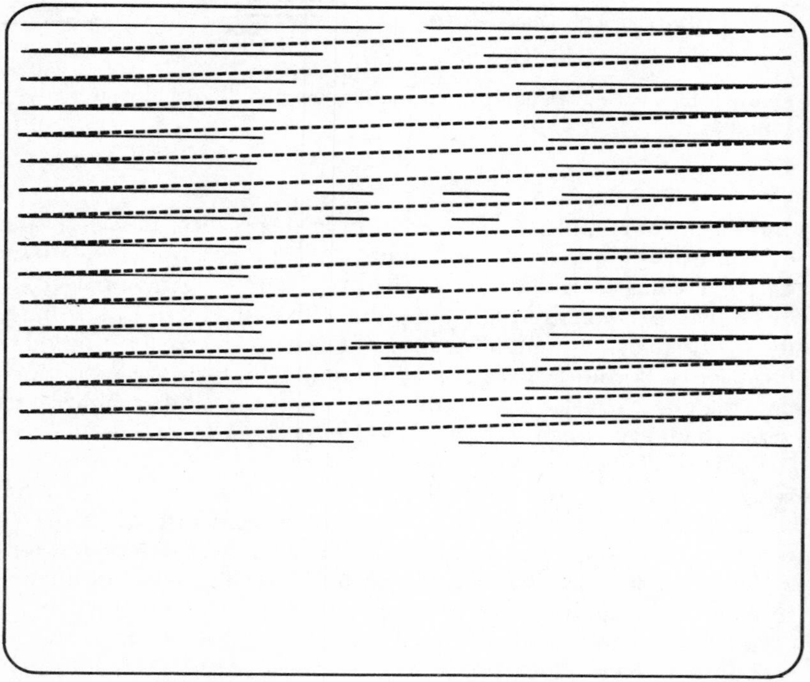

Figure 8.2. A video image is formed by a fast-moving changing dot of light

nents and adding the carrier at the transmitting end, and doing the reverse in the tv set, takes quite a lot from the quality of the broadcast information. A computer monitor can give a better picture as it takes in the pure luminance and chrominance signals direct from the computer. (Most monitors do not have a speaker, to make things even simpler; a computer's audio output feeds a separate speaker near the keyboard or in the case.)

A single video frame contains a huge amount of information because it contains in effect some half million cells (pixels, or picture cells), each of which needs brightness and red/green/blue control. To produce a screen image as good as a broadcast colour tv picture would need around half a megabyte of data in analog form, or several times more if digital. The latter would involve more storage than microcomputers offer, far more than a typical floppy disc too. People use various means to get round this problem; the normal way to show computer graphics is to reduce the resolution of the output greatly by treating a block of pixels as the unit.

Lack of enough storage to handle high quality pictures is a major drawback of most current computers. Other techniques of linking computers and video are therefore applied. We will return to them shortly, but first we need to consider closed circuit tv (cctv), which involves making and using video material on a local scale.

You may know about the hardware that you can use with a tv set or monitor in a closed circuit system. The basic layout of camera, recorder and display appears in Figure 8.3. The uses of closed circuit tv in business include the production of video tapes for training, marketing and sales, as well as site surveillance, for security perhaps.

The quality of the cctv hardware now in the domestic market is remarkable and is quite suitable for simple business use. For a couple of thousand pounds you can obtain a system like that in Figure 8.3 and produce quite acceptable video material, in colour and with sound. A similar sum will buy you a good security system with several cameras and displays, in black and white and without sound or a tape recorder.

The basic cctv unit of Figure 8.3 is quite good enough for simple internal communications films. Internal (or corporate) communication is traditionally by way of notices and news sheets, but video tapes for the same purpose – keeping all staff in touch with what is going on – are now quite common too. Training is another important use of cctv: people learning new skills, such as dealing with clients, can be taped with a basic cctv system so that they can later study themselves in detail with the training staff.

For sales and marketing, however, the films that result from the use of a simple cctv pack are far too amateur for the sophisticated viewing public. In such contexts you need (at least) two or three cameras with proper mobile stands; a tape recorder that allows editing; hardware

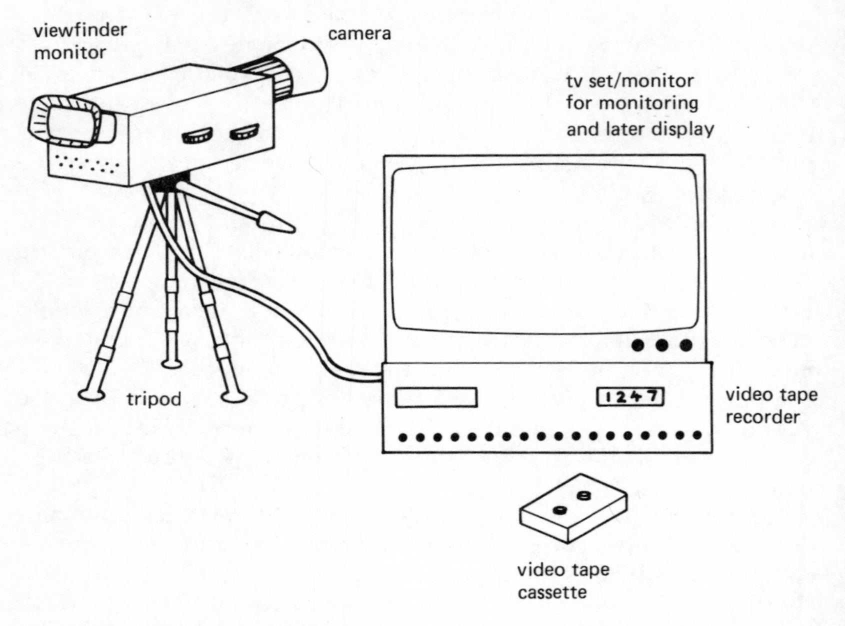

Figure 8.3. The basic closed circuit tv system comprises camera, recorder and display

such as a mixer, caption system and a simple special effects unit; and trained production staff. Large companies often have their own video studios and teams; smaller ones will turn to special firms when they need quality material. Either way, the use of video in business is widespread.

8.2 Video discs

In the same way as the audio market offers discs as well as tapes, so these two media are available for video and the features are much the same; however, as far as marketing is concerned, it is very relevant that in the audio field discs appeared long before tapes, while the reverse is the case with video. In both cases, you can re-record on tape, so tape is a read and write medium but disc material is read-only. In both cases too, access to a particular item on tape requires winding through from the start (serial access) while you can find material on disc by direct access – going straight to it (as long as you know where it is). Figure 8.4 compares the two media; it does so for video, but the picture for audio does not differ greatly.

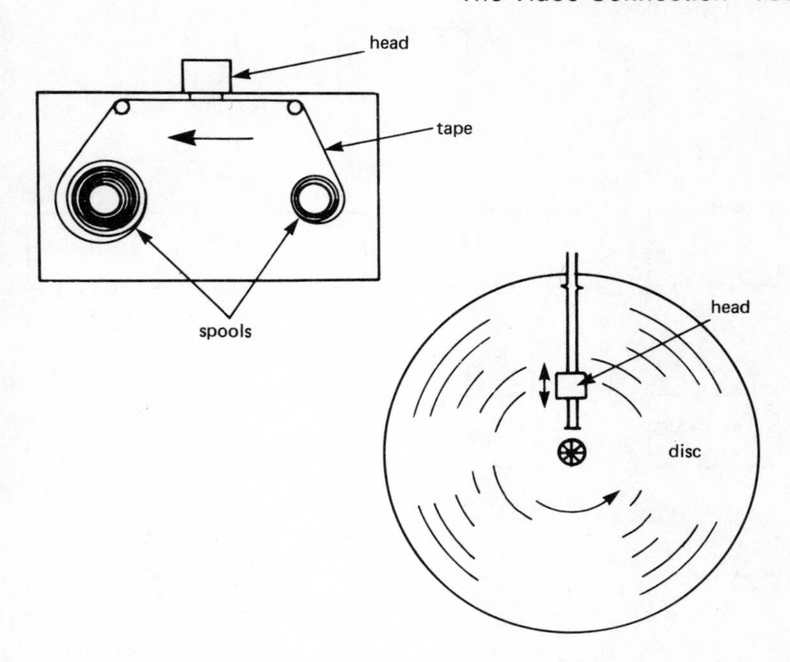

Figure 8.4. Video tape, like audio tape, offers only serial access, but you can write to it; video discs, like audio discs, allow direct access but are read-only

Video technology is newer than audio, and as a result there are still problems of incompatibility. (In fact, video discs are not *very* new – John Logie Baird first designed some 60 years ago, and they were on sale in the 1930s.) Two main video disc standards exist for the pal hardware used in Britain – the two in the centre of the bottom row in Figure 8.5.

The video high density (vhd) system uses a read head that touches the disc surface and detects variations of capacitance as it slides along. Two spirals of shallow pits cover the surface. One set keeps the read head on course and the other stores the data in analog (or, in some cases, digital) form.

Laservision, the reflective optical video disc system, also uses pits in the surface. This time, though, the read head glides over the surface without touching it; a laser and photo-cell in the head detect the pits and the lands between them, and measure their sizes by reflected light. Again this gives an analog or digital output, depending on the system.

The two video disc techniques found in Britain are totally different; in use they contrast in various ways. The vhd format allows half an

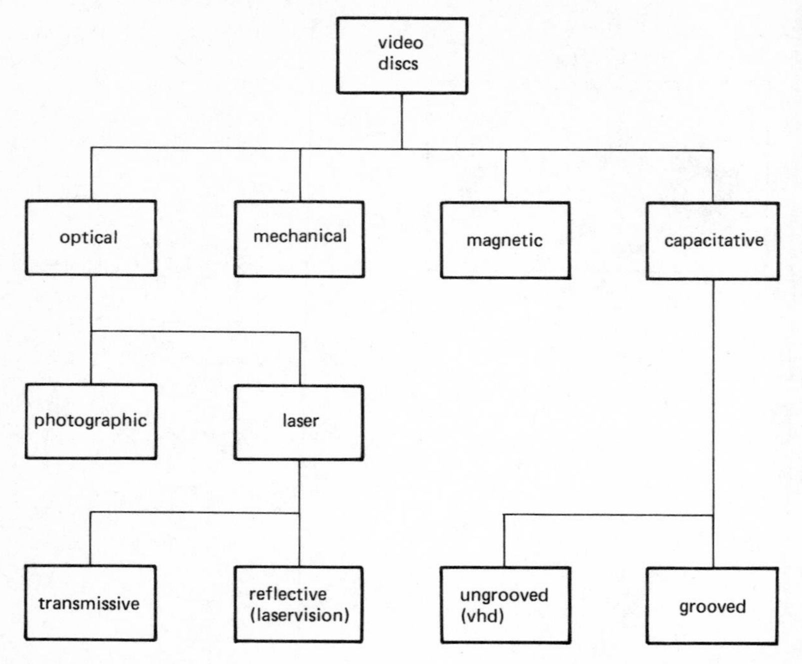

Figure 8.5. Several types of video disc exist, the two boxed being in use in Britain

hour of high quality video on each side. That's 90,000 frames in total, any of which you can access with no more delay than a second or two. However, the vhd disc stores two frames for each revolution; that is, when the disc goes round once, the head will access two frames. The result of this can be a blur or flicker when you try to view a single frame – you are really seeing two that alternate very fast. The final problem with vhd is that of wear; because the read head is actually in contact with the disc surface, there is a gradual degradation of image quality. A major advantage, on the other hand, is that a given vhd disc can be used in suitable players to give pal, secam or ntsc output; therefore a given vhd disc can be used all over the world.

Laservision (optical video) discs hold more frames, 54,000 per side, and do so as one rather than two per revolution. There is only one replay mode, giving 36 minutes of high quality video per side, but in freeze-frame access the image is absolutely steady. Now we have a system in which the read head does not actually touch the surface, so there is no problem of wear; you can scratch and smear the disc quite a lot and find no effect on output. A given laservision disc suits only one video format, however, so that producers must make different versions for pal, secam and ntsc colour output.

Despite the last point – a major drawback for video disc users as well as for the makers – laservision seems to be the more popular system in Britain at the moment. All the same, this field is still very young, so the situation may change in the next few years. The great success of the audio compact disc (Section 10.4) could have an effect in some contexts, for its technology is in essence the same as that of laservision. Thus players exist which can read both compact and laservision discs.

Video discs can clearly hold vast amounts of information. We saw earlier that a broadcast quality frame would need half a megabyte to store in analog form. This is more than most floppies can hold and larger than the main memories of most micros. Yet a video disc can carry around 100,000 analog frames; this means that its total data storage capacity is of the order of many thousand million bytes (GB, gigabytes). The potential for using video discs for computer backing store is therefore tremendous; one video disc can hold as much as tens of thousands of floppies or hundreds of hard discs. There is an obvious drawback in that current video discs are read-only, so the data that's stored on them cannot be changed.

One could envisage using a digital video disc (digital optical disc (dod), Section 10.4) as a form of read-only computer backing store, to hold for access programs and data that would never need to be changed. This is possible. The computer system would still need the normal read and write backing storage, such as standard floppy or hard disc drives. It would also support a video disc drive, costing (say) £500, and the computer would need to have just one disc for use in there to carry all programs and permanent data.

That disc would by no means be full. To store all the programs now on the market for the IBM PC (a very popular stand-alone micro) needs no more than a few hundred megabytes. A disc that holds all those would be mostly empty. Of course no single user would want to access more than a tiny fraction of those thousands of programs (they include over 100 word processors for instance). Yet video discs are potentially very cheap. A selling price of £100 would give good profits to the makers and fees to the copyright owners, but would still allow most interested users to afford a new version each year.

In fact the compact disc (cd) could beat the video disc as the high volume, read-only backing storage medium of the near future. One imminent technical advance could change that view, however: the erasable rewritable optical disc on which new information can be stored. If your video disc player is able to record (write) data as well as reading it, the system becomes very tempting indeed. In fact, with such a large volume of storage space at the computer's beck and call, writing over each part of the disc just once would still provide most users with years of service.

The last point leads to the concept of the write once optical disc (wood). When writing data to this type of disc, the system sets the laser brightness on high. At this setting the energy is enough to melt new pits into the disc surface; the head will be able to read these when the laser is on the normal low setting.

This suggests a possible near future scenario of the use of digital optical discs with a computer. The drive takes a single disc, and you buy that disc with all the programs you could ever want. The wide open spaces of the empty part of the surface can slowly fill up with your own data.

People have devised various formats of wood, although at the time of writing (early 1987) none has reached the market. As you might expect, it is the lack of agreed standards that holds progress back. These discs range in size from 50 mm to 360 mm across, and vary correspondingly in data capacity; more important, there is great variation in the methods of addressing the different locations and of holding the directory. All the same, the system has great potential. As well as being able to replace magnetic storage media for holding programs and data, text and graphics, woods may become strong in electronic document storage (eds).

Many organisations need to hold archives – copies of vast numbers of documents that start off on paper, as well as pictures on film. They include libraries (books and periodicals), insurance companies (proposal forms), medical centres (patient records and x-ray photos), and banks (cheques and paying-in slips). At the moment, the only alternative to storage on paper – bulky, dirty, and open to loss – is microform. Microform involves storage of the documents as tiny photographic images, either on rolls of serial access microfilm or on direct access microfiches, index card sized sheets. Microform is cheaper and more secure than paper, but electronic data storage (eds) on video discs could be far better still; it would not take up so much room, it would cost less, and it could be simpler to access by computer.

Turning a document into a digital signal is the principle behind fax (Section 7.3). This process of scanning and digitisation is not difficult. The problem in this context is the amount of data concerned. Even with the best techniques of compacting data, an A4 printed or typed page needs 50 kilobytes, while one that consists of a highly detailed colour image may need more than a video frame – perhaps several megabytes. Even a wood (write once optical disc) with its immense capacity may be able to carry only a few thousand electronically stored documents. This may be enough for a small business that decides to use eds, but it would still not help the big organisations.

While an optical disc can store the contents of several multi-volume encyclopedias, that's still only a shelf or two of the hundreds in even a small library. For such users of large archives, there will be a need to have access to hundreds or even thousands of woods on- or offline.

People are now working hard on the main two areas that need attention. These are jukebox units to carry a couple of hundred discs and insert any one into a drive on call, and methods of indexing the information to allow easy access from such a huge volume. There also remains a question. How long is the useful life of a disc? Estimates range from a decade to a century.

Meanwhile, the search goes on for optical discs you can write to as often as you wish. To do this requires a method of wiping out the tracks of pits that are no longer required, before using the high power write setting on the laser. Various techniques show great promise here; we can expect the optical disc to replace the magnetic disc in computer systems at all levels in the medium-term future.

The real target is still a long way off, however. This is the universal drive able to work with universally compatible optical discs. Such a system would allow one to record and replay (write and read) computer data, video material, documents, and audio, or any mixture of these. The data could be captured from cable and satellite links as well as from more conventional sources, and the system would offer as much to the home as to the office user. Figure 8.6 shows this. It may

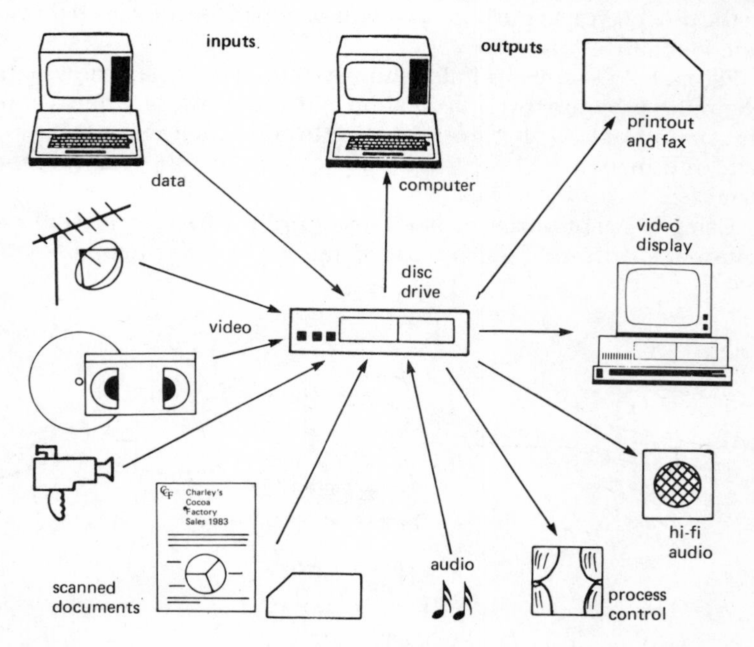

Figure 8.6. Optical disc technology may lead one day to a universal information storage and access system

well be that the compact disc is the format that succeeds first in this area, rather than the laservision disc. The technologies are much the same, but the sizes differ.

While there is great potential for the video disc as a medium for the straight replay of analog filmed material for marketing, much of the usage just described depends on the fact that information on any part of the disc surface can be accessed quickly. This direct access (or random access) feature is also the basis for interactive video.

8.3 Interactive video

Interactive video (iv) is a technique which could offer a great deal to training methods, and also to other areas of interest to business. It is a unique mix of interactive computer program and high density visual information on optical disc (video, or sometimes compact). In fact good iv programmes have been devised with the visual content on tape, but because of the need to spool the tape to the right place for each sequence needed, this requires a lot more care in planning.

The essence of iv is that software presents each chunk of disc material on the basis of the user's responses, eg to questions and menus. A simple system has the software on the disc and the computer in the disc player; the user works with a keypad like that used for tv set remote control.

Figure 8.7 describes a full feature system; the display shows either computer program text (information and questions) or video disc output, or both at once. It is even possible to add a modem and allow certain information to be brought up to date nightly from a central database.

Using iv is not intrinsically different from working with a piece of computer software. Take the case of training material: in this situation,

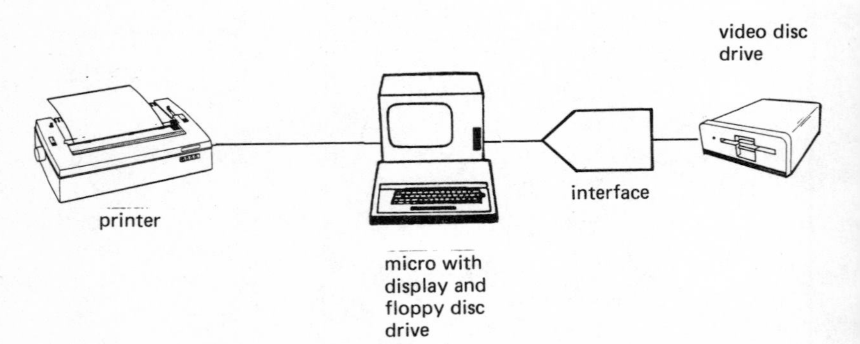

Figure 8.7. Interactive video allows full integration between an interactive computer program and high density information on video disc

a computer program may offer, perhaps by way of menus, a number of areas and topics to explore; it would then present screens of text and computer graphics as required; maybe the user then works through a series of questions and, at the end, the program displays results and comments. The system may also store each trainee's results for the tutors to study.

With interactive video for the trainer to call on, the quality and versatility of the approach become much greater. Now a wealth of broadcast quality– video– graphics and film material are there, to add to the total information content and the efficacy of the training. Think of any subject in which training is needed, and imagine how well an hour or two of flexibly chosen video sequences and tv quality stills could improve a computer-based training program, all with high fidelity sound as required.

A second major area in which interactive video can be of value (other than in outstanding games) is sales. The disc could include shots of all your products as well as sequences showing them in use; with computer-generated menus, text and questions to guide the user to the video material of interest, such a system would be easy and fun to use, and very effective in its task. In much the same way, people now apply iv to information presentations in exhibitions, town centres, schools, and libraries.

A third use is at the point of sale (pos). Here an interactive video unit allows the shopper to browse through details of the lines of goods on offer and eventually to select a few to look at.

Interactive video is better than conventional video programmes in all these contexts, in that its sequence involves branching under user and software control, rather than being linear. In any particular case, great chunks can be left out, while other parts can be repeated, perhaps by still or freeze-frame or in slow motion, as often as required. Interactive video is better than a 'traditional' computer program too, as the amount of data online and the quality of the illustrations and sound are so much higher. Interactive video is a true product of information technology, a splendid marriage of two very different fields.

8.4 Into space

Recall that a tv frame involves something like half a megabyte of analog data and that a tv channel carries 25 frames a second; thus the channel has to transfer information at a rate of millions of bytes a second. In technical terms, this needs a large bandwidth, and for technical reasons (as well as those of cost), it limits the number of tv channels in a region. Broadcast tv – sent out in all directions from a central point to whatever viewers there may happen to be – does not, therefore, give a large choice.

Two new technologies are changing that picture: the use of cable (which we touched on in Chapter 7), and satellite tv. Both will much increase the choice of video channels for home viewers. Of interest in this context are their potential for faster and cheaper computer data and other information transfers. We'll look at satellite tv first.

Satellite tv depends on the concept of the geostationary communications satellite. This was first proposed decades before Sputnik (the first artificial earth satellite, launched by the USSR in 1957). The geostationary craft enters orbit in such a way that it goes round the earth in 24 hours; thus it appears to hover above the same place on the planet's surface. As a result it can act as a fixed tv transmitter, but one that covers a very large region. Signals are broadcast to it from a tight (narrow) beam transmitter as in Figure 8.8.

A modern communications satellite has the power to relay many channels of information in this way. Current models can handle tens of thousands of telephone conversations or computer data transfers, or over a hundred tv signals. With more than a dozen such satellites now in service round the world, there has been huge progress since the system started a couple of decades ago. International speech and digital

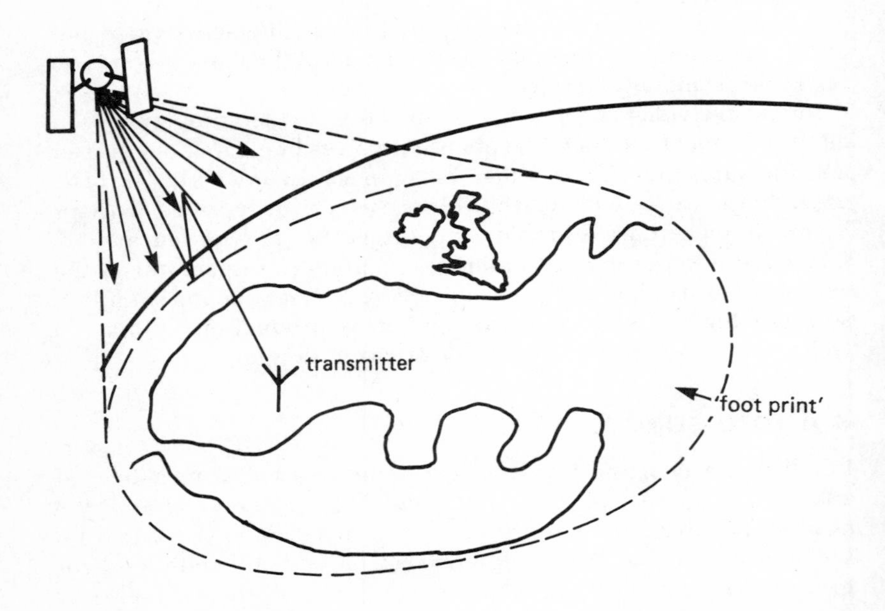

Figure 8.8. A geostationary satellite can beam programme material to a large area of the earth's surface

data telephone traffic depends more and more on this technique, and there is growing day-to-day use by the tv broadcast companies.

The broadcast companies use it mainly to vary the diet of the viewing public at the moment. News material and coverage of major sporting events come from other parts of the world by satellite, and are then sent out as part of normal programmes. However, the still novel direct broadcast by satellite (dbs) approach is gaining ground, and this is what can really widen viewers' choice.

In this case, viewers buy a dish aerial and set it up on the roof or in the garden, pointing accurately at a geostationary satellite. With the aid of a powerful amplifier, they can pick up channels broadcast by the spacecraft and can choose for themselves what they view. There are still all sorts of financial, legal and technical matters to sort out, however, such as how the viewer should pay, who should monitor content, and what video standards should apply. One way out that makes things simpler for the viewer involves cable systems.

8.5 Cable tv

The delivery of broadcast material to homes by cable has a long history. The need first arose as a result of problems of poor signal reception in certain areas, and the solution was obvious. At some central point a really good aerial gathers the signals; it then routes these on demand to the cable network clients. There are still some parts of the country, such as remote and hilly regions, where this is the only way to get decent broadcast tv reception, while for aesthetic reasons it is common in hotels and blocks of flats.

Once there is a cable system there is the opportunity to use it in other ways. The system providers may add extra video material to the broadcast programmes they pass on; for instance, video films, live and recorded community tv, and programmes received by satellite from elsewhere. Indeed, in some places by law the cable operators have to supply dbs material, and charge users for viewing it.

Two aspects of the use of a cable network in a residential area are of special interest to business. Both arise from the fact that there could be a lot of spare capacity on the cable (whether it be standard co-ax or optical fibre); this means that high volume two-way traffic is possible. The first spin-off from that is interactive tv. This gives a promise of the video equivalent of the radio phone-in programme: viewers with a video camera or a video phone can be interviewed in a programme or can contribute to it in other ways. Using no more than a simple keypad, they can vote too – perhaps choosing the ending of a film; giving their views on current affairs, programmes and advertisements; taking part in quizzes or market research.

The second spin-off is that channels can be set aside in the cable for such uses as teletex (Section 7.2), teleshopping (as mentioned for Prestel in Section 10.2), teleconferencing, and videotex (Section 10.3). There is no reason why a cable network that feeds every home, office, school and other building in an area could not provide telephone and computer data channels as well as video links. The limit is not so much the capacity of the cabling or the sophistication of the hardware, but the way the cable network is laid out. While it is cheaper to provide a tree system as in Figure 8.9(a), the switched star of Figure 8.9(b) allows a much greater volume of two-way traffic.

A video phone system has long been a dream of communication designers and trial systems have started in a number of countries. The instrument includes, as well as the keypad for 'dialling' and the microphone and speaker for speech, a fixed focus video camera and a small screen. It looks something like that shown in Figure 8.10, although there are also designs which incorporate a microcomputer for dual use either as a stand-alone system or as a terminal on the telephone network.

While it may be nice to see, as well as hear, the person with whom you are making a phone call, the video link can also offer the ability to

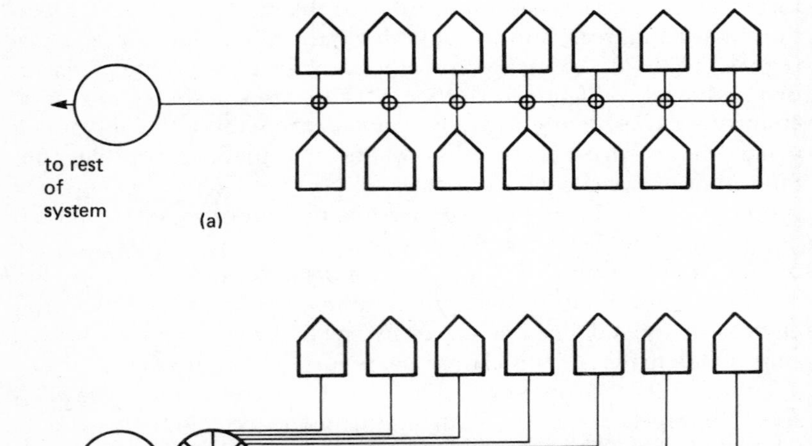

Figure 8.9. The design of a cable network affects how well it can carry telephone and interactive video services

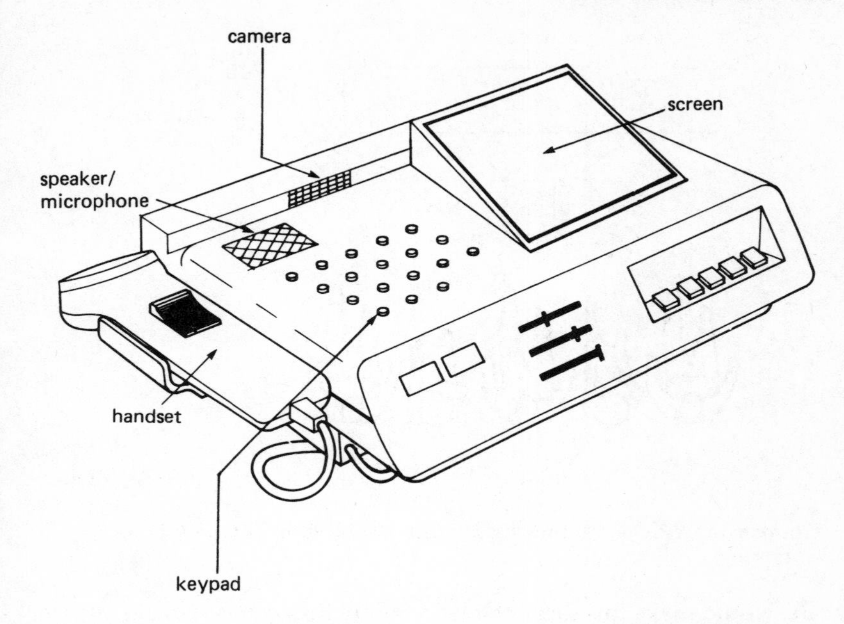

Figure 8.10. A video phone contains the elements of closed circuit tv as well as the components of an intelligent voice telephone unit

let him or her view at least simple documents and drawings you want to discuss. The costs of the network hardware able to handle two-way information transfer at the rates needed for video are, however, high; this is a major barrier to progress in this direction as operators are not certain that their investment would be worthwhile. It may be that slow-scan tv could come to the rescue here, this being a technology that is well developed for such purposes as site surveillance. A slow-scan tv signal transfers a complete frame over several seconds instead of a fraction of a second. This means that the rate of information transfer is much lower, so the bandwidth required is far less. For the purpose of a video phone link, that low transfer rate is mostly acceptable.

It would, in the same way, be desirable to extend the concept of videoconferencing. At the moment, videoconferencing as a public service requires the booking of a special studio (and its staff) at each end. Figure 8.11 shows how this works. The system is rarely used to link more than two such studios; with just two, the charges are high, even if they cost a firm less than sending several people on a long journey. A switched cable network able to carry two-way video, even at slow-scan

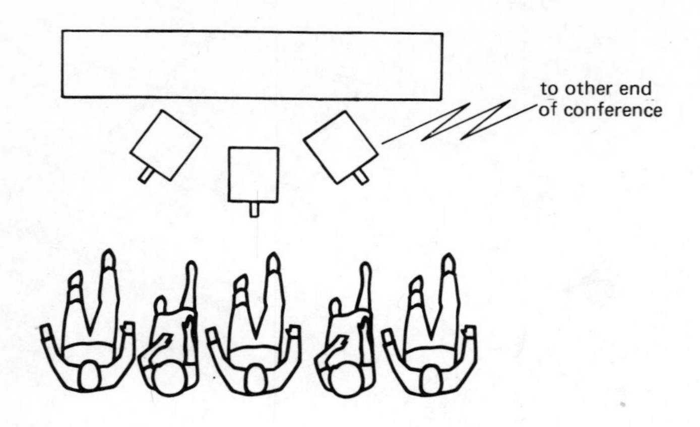

Figure 8.11. Videoconferencing is costly at the moment, so it is not common

rate, would make this form of teleconferencing between desks simple, common, cheap and effective, at least once the hardware is in place.

To return once more to the theme of the wired society of the global village, we can expect that in the next century it will be common for people's living and work units to be linked by high capacity cable. Then the high volume two-way transfer of information will become cheap and common. This will include video material as well as live speech and conference video and computer communication. Links to interactive video systems for learning, information and gaming will be the norm.

The business use of video is growing fast. In a recent survey, nearly two-thirds of firms indicated that they either use video or are planning to do so. They work either with their own facilities or by calling on specialist production companies (of which there were a thousand in Britain in early 1987). Over 80 per cent of users have produced training programmes on video, while two-thirds employ video for marketing and sales in one way or another. Forty per cent find video of value for corporate communication, keeping staff in touch with what is going on. Video disc, with which only 4 per cent were involved, has only just started to make an impact, but a quarter of the firms have begun work with interactive video (often tape-based rather than with disc). As cable systems spread, it is certain that commercial usage of video in these areas will grow to become near universal. Just think – video junk mail each time you switch on your IT workstation.

9 Desktop Publishing

In this chapter we come back to a new, but fast growing, area of computer usage in business. It involves working with a package of suitable hardware and software, in order to prepare high quality layouts of text and graphics on paper ready for printing.

The prediction that information on costly, bulky, dirty paper would give way to that on some other better medium first appeared when microform, in particular microfiche, started to become common, and when microform readers became cheap (see Sections 8.2 and 10.1). Despite the clear advantages of holding documents (such as catalogues, books, reports and periodicals) on film in this way rather than on paper, the microform revolution never truly took off.

Similar predictions have become common once more in the 1980s, with the spread into every business and many homes of the personal computer and other modern forms of IT hardware.

9.1 Electronic and traditional publishing

Electronic publishing involves putting the information concerned into computer backing store (magnetic or optical) in a suitable form, so that interested people can access it through a communications link. The caller sees a menu– contents list– after logging on to the database (as it is in effect), and can then work through to obtain the material of interest.

The most well known public electronically published database in Britain is Prestel, covered in the next chapter. At this stage, however, it is worth noting at least the advantages and disadvantages of electronic publishing over the good old paper-based variety.

Electronically published information is easy to keep up to date, even (if need be) at minute-by-minute intervals, as with stock exchange prices for instance. It is easy to design the software to allow access in a number of useful ways, and it is easy to bring in a complex but flexible charging system.

On the other hand, electronic communications is not a mature technology; it is still slow, fiddly and novel, so that users don't like it as much as they may in a decade or two's time. A second barrier is that cost can build up quite fast; you need practice to learn how to get through electronically published material to find and copy what you want quickly. There are plenty of hidden costs to finding information the old way– those of people's time and trouble in particular– and the information found is often out of date. Yet people are used to traditional methods, however time-consuming they may be, and however doubtful the information obtained. Indeed, people like paper: they like holding it, owning it, browsing through it, piling it up on their worksurface, shelves and floors.

Electronic publishing will become the norm in business before it is common in other areas of activity. Even so, the change will take a long time yet, and in the meantime we shall still rely on paper in many areas.

In the context of business information transfer, paper publishing has an additional problem to those mentioned above, namely that it takes a long time for material to be published. Very roughly, the production time is of the same order as the material's lifetime: a book whose information is written to apply for several years may be two or more in the making; much of the content of a daily paper takes a couple of days to reach the streets. Production takes at least as much time as origination, ie preparing the material in the first place. If one could reduce the production time, the material would be that much fresher when it reaches the reader.

Desktop publishing can make a significant contribution to cutting the production time of material, so that schedules then depend mainly on organisation. To see its significance, here are the main stages of getting a document ready, such as a report, brochure or house magazine.

1. Preparing and editing the text.
2. Drafting and producing the illustrations.
3. Printing the text as a master – typesetting.
4. Planning and working through the layout of the pages.
5. Making the masters for printing.
6. Printing.
7. Binding.

Word processing (Sections 3.3 and 6.4) has made a great deal of difference to the first stage, of course. Using word processing software, the author(s) can now plan, draft, edit and polish a document faster than before. This is because there is no need to retype each main version. As a document typically goes through three or four main versions, this is very significant.

Art and graphics software (Section 3.7) makes producing non-photographic illustrations a joy too. The laborious manual work that needs a highly qualified studio artist is moving into the past; almost anyone can now run up professional line diagrams, charts and graphs in a short time with the aid of a computer.

The next stage, typesetting, involves using special costly equipment to produce text in high quality form. It can take up a lot of time and the output needs careful checking. Like the previous stage, it is therefore traditionally the work of specialist staff. Even large publishing houses do not carry out this work themselves; rather they send it off to a bureau – and then they have to put up with the inevitable delays that follow.

The fourth stage in the list, handling the layout, is yet another that needs a lot of experience and time. Layout work involves cutting up the typeset master text and arranging it on sheets; the headings, page numbers and illustrations need to be of the right sizes and in the right places. It is not as easy to do that as it sounds: the final pages should be uniform and pleasing to the eye; text should be continuous (without too much of the 'Now turn to page such and such' syndrome); everything required should be checked as present and in a suitable order; there should not be an excess of blank space.

The layout people will also often make the masters (artwork) for printing, usually with the aid of a device called a process camera. Printing needs costly specialised hardware that only the larger firms will have on their own premises, and the same applies to binding.

Preparing material for publication is a lengthy, complex and time-consuming affair. For the people in charge, such as the editor of the document, it can be a nightmare as deadlines approach and go by, and because so much forward planning and replanning are needed. Figure 9.1 provides a graphic summary – much simplified – of this traditional publishing sequence.

9.2 Disc to type

Information technology has lately given us typesetting from disc as one way to reduce the delays involved in traditional publishing. Let's expand a little on the relevant stages – 1 and 3 – of the old approach, before going into that.

In the old days (and to some extent now), text for publishing would be sent by its author to the editor in the form of typescript. After the editor had wielded the red pencil to bring it all into a suitable style, the sheets would go to a typesetting firm. Quite possibly a fair copy would have to be typed up first, especially if the number of changes was high.

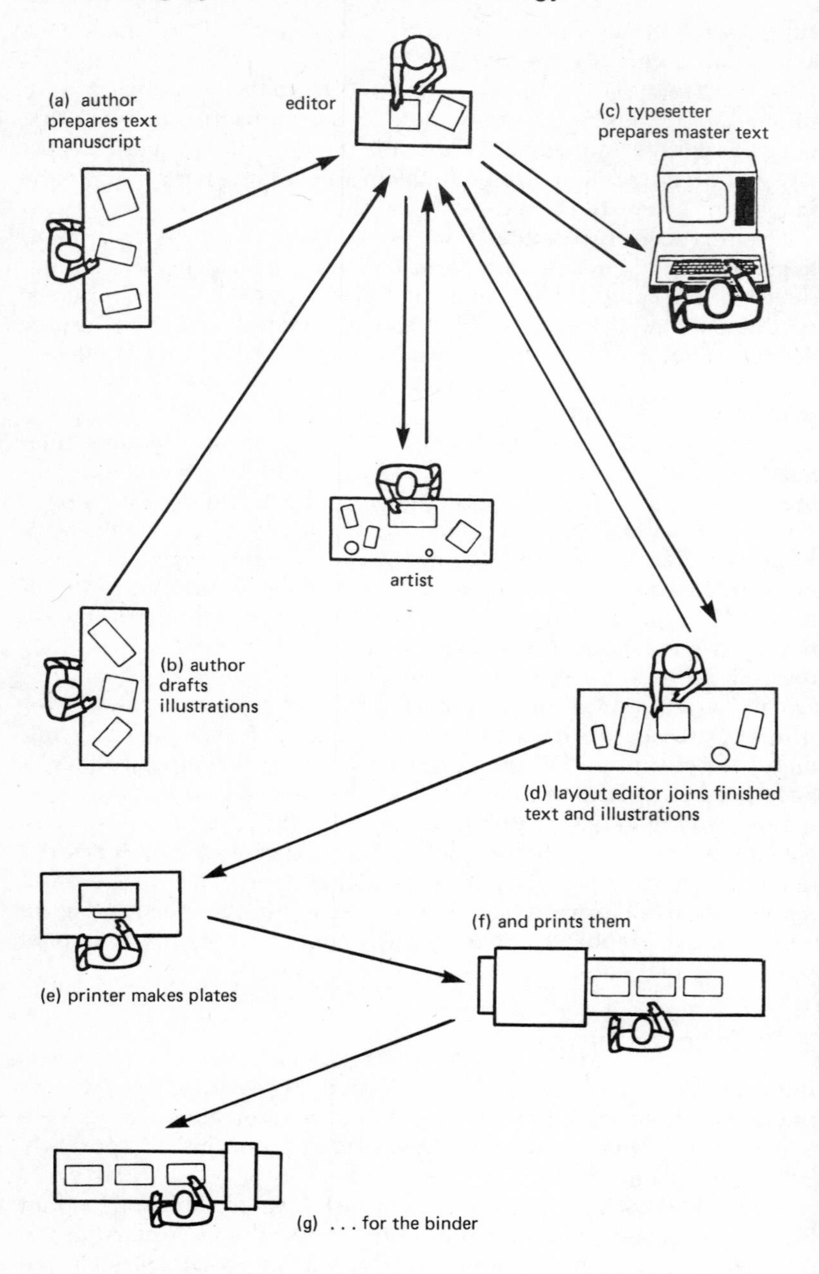

Figure 9.1. The various stages of traditional publishing involve cost, time and special knowledge

The typesetter would also use a keyboard; he or she would enter the text into the setting machine, using the special codes needed for effects such as line lengths, indents, highlights (bold and italic, for instance), typefaces and typesizes. The machine would print the result out on special paper, and that copy (the proof) would go back to the editor, and perhaps also to the author, for checking (proof-reading).

The typesetter's next task would be to enter corrections and other changes and to obtain the final copy from the machine. This final copy would then go on to the layout stage.

Figure 9.2 shows all this as a flow chart; you can see why the whole process takes so much time. You can also see, perhaps, an obvious source of inefficiency – the text is typed several times. Each time a document is typed, errors can creep in, so there is a need for yet further checks.

As we have seen, word processing is a great boon for people wanting to put text on to paper. For the authors it means that a writing task need involve only one major keyboard operation, rather than two or three. If the editor can accept authors' copy on disc, there's the chance to save another typing operation, that of making the fair copy. Indeed, a number of editors already accept text on disc so that they can work on it direct. (This is true even with some who work for book publishers, although the lengthier time-scales for books allow much more leeway.) Some editors can now take copy in digital form through the telephone system, saving even more time. This approach is fast moving towards the norm in the case of news publication.

Typesetting from disc is the next logical step in this progression, but we shall first look at a halfway house. This is publishing material on disc, ie producing and distributing it in that form. The users then load the text as required from the disc into their computer systems, printing out what they want on to paper.

There have been several attempts to publish periodicals on disc for popular micros, but the most usual format is that of some kind of database. This is, however, somewhat restrictive, in that the 'readers' need not only the right hardware, but also a suitable database management package. Publishing data on disc has a number of advantages and disadvantages compared with putting it out as microform or through an electronic dial-in system, and as yet it is too early to see the trends.

However, if a publisher wants to see output on paper, typesetting for printing is still the norm. IT can help here too. If the typesetting machine can handle digital data on disc, the savings in time and trouble will be very significant. In fact, typesetting from disc is already growing very fast, with more and more printers able to work with it. The major barrier is the number of disc and text formats around, stemming from the many incompatible computers and their even more

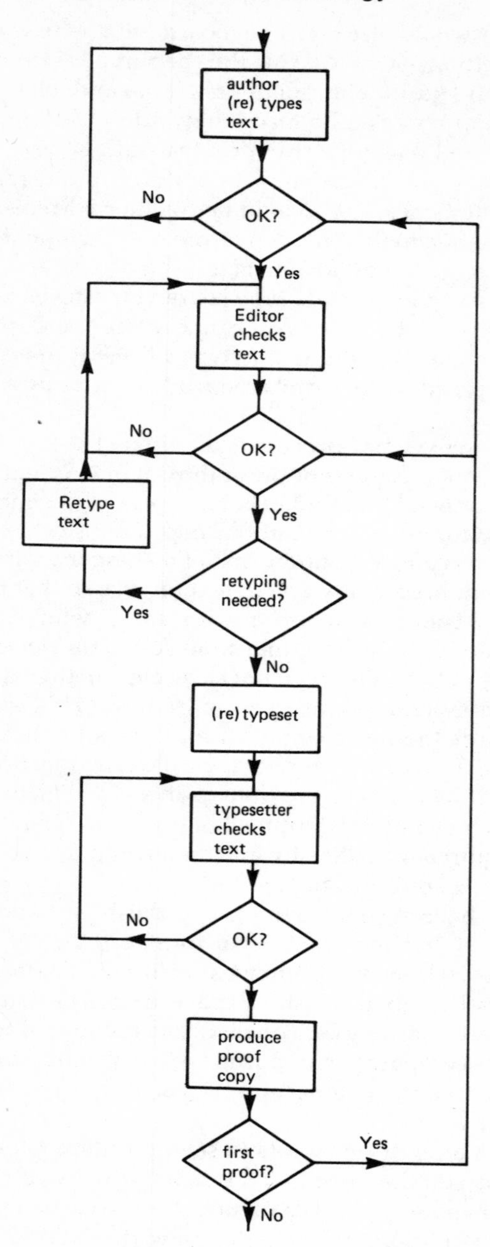

Figure 9.2. Traditional text preparation involves many stages, taking a lot of time

numerous word processor coding systems. A typical typesetting machine able to read discs must offer a menu of hundreds of such disc and text formats. Obviously it must itself be a powerful computer, able to translate any one set of codes into the instructions needed for typesetting.

A cheaper approach is to expect the provider of the disc to code the contents for typesetting. This is not too hard, as such features of a word processor as search and replace can help. The industry is therefore moving towards an international standard of typesetting codes; its name is author's symbolic pre-press interface code (aspic). With these codings in the word-processed disc, typesetting is even more under the control of the writer and editor, and faster and more straightforward. In particular, there is less need to proof-read the material, as an extra stage of working with a keyboard has been dropped. Figure 9.3 shows, on the left, word processor output of text using aspic codes; on the right is the typeset material that is produced automatically from it. This is clearly a powerful system that is easy to learn to use.

Compare Figure 9.4 with Figure 9.2, and you can see the advantages of typesetting from disc over the approach of the early 1980s and before.

```
If you want a [t2]Chapter Three[t1] heading on each page, enter
[i2][t3]f1[t1][t2]dh[t1][t3]f2[t1][t2]Chapter Three[t1][t3]RETURN[t1]
[i1]at the start.  The heading is everything between [t3]f2[t1] and
[t3]RETURN[t1]; note you [i]must[r] close a heading or a footing
command with [t3]RETURN[t1].
```

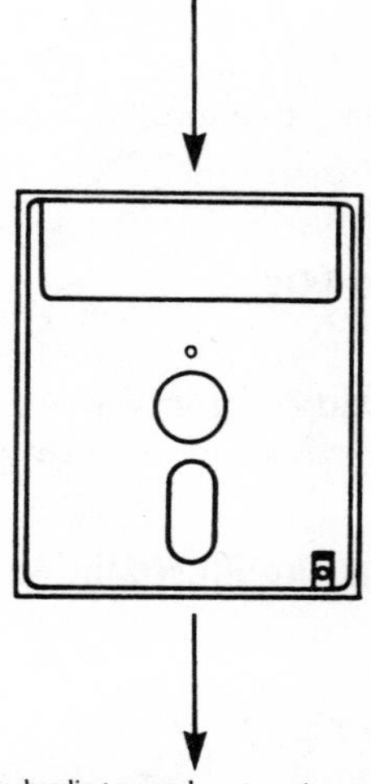

If you want a Chapter Three heading on each page, enter

f1 dh f2 Chapter Three RETURN

at the start. The heading is everything between f2 and RETURN; note you *must* close a heading or a footing command with RETURN.

Figure 9.3. A suitable typesetting machine can take coded material from disc and go straight to proper error-free output

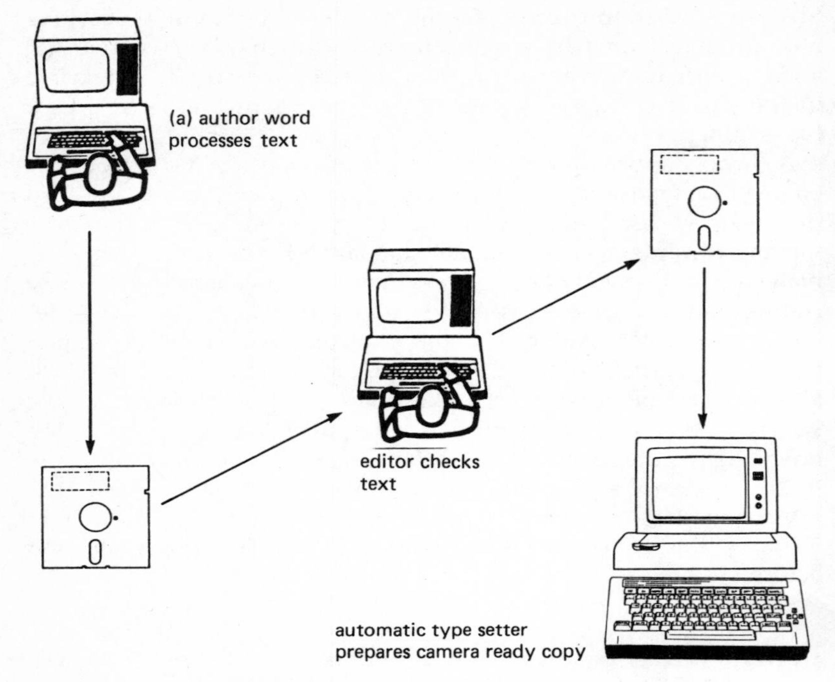

Figure 9.4. Typesetting from disc streamlines document production very significantly

With desktop publishing, however, you do away with typesetting altogether. Desktop publishing brings all the first five stages of the process into the hands of author or editor.

9.3 On to the desk top

Those five stages lead to the final printing and binding. In other words, they lead to the 'camera-ready' copy of the pages of the document. Here's the list again; it excludes only printing and binding:

1. Preparing and editing the text.
2. Drafting and producing the illustrations.
3. Typesetting the text.
4. Page layout.
5. Preparing the master pages.

Word processing gives us the power to produce perfect text (even if we can't achieve that power in practice). In the same way, art and graphics software help to make perfect illustrations. A desktop publishing program combines the two, so that the user can work on both aspects of visual information transfer at the same time. It thus covers the first two stages in that pre-publication list.

To make it fully able to carry out this task in practice, the system must also be able to handle photographs. This requires that the original photo be put into digital form in the computer's memory. Digitisation is the way to do this. It involves either scanning the original to make a digital signal (as in fax (Section 7.3) and electronic document storage (Section 8.2)) or storing the image produced by a video camera. Both methods need a hardware input unit called a digitiser, also an alternative name for a graphics pad, which is of use here as well. With a graphics pad, you can trace a fairly simple diagram in order to store it in digital form. Figure 9.5 shows all those methods of getting non-text material into a computer's memory.

In this context, the next stage now is to marry the two types of material – text and pictures – in order to lay out the pages of the document. Desktop publishing software has a layout option to handle this. With it, you view the blank page on screen, strip in the text material and then insert the illustrations. You can change the size of an illustration (in either direction or both) so that it exactly fits the space set by

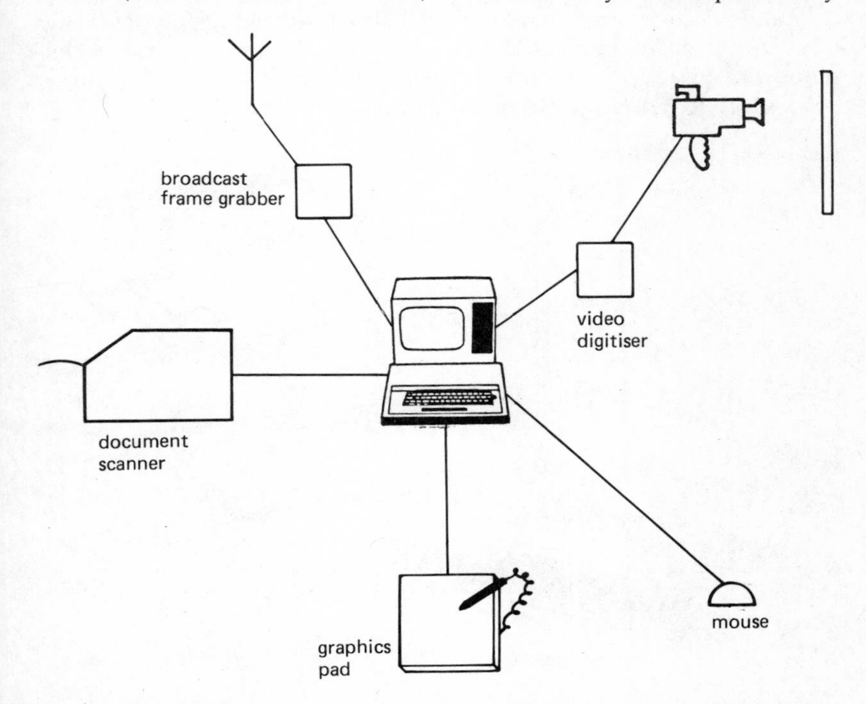

Figure 9.5. There are various ways for a computer to store a visual image in digital form

for it. It is just as easy to put borders round boxed material and to work with headings and footings, page numbers, typefaces and typesizes. You can also screen (shade) parts of the page so that they stand out from the rest, and the system offers full cut and paste features.

In so far as this kind of software is necessarily complex, a wimp environment (including the use of windows, icons and a mouse) is almost essential. Figure 9.6 shows a typical desktop publishing system set up; note the upright A4 aspect screen that makes layout (and word processing) so much more straightforward.

To the right of the figure is the hardware unit that really made effective desktop publishing possible in mid-1985. It is a page printer. Its ability to provide very high quality printout on your desk is the key: if the system can produce hard copy of a screen page layout that is good enough to act as a master for printing, then the first five of the seven stages of publication can stay under your full control and in your own premises. With a page printer this is possible. Not only does using this hardware save an immense amount of time, but it puts all aspects of the content and appearance of the document into the hands of the people who prepare it.

Figure 9.4 compared with Figure 9.2 shows the value of typesetting from disc over the more traditional stages leading to set type. In the same way, Figure 9.7 can be compared with Figure 9.1 for the whole process up to printing; Figure 9.8 shows typical output.

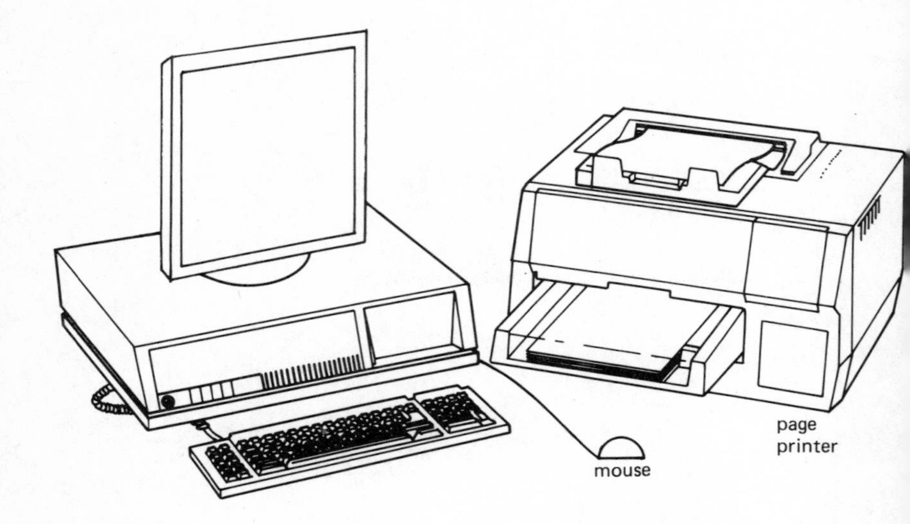

Figure 9.6. Desktop publishing often needs special hardware as well as complex software

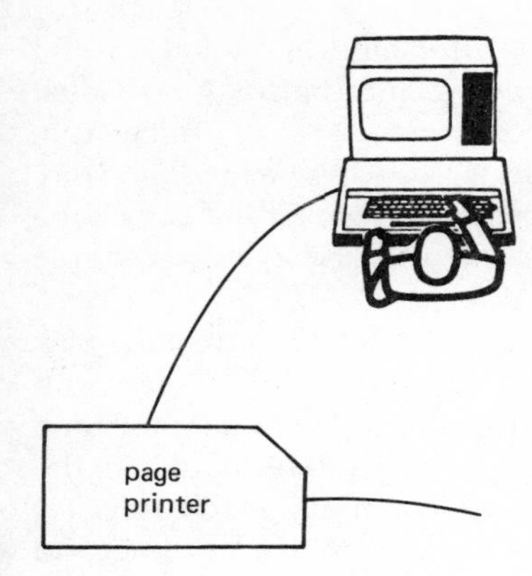

(a) author prepares and edits text
(b) author prepares and edits illustrations
(c) author prepares and edits layout
(d) author produces camera ready copy for printing

Figure 9.7. Desktop publishing radically streamlines pre-printing

Figure 9.8. The typical products of desktop publishing software are nearly as good as 'the real thing'

Why stop, however, at the end of the fifth stage, and send out the master pages to a specialist firm for printing and binding? Specialist printers are still able to produce finished bound work more cheaply than you can when the number of copies is more than a few hundred. However, the apparent cost benefit must be set against the extra time required – even an 'instant printer' normally requires at least a couple of days, whether you book the job or not.

For short runs, modern office equipment can let you finish the task yourself, fast, cheaply, and effectively. Current photocopiers can handle A4 sheets and make perfect copies at not much more than twice the cost of the paper. Some can copy both sides and collate the output (stack it in order); this means that you can put all your master pages in at once, press the right buttons to program the machine, and leave the system to get on with it.

If you want to handle long print runs yourself, look at office offset machines. These are a far cry from the traditional office duplicator, though the function is the same.

Do-it-yourself binding is easy too. The most straightforward approach is to use a long-arm stapler (if, for instance, your copier has reduced the A4 originals to A5 pages, two on each sheet). Other simple, cheap binding systems use plastic clips, plastic combs, or pre-printed binder covers with glue along the inside of the spine.

You can work on your report or brochure at all stages, therefore, using your own resources, expertise and effort. It will be as professional as you want to make it, and if it isn't ready when you want it, there's only one person to blame. Outside printers win on one score, though – they can still deal with colour much better; agreed, there are now colour computer printers and colour copiers, but in-house, full-colour desktop publishing is still a system of the future. Also, note that professional printing machines work at resolutions two or three times higher than most current models of page printer offer; you will still need to call on the former when you are working with material that involves very fine detail.

Publishing your own literature can progress in two very different directions, therefore. Full-colour, full-resolution desktop publishing is one, and we can expect to have this at reasonable cost within a decade. Electronic publishing is the other. For this to be effective, we need a public cable network that will allow people to log on to your computer and collect the material on offer at a reasonable information transfer speed. It will probably also be a decade before we reach that stage. Meanwhile publishing on disc – whether for computer or video player – may keep firms' heads above water.

These approaches to in-house publishing are the newest areas of interest to the IT-based office; for many firms they may also be the most exciting. The excitement comes as much from the thrill of learning new skills as from the control from start to finish of the complex and novel publishing process. The skills in question are well within the grasp of an intelligent secretary, so electronic and desktop publishing, publishing on disc, or setting to type from disc, need not provide more cases of IT adding to the manager's own workload.

The examples used in this chapter – reports, brochures, house magazines – are in fact only the tip of an iceberg. Desktop publishing (and, in theory but not in practice, electronic publishing) lets you handle any document that involves text and/or graphics and/or special layout. Some more examples are advertisements, certificates, mail shots, manuals, menus, notices, plans, posters, printed stationery, specifications, and training units. Most firms produce a huge amount of print work; IT can offer a great deal in that area.

Indeed, there are cases in which use of these techniques has led companies to turn the tables neatly. In the old days they would send their print work out to studios; now they offer to produce other people's literature by in-house desktop publishing. After all, if you have spent a lot of money on special hardware, software, and staff training, it makes sense to offer a service to other firms if you don't use your package full time.

We'll close with a brief checklist of desktop publishing features. The ideal current system, able to meet most needs, would offer all these, on screen as well as on paper as appropriate.

Text

- Wide range of fonts (type styles, including foreign alphabets), with various typesizes and highlights.
- Full range of accents and special symbols, plus ability to create and store your own new characters.
- Subscripts and superscripts, perhaps at two levels.
- Spelling checking.

Text layout

- More than one column.
- Proportional spacing with or without justification.
- Fine adjustment of line and character spacing.
- Ability to centre lines of text.

Graphics

- Ability to pull in non-text material from a range of sources, including libraries of component designs.
- Sprites (large graphic characters); a range of standard ones and ability to add your own to the library.

- At least eight levels of shading to represent coloured material.
- Flexible variation of picture size in both directions.

Page layout

- Library of standard and user-defined layouts.
- Full cut and paste.
- Automatic control of widows and orphans (lone lines of text at beginning or end of columns).
- Fine adjustment of all four outside margins and of internal ones in the case of matter set in columns.
- Wide range of borders, ruled lines and boxes, including ability to vary line thickness.
- Range of screens for highlighting blocks of text and illustrations.
- Ability to magnify any section of a page for fine control.
- Ability to reduce a page to fit a screen that is not A4 in aspect.

Document layout

- Automatic control of headings, footings and page numbers.
- Distinction between left and right pages.
- Full cut and paste between pages.
- Control of widows and orphans from page to page.
- Justification to top and bottom margins.

General

- Good wimp environment.
- Automatic generation of a contents list from the document's headings and subheadings.
- Automatic indexing.
- Clear page description language for programming such things as layout.

Here, without doubt, is an area where 'fools can rush in'. Don't forget, though, that the desktop publishing market is a really new field of IT. It is therefore one in which prices are falling fast at the same time as features and systems grow. Shop around *and* take your time, therefore.

10
Databases

In practice, the term database has two somewhat distinct meanings within information technology. In Section 3.5, we saw how special database management systems (dbms software) can help an office to organise many kinds of information on a fairly small scale. The more sophisticated and more recent relational database discussed in Section 4.5 has much the same task, even if it carries out that task in a way that more closely relates to 'real life'.

In the case of either of these types of database, the software's task is to allow the user(s) to enter, organise and access the information in question with as much flexibility as possible and without too much trouble. Database programs like these are exceedingly important. With them a computer is able to replace the clumsy use of the manual paper-based filing systems which take up so much space (and staff) and cause so many problems.

In a typical office, people use such software to handle customer, supplier, stock and staff files. These may be integrated to an extent, as appropriate, perhaps to allow more straightforward accounting and auditing.

In this chapter, we shall explore the second kind of database; it holds very large volumes of information for access by people other than the providers (those who create, amend and add to it). Such a distributed database – a form of electronic publishing (Section 9.1) – can be held within the office or outside it.

10.1 Options old and new

Any paper based filing system involves duplication of effort and many time-wasting activities. Paper is also slow to access, costly, dirty, fragile, open to loss, a bother to move around and a fire risk, but you know all that.

A well established alternative to paper, for archive files at least (those needing long-term storage and rare changes), is microform. Microform involves the transfer of documents to tiny photographic images. It has been around a long time: the first usage, in a military context, was over a century ago.

The technology of microform involves making a very small photographic transparency of each page of a document. The image may be monochrome in the case of simple documents, but if you want to store copies of complex material, such as colour-coded plans and colour photos, that will not do, of course. The other half of the system involves the hardware needed to access any such image once produced. For this you need a microform reader; here a powerful optical system projects a view, once again full size, on to a ground-glass screen. Some readers also have printers attached, so that the users can go back to having pieces of paper in their hands. Figure 10.1 shows the structure of a system based on the microfiche format. A fiche is typically 150 mm by 100 mm in size, and can carry a hundred or more images of A4 originals (the whole of an issue of a magazine, for instance).

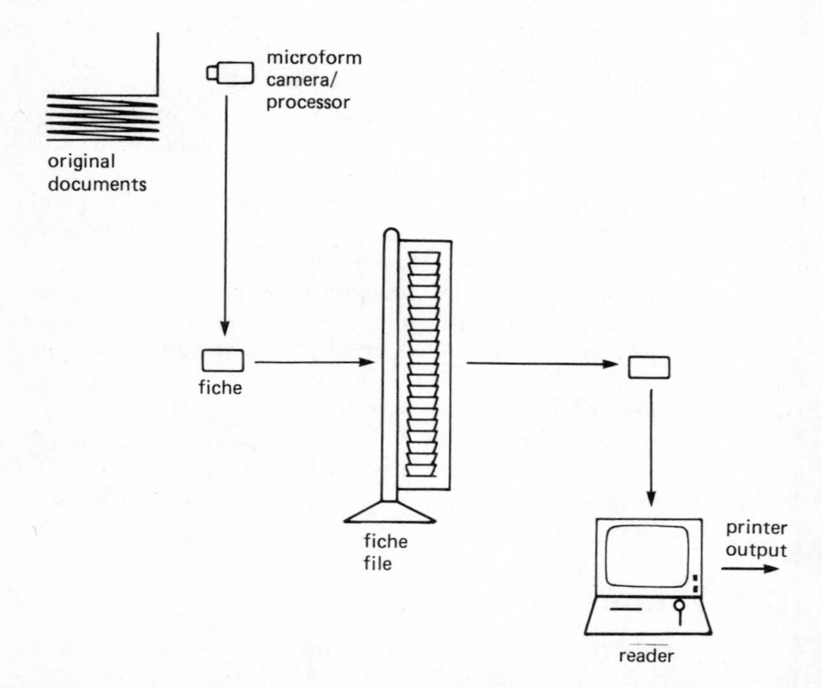

Figure 10.1. Microfiche, a common type of microform, may be fiddly in practice, but has major advantages over paper

As Section 8.2 explained, the main competitor to microfiche is microfilm (although many people use this word to cover all types). A roll of microfilm is tens of metres long, so it can hold images of a much larger number of documents than fiche. It is a serial access medium, while fiche offers direct access; however, only to few readers does that matter much in practice. Generally, people store microfilm in cassettes (cartridges) rather than on open reels. The advantage of this is easier and faster loading. Also, after looking at one image, the film does not need to be rewound.

There is a very big problem with all kinds of microform system (apart from the aperture card used mainly by architects– here a single large card carries a single microform image in a window in the centre). The problem arises when there is any need to change the image of a given document: it is not possible to reshoot that image on an existing fiche or roll of film, so if you want to update material in your microform database you will have to reshoot the whole fiche or roll, or work out a necessarily complex system of cross-referencing.

Microform *is* best kept for archive material, ie records that you don't need to change. Also it's fine for such uses as holding images of documents stored in date or number order, like invoices and statements. However, if there *is* a need to make changes to material held on microform, the best way round the problem is to use jacket microfilm. A jacket is a plastic sheet the size of a fiche; it has slots into which you can slide five or six short (12 image) lengths of cut microfilm. To update a record means either reshooting only a dozen documents or setting to with a pair of scissors.

Almost as big a problem can be the delay involved in producing the microform versions of each set of documents. Even if you do all your preparation – filming, processing, and mounting – in-house rather than using a bureau, there will be a period of hours (or even longer) during which you can access neither the original document nor the microform version. This is yet another reason why microform is best reserved for storing archive papers rather than current documents.

There are two ways in which modern information technology overlaps microform. The first is computer output to microform (com). Here the output device involves a cathode ray tube (crt): the swinging electron beam is under computer control as it creates tiny images on a microform film at the end of the tube. Thus, instead of having reams of hard copy, you end up with a much more manageable pack of microfiches for your computer output. Getting computer output this way is actually far faster than any conventional printer can work; add that advantage to all the others of microform over paper, and you can see why com appeals to firms with a lot of printout to store or mail. Catalogues and price-lists to be sent to dealers and agents are an obvious case where mailed com appeals.

The second area in which microform overlaps with the computer is in the access of stored images. With a microfiche or microfilm cabinet at one side and a reader at the other, you will not have much trouble working with images of many thousands of sheets, once you are used to the system. Indeed, you may have found this to be so if you use a library whose book details are on microform rather than in index card boxes. After all, each fiche or film carries a large clear label to state its contents.

Nevertheless, some firms use computers to store details of the exact location in the microform archive of each document. When the user enters the basic details – eg **invoice, ahmed, august** – the software displays the location(s) concerned on the video screen. A database about a database, that is. One can go even further and automate retrieval, with the system putting a given image on screen for you; this may be done by having a bar code by each image. All the same, microform archives are so compact and easy to use that manual access is almost always adequate.

The essence of IT in practice is to achieve the benefits of a properly organised electronic database, one in which the actual records are stored in digital form. While one can hold A4 documents on microform at (literally) 10 a penny, electronic methods can, in certain circumstances, be even cheaper still, as well as simpler to work with. Let's see how that works with Prestel, Britain's public electronic database *par excellence.*

10.2 Prestel

Excellent or not, this system has grown sadly slowly as far as the number of subscribers is concerned. There are many possible reasons for this, but they can't include a fault in the basic idea – France's newer equivalent is much the same in concept, but it is far more popular: the biggest network in the world, they proudly call it.

Prestel is a sort of network: a wide area network, or wan (Section 5.3). Each subscriber logs on using a keypad or a micro (which acts as a terminal), with data transfer through a modem linked to the public switched telephone network. After the system checks and accepts the log on code (a 10-digit number) and password (a four-character string), any of the hundreds of thousands of pages can be accessed, either through a tree-like series of menus or direct by page number or title if known.

The strength of Prestel is that the information held is up to date rather than encyclopedic. You can find out more about most areas of constant factual knowledge by using your own reference books or those at the local library. Prestel deals primarily with information that changes often. Here are some examples:

- adult education course details
- building society rates
- compact discs on the market
- discount travel fares
- employment agencies
- ferry timetables
- gold prices
- health information for travellers
- independent schools
- keeping fit
- life assurance schemes
- marine freight rates
- news
- official publications
- programs for computers
- qualifications
- recruitment agencies
- sports results
- theatre programmes
- unemployment figures
- vacancies
- weather forecasts
- yachts for sale
- Zimbabwean offices

When you first log on to the system, you see the general menu screen shown in Figure 1.5. By working through a series of (in most cases) no more than half a dozen or so increasingly specific menus, you can arrive at a menu from which you are able to find out about each of the above areas; probably you can see how that could be done from the main menu in most cases. In fact, one of the most interesting aspects of Prestel to the browser (and one of the more frustrating to the lost seeker after knowledge), is that there are many routes through the system to any given page. On the other hand, you can search Prestel by keyword rather than page number – typing *** muse**, for instance, will take you straight to the MUSE front page; you can also give names to pages you use a lot of access in this way. Figure 10.2 shows what you next get when you enter **21** (for 'Banking') and **22** (for 'Business') from the Prestel main menu.

Browsing through Prestel (as through any general subject database, such as a library or an encyclopedia) is great fun. All the same, by doing so you build up costs. Not only are there the phone calls to pay for (at local rates from nearly all parts of the country), but Prestel charges for its use in two ways. The first is by a rate of a few pence for each minute you are online during business hours (access is free out-

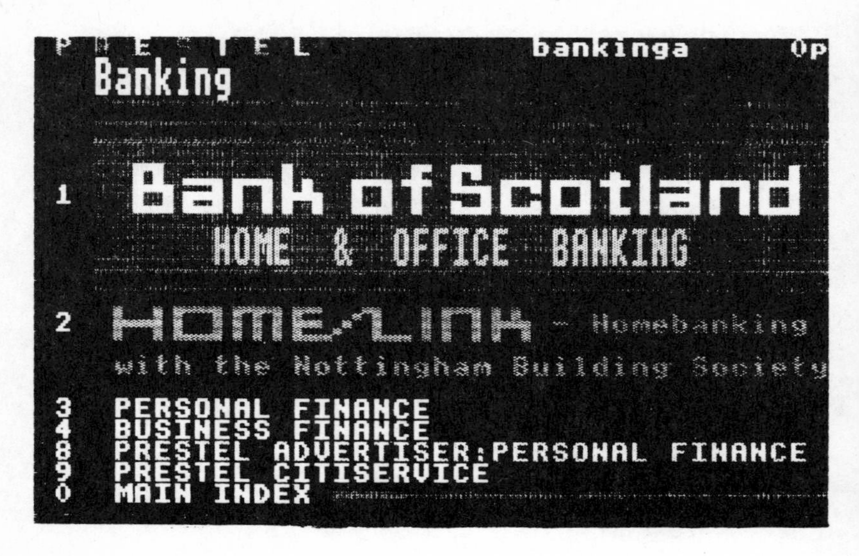

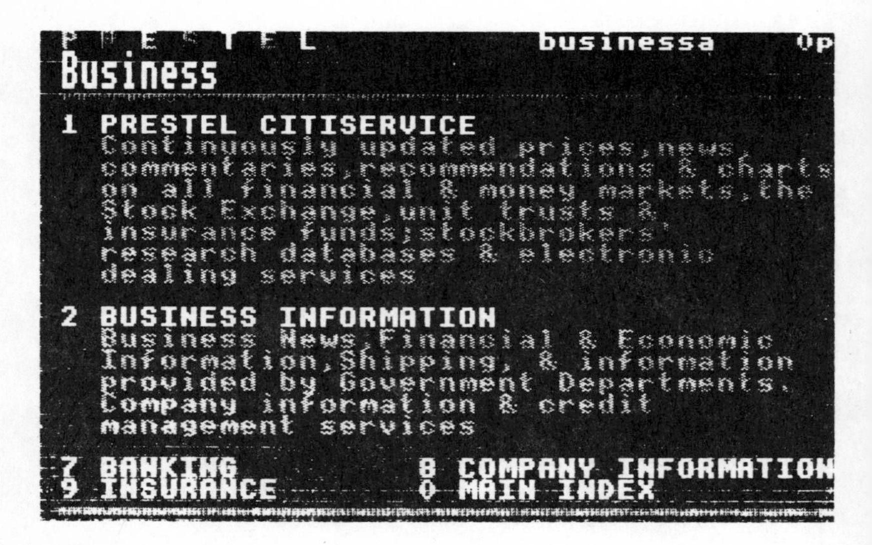

Figure 10.2. Here are two second-level menu pages; they are that much more subject-specific than the Prestel main menu (Figure 1.5) from which you may reach them

side of those); the second is a page charge which can vary from a few pence upwards (though most are free). Each time you call a charged page to your screen, you will find that amount added to your bill at the end of the quarter. The bill also includes the time charges and the subscription (about a pound a week in early 1987). Prestel does not, however, add the cost of using the telephone lines to your account – that goes on to your phone bill in the normal way.

From the story so far, you may think that Prestel is no more than a very large teletext system like Ceefax and Oracle (see Section 10.3). This is not the case, however. Teletext is a serial access database; when you call up a certain page, you must wait for it to flash by so your system can grab it for you. Prestel, with thousands of times more pages, can't possibly work like that. It has to be direct access; it must be able to send you each page you want as soon as you call it up. The distinction between serial and direct access is not how Prestel and teletext differ intrinsically, though it relates to their true difference.

The true difference is that teletext involves one-way information transfer only, while Prestel is two-way – it is interactive. Figure 10.3 shows this point.

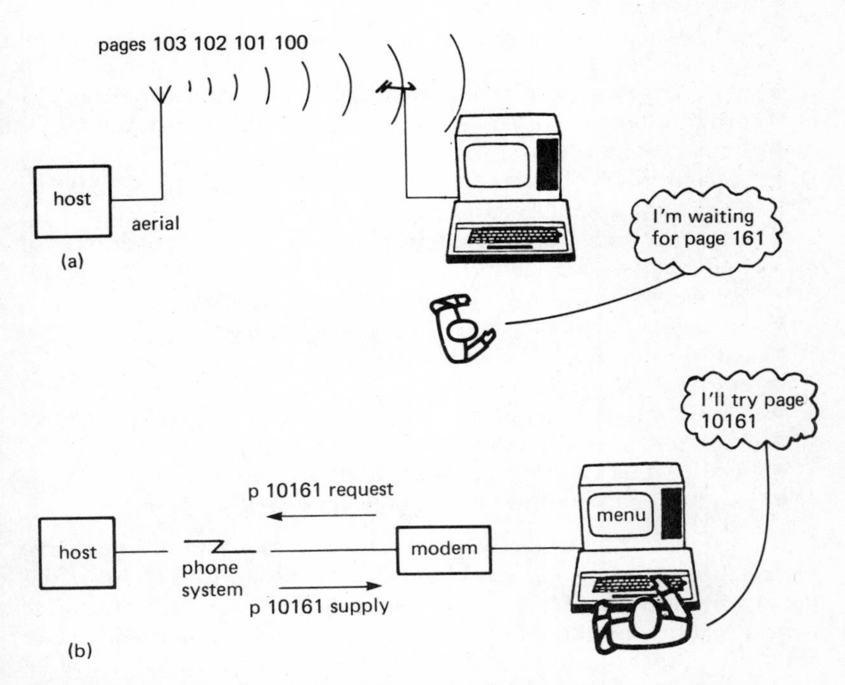

Figure 10.3. Teletext is a one-way information transfer, while Prestel is interactive, or two-way

The two systems also differ in the medium of information transfer. The type of teletext exemplified by Ceefax and Oracle carries information in broadcast tv signals. Therefore it *must* be one-way, as there's no method by which it could react to the needs of just one out of perhaps millions of viewers. Prestel (viewdata is the general name) uses the two-way telephone network for its information transfers; as long as a circuit can exist between the database on the central computer and a given user, then it can react to that user's requests.

Once one has the concept of interaction between user and system, one can see the potential of far more than simple page requests. Here's a second list of Prestel services, this time of those offered interactively, ie ones to which you can send information, as well as receiving it. You can:

- reserve an aeroplane seat (telebooking)
- carry out banking transactions (telebanking)
- hire a car (telebooking)
- chase up debts (electronic mail)
- work through objective tests (teletraining?)
- send flowers to an absent colleague (teleshopping)
- play games (telegaming)
- get advice on specific higher education courses (teleconsultation?)
- get prospectuses from independent schools (teleordering)
- order a delivery of jam and other groceries (teleshopping)
- book a hotel room in Kirkcaldy (telebooking)
- . . . and lunch at a nearby restaurant (telebooking)
- send a message (electronic mail)
- put up a notice on a 'bulletin board' (a sort of broadcast – or published – electronic mail)
- get details of Open University courses (teleordering)
- arrange a parcel special delivery (telebooking)
- compete in quizzes (telegaming)
- bet on a race (telegambling?)
- send a telex (a sort of electronic mail)
- explore US viewdata systems
- record your views of current events (televoting)
- send wine to another absent colleague (teleshopping)

Join those two lists of one-way database accesses and of interactive information transfers respectively, and you get some idea of the potential power of Prestel. Many of the tasks in either list would otherwise need a visit to a high street or city centre shop and a wait in a queue, or at least lengthy long distance phone calls or correspondence – even if they were not quite out of the question. With Prestel you can deal with each by pressing a few keys, or by filling in a simple form on screen and if need be typing in a credit card number.

There are perhaps three main reasons why the number of Prestel subscribers has only lately entered six figures (with almost as many home and school users as members in business). First, people are often quite content to get by with standing in queues and trying to phone long distance – the old ways seem the best. Next, while we all know that Prestel costs money, it is not so easy to work out how much (or how little) an access and search for information does cost (especially in comparison with that time spent in queues and on long distance phone calls). The third reason is that it takes a while to get to know how to use Prestel with speed and efficiency. Using the published directory (which comes free each quarter) and building up your own lists of often-used pages and mailbox numbers helps a great deal – but only practice makes perfect with Prestel.

Using a micro rather than a simple keypad or dumb keyboard helps too. With a micro you can prepare a message offline and store it on disc; when you have logged on, you can then send the message off into the electronic mail system much more quickly than you can type it. On the other hand, with a printer online, you can dump Prestel pages from screen to paper for later study and filing.

Prestel *is* splendid, but it does seem to have barriers in practice. What can we learn from France? Free or very cheap hardware and software and access to material not to be obtained elsewhere – these are part of the story.

10.3 Other videotex systems

Prestel is Britain's main example of viewdata; the one-way system of database access exemplified by Ceefax and Oracle is teletext. Both viewdata and teletext are types of videotex, a term covering any way in which a number of people widely spread out can obtain information held in a central electronic database. In the last section we saw how the two main types, viewdata and teletext, differ. They are much the same in being able effectively to distribute information that requires frequent updating (and that is why videotex often carries the name of distributed database working). The first of the two long lists of Prestel features given in Section 10.2 includes typical information of this kind; quite a few are offered by Ceefax and Oracle too. The table in Figure 10.4 shows how teletex and viewdata compare.

The way teletext works is very simple. At the transmitter, the system adds the pages of the database, one by one in turn, to a carrier radio wave; it starts again when it reaches the end. The radio signal thus transfers the endless sequence of pages through the whole broadcast

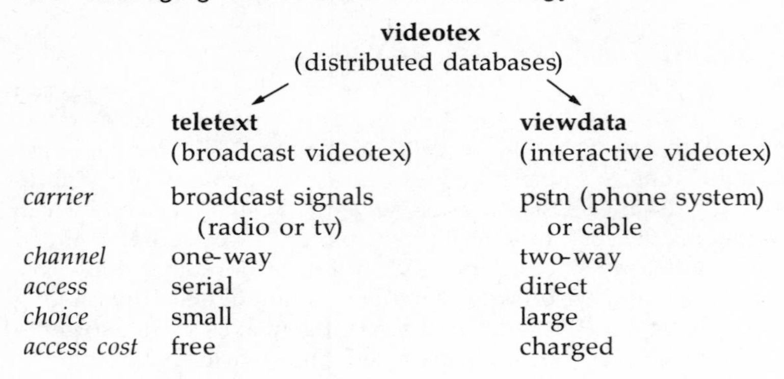

Figure 10.4. There are clear distinctions between broadcast videotex (teletext) and interactive videotex (viewdata)

region. Any viewer with a suitable decoder can capture the signal; using a keypad allows him or her to tell the decoder which page number to watch out for. When the signal that carries that particular page comes into the set through the aerial, the system 'grabs' it – stores it in its memory for display on screen. More complex (and more costly) teletext units have a little printer attached. The user can thus obtain a hard copy of any teletext page on demand.

As with Prestel, it is also possible to connect an interface between the decoder and a computer system. Not only does this let you obtain better printouts and save the most useful pages on disc, but it opens the way to telesoftware. This feature makes it possible for you to download programs (as well as 'conventional' information) from the database into your own computer. Because of the serial method of data transfer, however, a teletext database cannot offer very many pages. Do not think of telesoftware as a source of large volumes of high quality business software therefore; it is restricted on the whole to games and to fairly trivial educational programs in Basic for the BBC Microcomputer.

It would be entirely possible to devote a whole broadcast channel to teletext, and perhaps this will happen one day. At the moment, however, teletext frames take up some of the unused space in broadcast tv channels. The small amount of spare space that the system can use in this way restricts the rate of broadcast of the teletext pages to about four a second. That in turn restricts the number of pages in the magazine, because – recall the serial transfer – viewers should not have to wait too long to see a given frame. See Figure 10.5, however.

One aspect of that description may take you aback, in the light of comments made in Chapter 8. This is that the decoder actually stores

Figure 10.5. It is normal to transmit a teletext menu page, like this one from Ceefax, several times in each cycle of pages, so that viewers can see it quickly

the screenful of data that represents a teletext frame. This does not, however, need half a megabyte or more of memory as would be the case with a normal broadcast video frame (and that figure was for analog storage). Teletext uses great chunky pixels for its graphics, which is why curves and the edges of diagonals (Figure 10.6) appear jagged. This very low resolution graphics system means that a teletext frame needs just less than a kilobyte to transfer and store in digital form.

Prestel uses teletext graphics too; this is why a Prestel page that has come down a low bandwidth phone line takes less than a second to build up on screen. The viewdata systems in some other countries offer higher resolution – better pictures – and Prestel is exploring this too, in the form of Picture Prestel. However, until cable is common, with its great rate of information transfer (large bandwidth), really high resolution videotex of any kind is not likely.

There has been a long debate about the place of teletext in the future, with a big question being whether it will ever replace newspapers. The text in a newspaper is the same as that in at least a thousand teletext frames: a lot more than we now have on all four British channels combined. On the other hand, teletext offers much better colour than print, to make up somewhat for its poor graphics – but even so there is no contest at the moment. (Portability may not be an issue much longer, by the way; at the time of writing, it seems that pocket teletext receivers are shortly to appear.)

While teletext is of great general interest, therefore, its value in the

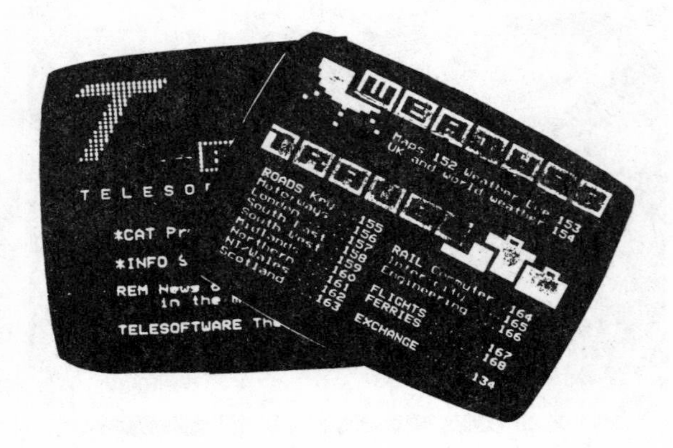

Figure 10.6. Teletext colour graphics are very low resolution, but a screen needs only 1K to transfer and store

business context is fairly low compared with that of viewdata, whose interactive nature and direct access to a huge volume of information give it much more potential. Indeed, because of this, many organisations have set up their own Prestel-style databases.

There are three types of system here: micro viewdata (closed circuit viewdata); special databases accessed via Prestel through gateways; and separate systems that can be accessed in the same way as Prestel. All three styles of database are identical to Prestel in their graphics system and tree-like, menu-driven structure. Therefore all three suffer to some extent from the restrictions of Prestel, including the use of single frames to hold separate fairly small chunks of information (a kilobyte can hold no more than about 150 words).

Micro viewdata is a very pleasant system for in-house databases held on a net and accessed through workstations. Suitable software allows you to construct the frames and their relations (routeing); it is available for many micros.

To construct a viewdata frame, you need to be able to enter text and also to handle the codes that let you use colour, flashing effects, double height characters, teletext graphics blocks, and the hiding of material that the user can reveal only by way of an extra key press. You design each frame, lay it out, and edit it; then you save it to disc with a list of the pages to which it should lead as a result of the different key presses offered in its menu (Figure 10.7). You can see that, as well as planning the frames, you need to work out the whole tree structure, of which Figure 10.7 may be just a tiny part.

There are three notes to add about routeing, making the links between the frames of a viewdata base. The first is to observe that it is not only possible, but also good practice, to plot several routes to a given page. Second, you must not leave a frame hanging at the end of a

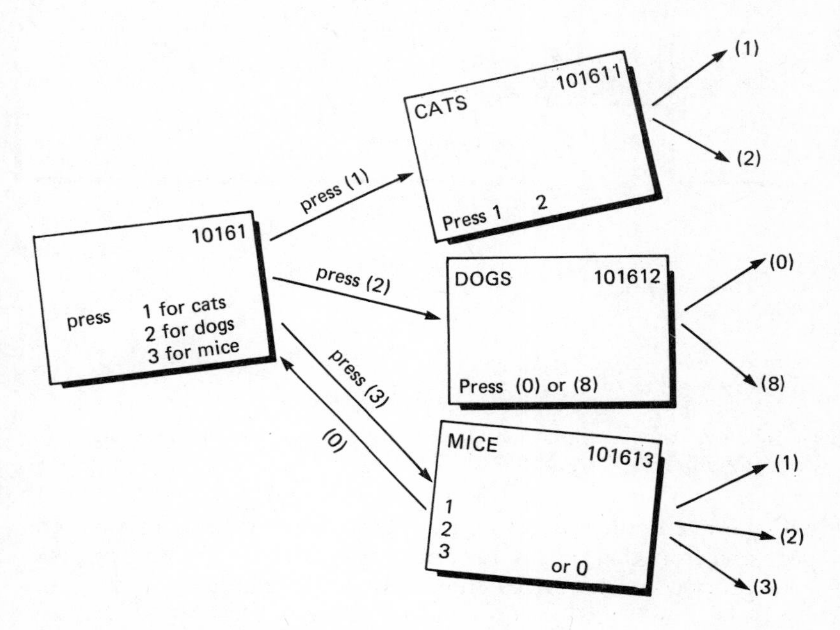

Figure 10.7. A viewdata frame offers options that lead to a number of other pages (unless it is at the end of a branch)

branch; if it leads nowhere else, at least route it back to a previous one. Both those points are shown in Figure 10.8. They may make route planning sound a hard task; but it is fun and easy enough to get into a routine with. There is a third point: you can route a set of frames into a closed loop round which the system passes automatically. This carousel style of working is not interactive, but it has its uses. These include displays of product details and sequences of pretty graphics frames that carry a very simple message; people use them at exhibitions and in foyers and shop windows.

To set up your micro viewdata base so that people can access it by telephone is a logical next step. Most viewdata programs allow you to design such a system. You will need a modem, and that must link the computer to a telephone line that has no other use (or at least has its access times published). When this is done, people can get in touch

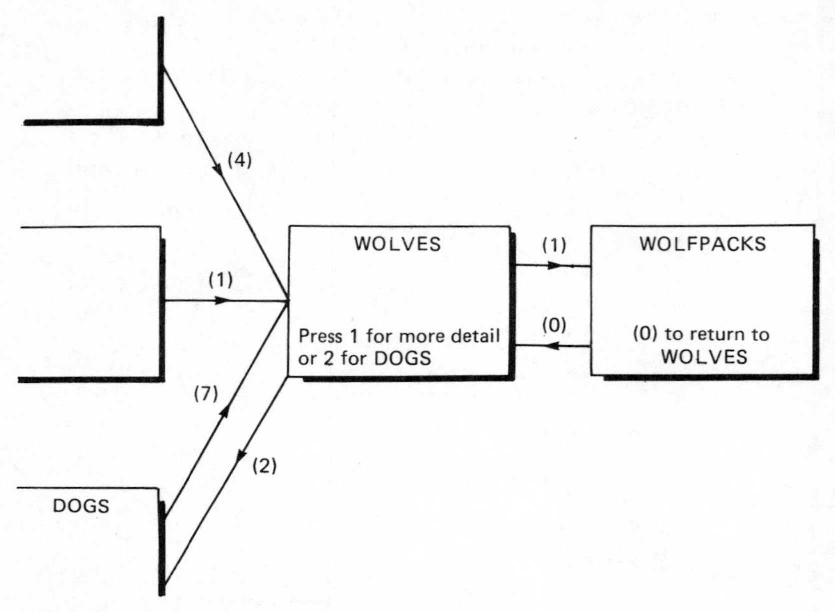

Figure 10.8. A given frame may lead to up to 10 others; it *must* lead to at least one other

with your computer whenever they want. They will reach your menu page and from that obtain, for instance, current details and prices of your products and services. Interaction is still possible, so the caller can leave a message for you, or order goods – teleshopping by electronic mail order. That means you can provide your own one-way electronic mail (two-way if you introduce a password system at the logging-on stage) and a teleordering service. Anything Prestel can do, you can do – if you have the hardware, software, time and patience, and if you have the staff to keep the pages up to date and to check often for the new orders and messages that have come in.

An alternative to this, if your database becomes really large and busy, is to join in with Prestel. Prestel offers a number of gateways to special databases. Users log into Prestel in the normal way and move to the gateway frame. They can pass through the gateway into the special database only if they now enter a distinct password. In other words, in most cases gateway databases are not open to all, but only to members of your closed user group (cug). The members may be travel agents who use the database for getting flight details and making bookings, for instance, or people prepared to pay to access masses of up-to-the-minute stock exchange information.

To the information provider (but not necessarily to the user) there are two kinds of gateway. One lets the user pass into an area of the Prestel computer database whose access is reserved for members of the closed user group in question. The other is a physical gateway, a link to a separate database held on a separate computer.

Thus, you may start out by offering your micro viewdata base to public access (or to customers or agents). Later you may decide to let Prestel provide a gateway as well as, or instead of, that. However, the data remains in your computer, so you can control its content with greater ease.

The term viewdata strictly covers all forms of interactive videotex. In recent years, however, there has been a tendency to use the term only for Prestel-style systems – those with the information organised into separate screen-sized frames built up from teletext graphics. There is, however, a second, highly important type of viewdata that in many ways offers more to business. This type doesn't much use colour graphics, nor does it use pages. Rather it allows the transfer in either direction of monochrome text in large volumes which scrolls down the viewer's page.

British Telecom Gold (BTG) is the best established system of this kind in the country. It started out as a subscription system for high volumes of electronic mail; (presumably) for this reason, some people call this kind of database an electronic mail system. It is far more than that, however; offering vast banks of information, perhaps general, or in a single special field such as nuclear physics.

Thus The Times Network for Schools is very strong on education; in that field, it has huge volumes of reports and other information there for the taking, as well as electronic mail that lets you exchange 'messages' of any length. Then there's British Telecom's Hotline, which is set up specifically for business users. Hotline in fact offers 19 separate databases, some of which cost (early 1987) a pound a minute to access (on top of the £1000 a year general subscription). The databases cover such things as British companies (nearly two million are listed in detail), world-wide market reports, news and comment in IT, abstracts in electronics, US company news, and so on.

Compared with such systems as these – and there are many – Prestel starts to look very small beer. On the other hand, Prestel is much cheaper and simpler in use.

Hotline, British Telecom Gold, The Times Network for Schools and the rest of the high volume scrolling databases all exemplify the thriving field of electronic publishing. Electronic publishing also includes dial-in current affairs databases (electronic magazines) on a much smaller scale. All the same, for the time being it seems mainly the province of very large companies; perhaps only they can afford the massive hardware and marketing costs and the continuing huge effort of getting information into backing store and keeping it up to date.

All these systems certainly include electronic mail among the services they offer their subscribers. They do so in a competitive, rather than a cooperative way, however. Thus, it is rare to find you can use one system to send information to a subscriber on a second. This is an unhelpful barrier that, we must all hope, will soon fall.

In theory there is a link in telex, because all these systems also allow members to send and receive telex signals. Telex is, however, a crude method of information transfer; also, you need to know the 'address' of the person or firm you want to contact. It is therefore very fiddly for subscribers to different 'electronic mail' systems to use telex for sending information to each other. Linking databases to allow the easy flow of information between subscribers is not technically hard, nor is it commercial bad practice. At the moment, however, the database providers do not like the idea; even when they do come round to a more helpful approach, a lot of work will be needed to provide a system of unique addresses and an adequate directory.

10.4 The compact disc

As we saw in Section 8.2, video discs – including the wood, the laser optical disc a computer can store digital data on (write to) – have huge potential in the area of database working of one kind or another. The same is true of the compact disc (cd). Its strength (to us, but weakness in some other contexts) is that it is digital only. The strength of digital data handling, in turn, is the great decrease of problems of data loss, noise, and wear.

The cd was first devised to store audio information – voice and music – in digital read-only form. A big advantage in comparison with video discs is that cd has only one format, one size (12 cm across) and one technology. The replay technology is in fact the same as that of the reflective optical video disc used in the laservision system; a laser in the drive reads the data held in the pits and lands on a spiral track, to which direct access is in effect allowed. A major difference is that, whereas the laser video disc stores its data in bytes (units of eight bits), cd does so in double bytes (16-bit words). This is not a barrier, however, and players exist which can read either compact or laservision discs.

The fact that only one world standard for cd exists so far is the main reason why cd is in advance of the video disc for read-only computer storage. Compact disc read-only memory (cd-rom) is likely to become common in the near future. With a cd able to store at least 600 megabytes at the moment, there is great potential here for database applications, particularly local online ones.

The strength of the concept is that you can link a standard (audio) cd player as backing store to a computer; all you need for a fast and high volume database management system, therefore, is the right link and suitable software. The database can hold any form of information that can be digitised. In particular, this includes computer programs, text, high resolution graphics, speech and music. The current 600MB limit gives about a quarter of a million pages of text. Sequences of broadcast video are possible too, of course, but these can only be short (as there isn't room on the disc for many frames at a few megabytes each); they must also come off in slow motion as the data transfer rate from cd is only half a megabyte per second. A video sequence stored on cd would therefore be like slow-scan tv.

Electronic document storage (eds) is another area in which cd-rom can offer a great deal. It can compete directly with microform for handling archives; the only problem is that it takes a lot longer to transfer information permanently to cd-rom than to microfilm or fiche. Then there is an interactive system rather like interactive video in principle, using interactive compact disc (cd-i). Again, though, recall that the current standard compact disc can store only a minute or so of video and can play it back only at a slow frame rate. At present, these are severe restrictions on many of the more exciting uses of cd in information technology.

At the moment then, it is the use of cd-rom for online database storage that is of most interest. This is optical publishing, to which the optical video disc can also offer a great deal. Reference works, such as directories and encyclopedias, and abstract services are already appearing in this form. Financial records and other forms of archive can be stored this way too.

Of course, people are working hard – in different directions – to overcome the problems mentioned above. They may well succeed. For instance, some are trying to assess the use of computers with both cd and video disc online. Also, there are ways to reduce the storage space needed by a video frame to well below 100K. As well as that, it is possible to achieve a high enough transfer rate to allow full speed video (such as putting only changes in the picture into the signal for each frame rather than the whole picture each time). Such compression techniques as these may well lead to success. Indeed, they have done so already; one US company has been able to replay two hours of broadcast quality video from a compact disc. That's not bad, in view of the fact that an audio cd can carry only about an hour of hi-fi music.

However, all this activity is likely to lead to loss of that precious world-wide compatibility. There are rumblings of this already, with several major computer manufacturers claiming to be near to bringing out cd-rom units specific to their own systems. Is that worth it, when we can use video discs in compact disc size to carry any kind of information? It is certain that cd will become strong in the storage of data in all but video form, and there are plenty of exciting applications for that. It would be nice, though, to have a truly universal database medium.

The digital optical disc (dod) is a type of video disc specially designed for use with a computer. In the form of the 13cm optical rom (orom), in particular, it may soon compete directly with the cd-rom (12cm). The strength of the orom is an access time of well under a second; it takes perhaps only a tenth as long as cd to pull out a given chunk of data. On the other hand, the data storage capacity is less than half as much, well below 300MB. If current work succeeds in making it possible to write to an orom (as will surely happen), optical publishing could end up with three incompatible formats: the laservision type of video disc, the cd-rom, and the orom (perhaps rewritable).

The laservision disc is the largest (30cm) and can carry the most data (several GB); however its access time is long. Its value to publishers, therefore, is when very large amounts of data have to go on to a single disc and/or when the data includes moving video. The orom has the smallest capacity and the fastest access time (less than half a second). This gives it value in software publishing (including the associated documentation). Finally, cd-rom is best for large databases of text with or without graphics.

All three systems are, to repeat, forms of optical publishing medium. All three therefore compete with data storage on paper, in microform, and on computer-readable magnetic media.

Magnetic media (discs in particular) have almost entirely taken over as the way to hold data in computer backing store. However, in comparison with optical media they have only one advantage at the moment, other than being well tried and well known. This is that re-writing is easy and straightforward. To balance that, magnetic media have many disadvantages for long-term data storage. In particular, with their drives they are costly and prone to damage (and therefore to data loss); as well as that, they do not hold their data long, so that people recommend backing up every couple of years. It is widely expected, on the other hand, that optical storage will have a lifetime of several decades – some claims have been as high as a century.

It is worth noting here that optical storage also improves on magnetic storage in the field of cards that carry data on stripes. The magnetic stripe is well known in the case of credit and cashpoint cards, but it is delicate and can hold only a couple of hundred bytes.

Drexon is optical data storage in reflective film form produced by a photographic process and read by laser. The film is used on discs and tapes, and also on stripe cards. In the last context, the stripe can hold (at the moment) at least 2MB. Each Drexon card, costing only a pound or two, can therefore carry a good number of computer programs for use in an online card reader, while the recordable version (write once) allows a huge volume of personal data to go on to an identity card (for instance). That data can include digitised fingerprints and a photograph, as well as more obvious personal and medical records. Two MB of online data storage gives the Drexon card a lot of potential in the database field too; catalogues, manuals and directories come to mind as publications that could do with compact storage and easy mailing. After all, 2MB is several times the length of this book.

10.5 Bringing in the expert

What is intelligence? Hidden deep in many minds is a fear that computers will eventually become so 'intelligent' that they will take over the world. While such a fear may show a rather simplistic view of computers, it remains. A more useful fear would concern people's abuses of the already huge powers given by IT, but it is still of interest to consider what we mean by computers being 'better' than people.

Already computers are better than people in many ways. Any computer can churn out invoices or circular letters with fewer mistakes and at greater speed than any human. At least, it can do so once it is programmed and fed with suitable data. Any computer can crunch numbers of amazing size. At least, it could do so if someone told it how. Any computer with an encyclopedia on cd-rom online is far better than a person at finding a specific item of information. At least, it is far quicker at showing on screen all paragraphs in which the phrase 'information technology', for instance, appears. Quicker it may be at all such tasks, but discriminating it is not – thus the human user of a paper encyclopedia may be slower at finding something, but at least he or she will be able to reject references that are not of interest.

Similar comments apply to all uses of computers: they may be able to do tasks of varied kinds with aplomb, but they do so in a blind unthinking, uncomprehending fashion. How we can do the same kinds of tasks, with insight and inspiration and a feel for relevance and shortcuts, is not open to analysis; it is an aspect of our intelligence.

People have defined human intelligence in many ways. I find it useful to think of it as shown when someone does something for which there are no clear and obvious rules. Stringing words together to make a memorable poem; struggling to make sense of someone's handwriting; throwing out a quick opinion on a matter of current debate; using leftovers to make a splendid meal; deciding what to do in an office crisis; sketching a landscape; planning a novel test in physics – none of these involves set procedures, and none is predictable in detail or clear as to method: all show intelligence.

A machine can't do any of those things because a machine can do no more than follow the precise instructions given to it – and those instructions *must* be precise. Yet the computer world is now full of talk of artificial (or machine) intelligence. If it has artificial intelligence (ai) a machine should clearly be able to do more than follow precise rules; it should rather act with 'fuzzy' logic and thus carry out tasks in a more 'human' way.

Most computers in use so far follow algorithms, precise (but restricted) sets of instructions and rules. The goal of workers in ai is to replace algorithms by heuristics – rules of thumb rather than of logic. 'If it's getting cloudy, take a raincoat when you go out' is a heuristic. When this goal is reached, computers *will* be able to carry out tasks in a more human way. For instance, they will be able to react to (no, not 'understand') natural language rather than the current baby talk we need to use with them; they will be able to play games like chess with a kind of insight, rather than by using immense number-crunching power to assess all possible moves; they will be able to solve problems, rather than just long sums: they will appear to reason, rather than acting blindly.

To do such things, the computer must be programmed with those heuristics rather than with the precise rules of the 1980s; it must also be able to draw on a database of facts and relationships; and – very important – it must be able to extend its database, to 'learn by experience'.

In the context of this book, those last two points are particularly important. An artificially intelligent computer with a knowledge database is an expert system – in full, a knowledge-based expert system (kbes). People who work on such systems have the grand title of knowledge engineers.

An expert system, then, is a database of facts and relationships from which the software makes deductions rather as a human would. The content of the database is not just information, therefore; it forms a body of knowledge. If the database is big enough and properly engineered, an expert system can approach the standards of a human expert. That means being able to solve problems correctly and in a human way (apparently).

Expert systems of value exist already in a number of areas of interest; people use them, for instance, in branches of medicine, architecture, engineering, law and business. In each case, the knowledge engineers consult specialists (human experts) as to the facts, rules and heuristics to include in the database. Often they put in probabilities too, to allow the output to list possible solutions to the problem in order of likelihood. When that has been done, the computer carries an expert system. This means that when problems within its field are entered in the right form, the system should be able to come up with reasonable solutions.

- 'Should I sell those shares now, or wait a couple of days?'
- 'What is the best price for this product?'

- 'I have this pain – what is the matter with me?'
- 'How can I ensure all the field staff get my message tonight?'
- 'Is this particular product exempt from value added tax?'
- 'What is the best circuit to use this chip to do such and such?'
- 'Is there likely to be gold in them thar hills?'
- 'What communications system should I install in my office?'
- 'How much discount can I offer this new client?'

Questions like these, although not put so bluntly, show the types of problem an expert system, once engineered, can cope with. If the database is set up right, and if the problem is correctly stated, then an expert system will actually give better solutions than any human could. This is because it carries, and correctly works with, the knowledge of a number of leading human experts in the field. It does not have insight, though, or show inspiration.

Don't confuse this type of system with programs like the famous Eliza (so well described in David Lodge's book *Small World*). Eliza can appear to be intelligent by reacting in a guided way to inputs, so getting involved in long 'conversations' with a 'patient'. Thus, any time the patient mentions his or her father, the program would reply with a question like 'How do you feel about your father?' All the same, Eliza learns nothing, infers nothing, can come up with no answers or diagnoses.

There are many stories about business people (and others) who expect too much of their computer. On unpacking the box and switching on, they type in some such question as those listed above. Rather than responding with an answer as a guru might, the computer reacts with 'Mistake' or a message of that kind. That's because the system has not been programmed for the required purpose and does not carry the information it would need. Computers are not intelligent – and nor does giving them an expert system make them so.

How can you decide if you'd benefit from an expert system? If knowledge and knowledge-based skills are of high value in your business, a kbes is likely to be helpful. If someone with years of unique experience is leaving, and you don't know how you'll manage, distil his or her wisdom into a kbes with the aid of a knowledge engineer. If you can't keep in mind all the factors that relate to a given problem, so that mistakes from faulty memory could cost you dear, invest in an expert system. In each case, you gain a highly useful tool, but it remains a tool and not an intelligent adviser.

It may be the case that the expert system you'd like is already on the market, so you may be able to buy in this software expertise ready-packed. If you do that, make sure the system has an 'explain' option. This means that you can ask it to 'explain its reasons' for its claims. Also, you will need to be very clear about what it can't do, as well as what it can. It is useful to realise that having a bureau design a kbes for you need not be very costly; it depends on how novel the database must be, and how wide. Keeping within the range £1000–£10,000 is quite common.

As expert systems become more widely used, the question of their actual intelligence will be more and more often asked. Can an intelligent computer make mistakes? Should an intelligent computer have rights, or be able to vote? Can a patient sue the machine if it carries an expert system that gives the wrong diagnosis as the most likely? An expert system in the field of expert systems could design a better expert system than itself. Could this go on so that we end up with expert systems that know everything and can make no mistakes? If we do, would these systems 'rule the world'? This is indeed a fascinating area, but it can overlap with science fiction rather than with IT fact.

There are areas of ai other than knowledge-based expert systems. The ability to understand, and to reply in, natural language is a very important one, as is the ability to do so using speech input and output rather than keyboard and screen. If a computer can be given a good grasp of natural language rules and heuristics, it should be able to translate between human languages with minimum error, although in practice, this is a fearfully tricky task. It could also be used for the automatic monitoring of suspects' telephone lines, a '1984' outcome that we would be much less happy to welcome.

From artificial speech we lead naturally on to artificial vision. Here, under the title of pattern recognition, is another important area of ai that, finally, brings us to robotics. The future will bring machines that really can replace people in many areas of manufacturing. Able to see and decide what to do on the basis of what they see, future robots will be much more flexible than those we have now. But intelligent? Perhaps an important question in that context concerns how much intelligence the replaced humans had to bring to bear on their work. Drudgery does not require intelligence, after all.

10.6 Information in the global village

The 'global village' theme touched on once or twice is a view of a future world in which all people have cheap and effective access to the information they want and need. Various scenarios could allow that to happen; all depend on the universal availability of the right kind of hardware and software and on cheap and trouble-free methods of high-volume information storage and transfer.

Cable and satellite links can provide that without doubt, while developments in hardware are certain to continue their amazing pace. As for storage, progress with floppy magnetic discs is leading to capacities as high as 100 MB; it is also likely that hard discs, digital audio tape (dat), and video storage media will show an increase in storage density of the same order – a thousand times, in other words. Thus, within a decade, any computer user will be able to have as much information locally online as he or she may wish.

We can also expect continued miniaturisation, with its spin-off of increased reliability, reduced costs, and reduced power demand. This is so, not just in electronics, but in areas such as electric motors. (There are now some able to fit on to chips with their control circuits, so are as small as a tenth of a millimetre across.) Superconductivity can make electric power demands negligible within equipment as well as in network links, while bioelectronics may bring people and machines much closer together. On the software side, we can look forward to highly integrated facilities within artificially intelligent systems, as well as the ability to process large quantities of data using a number of programs at the same time.

Some of those developments will first affect the world of the large organisation, where the needs are highly concentrated and finance is less of a problem. However, they will rapidly spread to the small business, to education and training, and to the home.

Indeed, a scenario at one extreme of the spectrum sees each work, leisure and living unit linked to a global cable network. In the unit – office, school, shop, home, pub – is an adequate supply of intelligent workstations. Current progress in artificial intelligence and true concurrent processing could lead to those being non-local. By this I mean that speech synthesis and speech recognition could reach the stage that, wherever in the unit you happened to be, you could talk with the 'workstation' in the same way as talking with the person standing next to you.

All this could lead to psychological problems, of course: the thought of a room full of people all chatting away with their IT systems may bring to mind a cocktail party – not the best situation for a thoughtful and useful interaction. Apart from that, it might not always be the most suitable way of getting information to the system and out of it, and other forms of input and output would sometimes be better for security reasons anyway.

Of course there would still be a need for visual displays so that one could study tables of information, look at views of products or places, and see data in text or graphic form. But the visual display might take the form of a large flat wall unit, able to show broadcast and recorded tv; the person across the world with whom you are having a phone call; frames from any of a range of videotex databases; documents from microform archives or an eds system; restful scenes from your library of pet landscape photos; or computer-generated graphics to match your mood by a kind of living wallpaper. The software driving the display would of course offer windows (a split screen feature in other words) in all these contexts, so you could keep an eye on, or work with, information from various sources at once. That cable system has a lot to carry!

The vision at the other end of the scale is one where each unit is, on the whole, self-sufficient in information. There would be much the same hardware, but in most cases access to it would call up information on the unit's own bank of chips and discs. The social view behind this particular scenario involves the idea of the village in a true sense, that in which people relate to each other in a tight local community rather than in the world as a whole.

A major question is how well IT will be able to reduce the stresses that seem almost inherent in the current style of living and working. One major way to reduce those stresses at work involves a much increased degree of telecommuting. Here the need for local and long-distance business travel falls as information transfer – communication – becomes faster and cheaper. Working from home or from an 'office' just down the street is no problem if that global cable network is set up. Better expert systems, universal and fast electronic mail, interactive video, electronic and desktop publishing, fax – better versions of most things we've looked at – should *all* reduce the need for face-to-face meetings.

There are many possible visions of the medium and more distant futures in which IT plays a crucial role. In the meantime, hardware, software, machine intelligence and communications links will all continue to develop, cheapen and spread – and they will do so almost independently of social systems. Future scenarios, then, will be a result of how people decide to use what is on offer, rather than of changed technology as such. The criterion of choice should always involve giving all the people concerned a fuller life: less drudgery, less boredom, more freedom to do things in their own way. This should be so wherever we end up in that spectrum of IT futures. Managing with IT should not mean just coping with it, but using it as a positive aid to dealing with your enterprise needs effectively.

How will *you* manage with information technology?

Appendices

Appendix 1
Glossary

This glossary includes the main technical terms used in the book and those likely to be found in treatments of this field at a similar level. The entries are only for initial reference – this is not an encyclopedia. However, the material should provide enough information to help you in your reading and understanding of more detailed explanations elsewhere. Please also refer to the index.

abbreviated dialling The facility to code telephone numbers so the user can call them by pressing just a couple of keys.

access The retrieval of information from whatever stores it, eg a chip, floppy disc or video tape (see also serial access and random access). Access time describes how long a system takes to find a given packet of data. As a verb it means to get access to. Access to a computer system may be open to anyone who knows who to work it; on the other hand, it may be controlled by formalities like subscriptions, logging-on procedures, passwords and so on.

access time Describes how long a system takes to find a given item of data in backing store.

accounts An important area of business computing, in which the software greatly helps the keeping of accurate and up-to-date financial records.

acoustic coupler This type of modem is designed as a cradle for a telephone handset, linked to a computer through a cable. The coupler turns computer information into sound signals and vice versa. This method is not as fast as using a standard modem, and is sometimes unreliable, but couplers are cheap, portable and more flexible in use.

acu Autodialler – automatic call unit.

adc Analog to digital converter.

address A number, label or code that identifies a particular location in a computer memory or on a disc. Also a verb: a processor addresses a particular area when it directly reads information from it or writes to it.

aerial A structure, also called antenna, that captures or transmits long electromagnetic waves – eg a television aerial and a mobile phone antenna.

ai Artificial intelligence.

algorithm A way to describe the method of solving a problem as a logical series of steps; may be in words, as a chart, or in pseudocode.

alphanumeric An alphanumeric character is any letter, number or symbol on a keyboard. The US form is alphameric.

am Amplitude modulation.

amplifier A device to increase the strength (amplitude) of an analogue signal.

amplitude Technical word for signal size, with the amplitude of a signal relating to its strength.

amplitude modulation (am) Method of encoding an information signal on to a carrier wave by varying the amplitude.

analog Refers to many real world quantities (eg time, temperature, pressure, weight) that vary smoothly in value, rather than in the steps of digital (numeric) form. Digital computers can handle such information only by assigning numbers to it. This usually means translating it into bits, binary 0s and 1s.

analog to digital converter (adc) A type of device for converting analog information (eg of time or temperature) into digital form. Such converters allow digital hardware to link to analog systems.

animation The arrangement of a sequence of separate pictures, eg video frames and computer graphics, made to follow each other so quickly they appear to the viewer as continuous movement.

answer back Special code sent by a telex machine, for instance, to show that a message has been received.

antenna Aerial.

aperture card A type of microform, in which a large card carries a single frame in a central hole.

applications program Software that applies a computer to a real world problem, such as handling accounts or driving a robot.

architecture The logical (effective) layout of a circuit, system or cable network.

archive A form of data held to meet long-term needs (perhaps for reference), that will not need to be changed.

array A list or table of numbers or words laid out in an orderly way to allow easy access; a form of network.

artificial intelligence (ai) Some computer software displays intelligence in the sense that, if humans were to perform the same task, you would describe them as intelligent. For example, an ai program may add to its 'knowledge' from previous runs; interpret the meaning of a question from its context; prove mathematical theorems; or diagnose diseases or electronic faults. Machine intelligence is sometimes the phrase used (see also expert systems).

artwork Originally, graphics in a form ready for printing, but now often used for any kind of material ready for printing.

ASCII American Standard Code for Information Interchange: an internationally accepted system for coding characters for processing and transfer. For instance, the ASCII code for the letter 'A' is 65 (in base 10) while that for 'B' is 66. (In binary form these codes are 0100 0001 and 0100 0010 respectively.)

aspect ratio The ratio of the width to the height of a single frame or screen. For instance, video pictures are four units wide to three high, while film and 35mm transparencies are three units wide to two high. Most media have the same aspect ratio as television sets, though standard paper is 7.1 units wide to 10 high.

aspic One of several systems for coding layout and heading instructions so that a disc containing word processed text can be inserted directly into a typesetting machine to produce camera-ready pages.

assembler A program that translates

assembly language instructions into machine code.

assembly language A low level programming language that uses coded versions of English words to give instructions to a processor. The assembler automatically translates these into machine language. Assembly language is harder for humans to work with than high level programming languages like Basic.

atm Automatic teller machine.

attenuation Loss of strength of a signal while it travels over a distance, as in a sound getting fainter with distance from the source.

audio Concerns sound waves in the audible frequency range (roughly 20Hz to 20,000Hz), or electrical signals in the same range and equipment to handle them.

audit trail A printout report produced by some accounts software that shows what happens to a set of transactions.

authoring language A very high level programming language designed to speed up and simplify the job of writing applications software for computer-based systems. Authoring (or author) languages may also have special editing facilities and software tools to enable people who are not professional programmers to write their own software, eg for training; they are then sometimes called authoring systems. People often use modern authoring software for the control of presentation systems that include video tape or video disc.

autodial A facility allowing automatic calling of telephone numbers that have previously been stored, on receipt of simple codes. The device that offers the feature is an autodialler, or automatic call unit (acu).

automatic teller machine (atm) The cash dispenser in the wall of a bank or building society, that offers other services as well as money; also called auto-teller.

automation Putting processes under the control of machines rather than of people; this includes robotics.

background A processor can divide its attention so as to do several jobs at the same time. The simplest form of this time-sharing is where one job (like a spreadsheet) is worked on 'in the foreground' while another (like printing out some text) takes place whenever there are no other demands on the processor, ie in the background.

backing Backing store is external memory that supports and communicates with a computer's internal memory. Back-up equipment duplicates crucial items in case of breakdown. Thus people keep back-up discs in case of loss of or damage to the originals. To back up a disc is to copy it in its entirety.

bandwidth A measure of the information-carrying capacity of a communication channel. The higher the frequencies used, the more bandwidth may be available (see also broadband and narrowband).

bar code A pattern of printed lines (often seen on library books and items for sale) used for direct input of data to a computer with a bar code reader.

base station The unit in a cellular telephone network that handles the calls within a small area (cell).

Basic Beginners' All-purpose Symbolic Instruction Code: a very popular high level programming language, almost universally available on microcomputers, but in many incompatible dialects.

batching Collecting together all messages for one destination and sending them off at the same time.

batch processing A style of computer processing in which various jobs are run in one batch, the opposite of interactive processing.

baud A unit of rate of transfer of information within or between systems. Thus telex operates at 50 baud; programs often load from cassettes at 300 baud; teletex operates at 1200 or 2400 baud. For most practical purposes, one baud is one bit per second.

Baudot The well established information communications code used in telegraphy and telex, with a five-bit word length.

bespoke Describes a system that is designed for a particular customer. Commissioning bespoke software is the opposite approach to buying a package off the shelf.

binary number A number written in the binary system, so built up only from the digits 0 and 1.

binary system A method of counting which uses only two digits (0 and 1) instead of the usual 10 (0 to 9); digital computers work in binary deep down in effect.

bioelectronics Such technology uses microelectronics circuits with biological materials or with biological systems. Thus a biosensor is a sensor that handles some physiological input, such as blood sugar content.

bit A binary digit, 0 or 1.

board A circuit and a set of chips on a printed circuit board, added to a hardware device to provide extra features.

boot Programs can be made to load and run automatically on switch-on, so the system boots itself–'pulls itself up by its bootstraps'.

bps Bits per second, a measure of information transfer rate (see also baud).

branching A method of passing through a course, program or database by a route that depends on inputs, rather than by a fixed route (linear).

bridge A hardware and software link between, for instance, two networks.

British Telecom (BT) The United Kingdom's main telecommunication system provider.

British Telecom Gold (BTG) A major British interactive viewdata base, with a strong electronic mail component.

broadband (wideband) Describes a communications channel with plenty of bandwidth, usually taken to mean at least enough to transmit television signals at normal speed (contrast narrowband).

broadcast A process of distributing signals one-way to a wide audience, often by radio or television, usually financed by some blanket method of payment or advertising (contrast narrowcast).

broadcast videotex Teletext.

BT British Telecom.

BTG British Telecom Gold.

bubble memory A compact and robust form of main memory which depends on storing information in magnetic 'bubbles' (domains) in a thin film of a material like garnet.

buffer A temporary store for information in transfer, eg for holding a text until a printer has completed the printout, thus releasing the processor for other tasks.

bug A mistake, in a system or program, removed by debugging.

bulletin board A communal electronic notice board that allows people to log on and exchange news, views, for sale notices, and wants. Some bulletin boards are commercial, while others are run by hobbyists. They can be a cross between magazine, notice board, and exchange and mart system.

bureau An agency that offers special high power services to a number of firms that can't afford, or don't need, to own the systems involved themselves.

bus A common path that links all the different parts of a computer system, such as a network allowing them to exchange data. Everything is linked to the bus at all times, but each device takes data from the bus, or puts data on to it, only when necessary.

byte A byte, a group of eight bits, can represent any keyboard character or control code. An eight-bit processor handles information in bytes (still sometimes called octets), therefore, and machines with more power deal with data in pairs of bytes or even larger groups.

cable Describes video distributed through wires rather than broadcast using radio waves. In areas with poor reception, a cable operator may erect a high performance antenna and distribute the signal by cable to people. A cable network over an area may offer a whole new approach to many kinds of electronic information transfer(see also closed circuit tv).

cad Computer-aided design.

call logger A unit that monitors a telephone system and keeps details of all calls made for later study.

cam Computer-aided manufacture.

camera-ready Describes material in a form suited for printing (by a process camera).

capacitance Ability to store electric charge; in some video disc systems, the varying capacitance between the pick-up (head) and the disc's data surface codes audio and video information.

caption camera A video camera with the function of sending signals that represent captions to a mixer.

card Board, but see also punched media and stripe card.

carousel A system that cycles again and again through a series of pictures or viewdata frames.

carrier wave A wave (often of light or radio) which carries an information signal by the variations of some kind (for instance, of amplitude or frequency) imposed on it.

cartridge Software on rom for some microcomputers is sold as a sealed plug-in cartridge. It is then easier to use than if on disc, or on a rom without the cartridge.

catalogue The place on a disc that carries a list of its contents; also called directory.

cathode ray tube (crt) In this device a narrow controlled beam of high energy electrons puts a visible picture of some kind on its screen. Monitors, tv sets and radar displays are based on the crt.

Cauzon strip Data for a computer, printed in robust and compact form on paper for reading by a special input device.

CCITT International Consultative Committee for Telephony and Telegraphy: a body that issues standards for telecommunications and data transfer for most countries outside the USA.

cctv Closed circuit television.

cd Compact disc: cd-i is compact disc interactive; cd-rom is compact disc read-only memory.

Ceefax A teletext service provided by the British Broadcasting Corporation.

cell A particular item in an array – eg, a data site in a spreadsheet, a unit of the picture on a screen (pixel), an area serviced by one transmitter in a radio telephone system.

central processing unit (cpu) Processor.

channel A path for communication – whatever connects an information source to an information receiver. A single complete channel may consist of several information transfer links and several units of hardware.

character Any number, letter, symbol or control code on a keyboard, screen or printer, the collection of all symbols that a system can process or display being its character set.

chat mode The design of electronic mail systems is to allow the sender to transmit a message to someone who may not be available until later. However, if both parties are online at the same time, they may also communicate in chat mode. This is a sort of typed-out telephone conversation in which each sees the other's words on the screen and can type in the reply immediately.

chip A tiny piece of silicon that can contain complicated electronic circuits.

chrominance That part of a video signal giving information about the colour of each cell of a television picture.

circuit switched public data network (cspdn) A type of exchange based telephone system specially designed for the transfer of data.

circuit switching Involves linking two devices directly using exchanges or switching centres, as in the public telephone network (pstn) and the cspdn (see above). Throughout the duration of a data transfer, the two parties occupy the switched circuit exclusively, even when there is no data actually in transfer (contrast packet switching).

clock A kind of clock, a chip that puts out pulses at regular intervals, controls the basic rhythm of a processor; it keeps the system's activities in step. Its frequency is millions of cycles per second (megahertz, MHz). Eight-bit microcomputers usually have a clock frequency in the range 1 to 8 MHz.

closed circuit tv (cctv) In such systems, video cameras pass signals either to a central point to be monitored by humans, or to a video recorder where they are stored for various periods (according to the application). The main uses are in security and for training (compare broadcast).

closed user group (cug) A group of subscribers to Prestel (for instance) who have access to the public pages but can also send information to each other privately.

cluster A star network.

cluster controller A device for handling access to a processor by a number of channels (see also multiplexer).

co-axial cable (co-ax) Wire with a sleeve of braided metal screening to prevent interference with the signal it carries, as with the wire that connects a tv aerial to the receiving set.

Cobol Common business oriented language: a high level programming language used widely in business computing.

code The process of writing out a computer program is coding; the chunks of program that result are code. Thus code generators are simply software generators. Codes are also a way of compressing information so that it takes up less space in a channel or a store.

com Computer output to microform.

command mode A style of system use in which the user controls the action by typing in commands (direct instructions) or command codes, instead of choosing options from a menu.

common carrier A provider of basic telecommunications facilities who takes no particular responsibility for the uses to which it is put.

communications software Programs that enable a computer user to transfer messages and data files over a distance,

often using a telephone link, perhaps with features like autodialling and help menus.
compact disc (cd) A 12cm disc, designed to store high quality audio signals; also able to carry hundreds of megabytes of digital data, leading to cd-rom, a method for putting very large amounts of data online to a computer in read-only form. Another field is cd-i (compact disc interactive), an approach rather like that of interactive video.
compatibility This rare quality in the world of electronic equipment is almost unheard of among microcomputers: even when people describe two systems as compatible, it may not necessarily mean that programs or data can be taken from one and fed straight to the other.
compiler A computer program that translates an instruction in a high level language like Basic into machine code, done as a once-and-for-all job, unlike an interpreter.
compression Cutting down the space needed to store, or the signal needed to carry, a given package of data (such as a video frame or an electronic mail message), various techniques being in use.
computer-aided design (cad) Software packages that help design work by giving good graphics, a library of standard sub-designs, modelling, analysis, and simulation.
computer-aided manufacture (cam) The digital control of machine tools and assembly lines in an integrated manner.
computer output to microform (com) A process in which microfiches or film are produced as direct computer output rather than having to be photographed from printout.
concentrator A modern form of multiplexer with its own processing power.
concept keyboard An input device of value to users who find a standard keyboard an obstacle. Instead of having to type out words letter by letter, the user presses the part of the surface that bears a picture or symbol representing a particular concept. The board accepts a variety of overlays, so can be adapted to different software.
concurrent Literally means occurring at the same time. Multi-tasking is a technique for making a number of programs seem to run in parallel, by letting them take turns at the processor. Concurrent cp/m is a version of the cp/m operating system designed for this purpose. In *true* concurrent processing, a number of processors linked together in parallel (as in a transputer) can really do different things at the same time.
conference call A telephone call in which more than two people participate.
configuration A particular configuration, or combination of equipment and software, makes up a working system. To configure a system is to modify it to meet some individual set of needs.
Confravision British Telecom's public video-conferencing system.
console The main terminal in a large system, for use by the chief operator, though the term sometimes loosely means any workstation.
consultant An expert (in theory) in some aspect of IT, with (in theory) no ties to any particular system or supplier, and therefore able to give (in theory) valid impartial aid and advice to a user.
consumables Anything you need a regular supply of, like printer paper and fuses.
continuous stationery Paper sup-

plied in continous form, eg fanfold, as opposed to separate sheets.
control codes Used to make screens and printers produce a variety of effects, like colour, margins, bold face and underlining.
control program Operating software.
convergence Describes technologies that were previously separate but are now coming together and making use of the same basic principles (eg digital coding of information) and sometimes even the same equipment (like video receiver/monitors and compact disc or video disc players).
corporate communication Meeting the information needs within a firm or group, such as by putting up notices, sending out circulars or a house magazine, or publishing the occasional video for the staff.
corruption Unwanted changes to data within a computer system or during transfer over a distance, as a result of software mistakes, interference or attenuation.
cpa Critical path analysis.
cpi Characters per inch, used to measure printer typefaces.
cp/m The nearest thing to a standard operating system for eight-bit microcomputers, always known by its initials; you can think of it as 'control program for microprocessors'. There are also 16-bit and network versions.
cps Characters per second, used to measure printer speed.
cpu Processor.
crash When a program stops before the end, we say it has crashed. Good software design should prevent this, and may then be called crash-proof. A head crash is when the read/write head of a drive touches a disc surface and causes damage and loss of data.
critical path analysis (cpa) A technique, now often used with the aid of a computer, to schedule the tasks involved in, and the resources needed by, a project.
crt Cathode ray tube.
cspdn Circuit switched public data network.
cug Closed user group.
cursor A symbol on a screen that shows you where you are, usually a square blob or an underline mark and often flashing.
cut and paste The technique of joining chunks of text and pictures together to make a camera-ready copy of a page for printing, now much aided by desktop publishing software on computers.
cycle time The delay between a teletext user calling up a page and its appearance on screen, caused by the time taken for the teletext magazine to cycle through all its pages.

dac Digital to analogue converter.
daisy wheel The print head of a type of letter-quality printer used with micros. The characters that can be printed appear as raised shapes on the ends of the spokes (petals) of the wheel, and the wheel spins to put the right ones in place in turn.
dat Digital audio tape.
data Generally, information without meaning, even if in the form of letters or numbers that you can read. Sometimes people restrict it to mean information after a system has prepared it for processing or transfer.
databank A collection – usually a large one – of data held in a computer, the term sometimes being used interchangeably with database.
database (db) A collection of information files organised systematically so as to make processing easy. Database management systems (dbms) are computer programs for designing a database, and allowing its use, normally by more than one person.
data capture The process by which a

computer automatically obtains data from its environment, or the process by which people obtain information so that it can be fed into a computer with few errors.

datafax A public fax system.

data haven A country where there are no restrictions on the processing, exchange and sale of data. Countries with data protection laws may restrict the export of data since their laws could be evaded so easily in data havens.

data processing (dp) Loosely, the handling of information; this usually refers in practice to the batch processing by computer of large volumes of prepared data, such as telephone bills or a payroll.

data protection Procedures and laws designed to ensure the privacy and security of stored personal data.

data skew When data pass through a parallel link over a long distance, bits that set off together do not always arrive exactly together. This lack of alignment is skew.

data subject Anyone on whom information is stored.

db Database.

dbms Database management system (see database).

dbs Direct broadcast (by) satellite.

debug To remove mistakes (bugs).

dedicated Specially designed for, or limited to, a particular purpose, as opposed to being programmable.

default The value or behaviour that a system assumes unless otherwise instructed.

demodulator A device that reconstructs an original signal from a modulated version, eg digital computer data from the analogue version received through a telephone system (see modem).

desktop publishing (dtp) With desktop publishing software a compact in-house computer system is used to produce pages of professionally laid-out text and graphics ready for printing.

dialect A variant of a programming language, eg Basic exists in hundreds of different dialects, all incompatible to some extent.

dialogue An exchange of questions and answers between a computer program and a user.

digital Anything that can be counted as separate numbers, the opposite of analog – a digital signal is step-like, while an analog one is wavy.

digital audio tape (dat) Magnetic tape on which analog sound signals can be stored in digital form, and therefore with very high quality and potential for computer backing store.

digital optical disc (dod) A video disc that carries its data in digital rather than analog form, so has potential in computer backing storage.

digital to analog converter (dac) A device that changes digital information into analog form, eg it may allow the output of a digital computer to control analog devices like motors and transfer to traditional telephone systems.

digital voice messaging The speech equivalent of store and forward electronic mail, voice messages being held by the host computer in digital form.

digitiser Any device able to give a digital output from some form of analog input. The term is most often used for graphics pads, for scanners, and for systems that capture a video signal so that it can be processed by computer.

direct access Also (less wisely) called random access, this describes how any part of a computer memory, back-up disc or video disc can be found quickly without having to work through from the start. The opposite of serial access (as in a cassette that has to be wound through from the beginning).

direct broadcast by satellite (dbs) Using a satellite to relay the signals sent to it so that they can be picked up in a large area by anyone with a suitable aerial.

direct connect modem A modem that connects directly to the telephone network, unlike an acoustic coupler.

directory Catalogue.

disable To prevent from operating; sometimes it is useful to disable a key (like a computer's <BREAK> key, pushing which may wipe out a program) or a device (eg a printer, if printout is not needed). The opposite of enable.

disc A flat circular sheet of material used to store information (US, disk). It may be hard (rigid) or flexible (floppy). Discs for computer data storage are magnetic; compact and video discs are non-magnetic.

disc drive A device that retrieves (reads) information from and records (writes) it to a disc, working with discs only of suitable type, size, density and number of tracks.

disc operating system (dos) A computer program that controls the storage and access of data on discs.

disc pack A stack of hard (rigid) magnetic discs.

diskette A floppy disc; a term mainly found in the US.

distributed database Has its banks of data shared between several computer systems. Sometimes used to describe an electronically published database.

distributed processing The generic phrase for using either intelligent terminals with a mainframe or mini, or a network system.

documentation Printed instructions and manuals that are vital if a user is to get the best out of any system; an important (but often neglected) part of a package.

dod Digital optical disc.

dongle A cartridge containing a chip that you must plug in to a computer before you can work with the software – it thus protects against illicit use.

dos Disc operating system.

dot matrix Describes a printer that forms characters from a matrix (grid) of dots; the more dots possible, the better the shape of the character.

download Transfer of data from one computer to a smaller one, typically from a mainframe to a terminal or from a network to a workstation.

downward compatible Able to work with hardware or software that is simpler or older.

dp Data processing: large firms often have separate dp departments with dp managers in charge.

Drexon Drexon film is able to carry digital data at high density so that a laser can read it for input to a computer system. Its uses are on video discs, tapes and cards.

dtp Desktop publishing.

dual sound With two independent sound tracks, so that the same video material can be viewed with a choice of sound track (perhaps in different languages or aimed at different levels of audience), or the second sound track can be used to provide stereo output.

dumb The opposite of intelligent; describes a device with no processing power of its own.

dump To copy a block of computer memory somewhere else, eg to a printer (thus a screen dump is a printout version of the screen display) or to backing store.

duplex A communications link is duplex (or full duplex) when both parties can send and receive at the same time (contrast half duplex and simplex).

edit To improve, cut or rearrange material, such as text, programs or video tape. An editor is a device or program to help you do this.
eds Electronic document storage.
eft Electronic funds transfer.
8-bit systems These deal with information in eight-bit chunks – or words – ie they process or transfer one byte at a time (see also 16-bit systems).
electromagnetic waves Vibrations of electrical and magnetic energy that travel together between two points. The electromagnetic spectrum is the full range of electromagnetic waves, usually classed by frequency or wavelength.
electronic document storage (eds) Holding copies of documents (pure text or with graphics) in a form that can be accessed by a computer, such as on some kind of disc.
electronic funds transfer (eft) The transfer between computers of data that represents sums of money.
electronic mail A method of transfer of information across a distance using cable, telephone lines, broadcast waves or satellites. Confusingly, some people also use the phrase to describe scrolling interactive videotex (viewdata) systems like British Telecom Gold.
electronic office Jargon used to describe an office in which there is much use of new information technology.
electronic publishing Preparing and storing documents (pure text or with graphics) so that other people can access them by computer, eg through a communications link.
electronics The technology of systems that involve small electric currents.
electrons Sub-atomic particles with negative charge that carry electric current in a metal and also make up the beam in a cathode ray tube.
emulation Making one device behave like another.
enable To make a key or device operate, as opposed to disable.
encryption Converting electronic data in to a coded form before storage or transfer to make illicit access harder.
enquiry language A high level language specially designed for interrogating (asking questions of) a database, in particular that of an expert system.
enter To put instructions or information into a computer.
ephemeral Not permanent, eg a computer's ram is often ephemeral – its contents vanish when you switch off.
eprom Erasable programmable read-only memory; a rom chip which you can load with a program that you can later erase. Usually erased by shining ultra-violet light through a circular window over the chip. Eproms are a useful way of distributing firmware that is still being developed and refined.
ergonomics The study of the relationship between the design of equipment and systems and the comfort and efficiency of the people who use it.
exchange Switching centre in a public telephone network, for instance.
execute The stage when a processor actually carries out the instructions in a program.
executive A type of operating software.
expert system The name given to software that builds up expertise in making judgements and displays artificial intelligence. Some expert systems can converse with humans in

a relatively natural way, and some can explain and justify their line of 'reasoning'. So far, the most successful expert systems tend to operate in a restricted field of knowledge; these may be called knowledge-based expert systems.

extension A telephone handset without its own direct line to an exchange.

external memory The storage of information outside a computer, usually in magnetic form such as on disc.

facsimile transfer Fax

fax Facsimile transfer (or telegraphy), in which the entire content of a sheet of paper (including diagrams, letterhead, signature and so on) is scanned, coded and sent to a compatible remote terminal connected by a telecommunications link.

fdm Frequency division multiplexing.

feedback The transfer of information from the output of a device or system to the input in such a way as to control the action of the device or system.

fibre optics The use of ultra-thin flexible strands of very pure glass to carry information at high speed.

field One complete scan of a television screen, covering every alternate line; two interlaced fields together make a single frame. The term also refers to a single item of information in a database, such as a name or address; each field may need a large number of bytes to store its information.

file A collection of instructions, text or data held in a computer's memory or backing store. A text file might be a short letter or a book chapter; a data file could consist of a handful of items or a hundred thousand.

file manager A program to help the user create, edit and update files of information.

filename The name by which a computer system knows a file, perhaps an abbreviation of the one by which the user normally refers to it.

firmware Intermediate between software and hardware, firmware instructions are fitted in to a computer semi-permanently, usually in the form of rom chips.

floppy disc (floppy) See disc.

flowchart Method of showing the logic of a computer program or the sequence of operations in a system using boxes joined with arrowed lines.

fm Frequency modulation.

footprint The area of the earth's surface with which a satellite can communicate, or the area of a surface that an item of equipment occupies.

format The format of a piece of text means its headings, spacing, layout and margins. The format of data means its arrangement in a file, on a disc or on a screen. The format of a video tape or video disc includes its physical size and colour standard. As a verb, to format a disc is to prepare it to receive information in the form suited to the system in use; this process deletes any information which was on the disc before.

fourth generation The imminent style of computer use, with vlsi electronics, parallel processing and human/machine communication by speech, and with software giving freer use of natural language than at present.

frame A complete video picture, made up of two fields; in videotex, a single screenful of information; in microform, a single image.

frame grabber A device that captures a frame from a television signal and turns it into digital form so that a computer can store, display and manipulate it.

freeze frame A single frame from a moving sequence held motionless on screen, though not designed to be viewed in isolation (contrast still frame).

frequency The number of cycles of some repetitive action performed in a second, measured in hertz.

frequency division multiplexing (fdm) A method of sending several signals down a single communications channel by letting each source use a different frequency.

frequency modulation (fm) A method of encoding information on a carrier wave by varying its frequency.

front end The interface between a hardware and/or software system and its user.

function keys Special keys on a keypad or keyboard that do certain operations at a touch. Sometimes their actions can be defined and redefined by the user, so that the same key which justifies text while word processing might also recalculate a spreadsheet, for instance.

gateway A link that allows certain network or viewdata users access to external computers and their databases.

GB Gigabyte.

generation It is useful to describe the history of the modern computer in four stages or generations. The processors of the first (1940s and 1950s) were based on valves; those of the second (1960s and early 1970s) used transistors; those of the third (current) have chips; while people expect the hardware of the fourth generation (1990s) to involve a number of processor chips working in parallel.

geostationary If a satellite circles the earth at a height of around 36,000 km (22,000 miles) it takes 24 hours to complete its orbit. It therefore appears to hover over the same place on the earth's surface and is then geostationary.

gigabyte (GB) Around a thousand million bytes (actually 2^{30} or 1, 073, 741, 824 bytes).

gigo Short for garbage in, garbage out – a long-standing cliché about using computers.

gips Giga-instructions per second: a measure of the speed of a computer processor in units of a thousand million instructions a second.

global village Jargon phrase to describe a possible future in which everyone has access to cheap powerful IT systems linked to all others, so allowing close world-wide contacts and information transfers.

graphics Pictures that a processor can draw on screen or print on to paper. The higher the resolution of the output device the better the picture. Business graphics software allows the user very simply to build up high quality graphs and charts from sets of data.

graphics pad A form of digitiser, an input device on which the user traces a shape that appears on screen and is coded in digital form for the computer to process and store.

hacker A computer enthusiast, especially one who breaks in to public and private databases. Hacking is sometimes just for fun and sometimes to show how vulnerable the databases are; occasionally it has criminal intentions and effect.

half duplex A communications line is half duplex when both parties can send and receive information, but not at the same time (contrast duplex and simplex).

handshake The protocols by which two intercommunicating systems or devices check each other's readiness.

hard copy Printed output – jargon

for printout.

hard disc A high speed, high density form of external computer memory that can hold much more information than a floppy, but if fixed in the computer (as is common), can't easily be duplicated for back-up.

hardware The equipment that makes up an IT system as opposed to the software that drives it.

hdtv High definition tv.

head The part of a magnetic disc or tape drive or of an optical disc or tape player that allows transfer of data between the storage medium and the system.

hertz (Hz) The unit of frequency, one cycle per second. Radio frequencies are often quoted in kilohertz (thousands of hertz), while processors usually have clock frequencies measured in megahertz (millions of hertz).

heuristics The fuzzy rules of thumb that guide certain artificially intelligent systems.

hierarchy An arrangement in which there are several levels, with higher levels more general than lower ones. Hierarchical databases represent the relationships between different levels in their structure.

high definition tv (hdtv) A planned international standard for the video systems of the 1990s that offers much higher definition than the current (eg 625 line) ones.

high level (programming) language A language like Basic or Cobol, in which instructions are written in words resembling English for subsequent translation into machine code.

high resolution graphics Computer-generated pictures with a lot of detail, which can, for instance, show smooth curves – at least 500 by 500 pixels.

host The central storage computer in an electronic mail or viewdata network.

hybrid Describes a computer whose architecture includes both analog and digital circuits; a network with a mixture of star, bus and ring sections; a video or compact disc that carries a digital version of analog information or vice versa.

Hz Hertz.

ic Integrated circuit.

icon A picture or graphic symbol that represents a particular function, for instance, a rubbish-bin icon to let you delete a file.

information That which adds to knowledge, data with meaning.

information provider (ip) An individual or organisation providing data for a database, usually in the context of viewdata systems, but in general an electronic publisher.

information technology (IT) Includes modern methods of collecting, handling, storing, and passing information, as text, graphics or sound, in this book taken to consist of computing, electronics and telecommunications. The UNESCO definition is: the scientific, technological and engineering disciplines and the management techniques used in information handling and processing; their applications; computers and their interaction with people and machines; and associated social, economic and cultural matters.

inkjet The mechanism of a compact, fast, quiet printer which sprays tiny drops of ink on to the paper.

input Anything put in to a system; also used as a verb meaning to feed in. A keyboard is an example of an input device.

integrated circuit (ic) Chip.

integrated services digital network (isdn) A type of digital network that combines voice and data traffic at 64,000 bits a second, so as to allow a wide range of communications options. For instance, subscribers can call up information from a remote computer database using a data channel, and discuss it with a colleague using a high quality voice channel at the same time.

integrated software Programs designed as a collection so that the output of one can automatically feed into a second.

intelligence Describes the ability to do things unpredictably and/or without following clear rules, perhaps with insight and/or inspiration, plus the ability to learn.

intelligent device A stand-alone or peripheral unit with its own (local) processing power.

interactive Interactive communication is two-way so that what one party does depends on the response just received from the other, and vice versa. Interactive computing is the opposite of batch processing. Interactive videotex is viewdata.

interactive video (iv) A new communications medium combining features of computing with features of video presentation. Instead of viewing a programme (a linear sequence of pictures and sound planned in advance by the producers), users choose their own route through the material. They may view still or moving video, hear stereo or dual sound, or see and hear material and sounds generated by computer. Sometimes they may see and hear a combined effect such as computer graphics with video sound, or computer subtitles overlaid on to a video still.

interactive videotex Another name for viewdata.

interface The join between two things – a beach is the interface between sea and land. To interface two devices is to do whatever is needed to let them transfer data. Computer interfaces often involve software as well as chips, plugs and cables, and can be costly.

interference Loss or alteration of a signal caused by noise (other unwanted signals).

interlace The process of linking two video fields together to make a complete frame.

internal memory The main store for information inside a system can be of two types: ram and rom. Internal memory is faster in use than external memory, but more limited and expensive.

interpreter Software that translates a program written in a high level language like Basic, instruction by instruction into machine code, with the result that each line of an interpreted program has to be retranslated each time it is to be carried out (compare with compiler).

inventory software An advanced type of stock control software that offers some accounts features.

ip Information provider.

ips Instructions per second: a crude measure of computing power, especially applied to mainframe computers, though normally quoted in kips or mips (thousands or millions of ips).

ipss International packet switching service: an international network for computer communications that gives higher speeds and reliability than the public telephone network, often at lower cost.

isdn Integrated services digital network.

IT Information technology.

iv Interactive video.

jacket A type of microform holder which contains short strips of microfilm, making the contents simpler to change.

joystick A computer input device that consists of a short lever which you can move freely in any direction, often used in place of a keyboard with computer software and interactive video, and also known as a paddle.

jukebox A device that contains a bank of discs and can load any one into a drive or player.

justify Most typewriters produce text that is unjustified, ie has a ragged right-hand edge. Word processing software can rearrange the spaces automatically, justifying the text so that the right margin is straight.

K or **kB** Kilobyte, a thousand (strictly 1024) bytes.

kbes Knowledge-based expert system (see expert system).

key A button switch on a small keyboard called a keypad; a field through which one searches a file or database for specific types of data; or a string used to decode encrypted data.

key system A form of local telephone network whose users can each take on some of the roles of a switchboard operator and whose handsets offer a wide range of features.

keyword Some databases can be searched by keywords that 'unlock' their contents; the system knows each item by a number of keywords that convey the gist of what it is about. In programming, keywords are instruction words with a special meaning to the computer's programming language.

kilobyte (K) Taken to mean 1000 bytes (actually 2^{10} or 1024). Since one byte can store one character, a kilobyte can carry about 150 words of text.

kips Knowledge information processing systems: the name given to the next generation of computers to emphasise how different their role will be from traditional computation and data processing.

knowledge engineering Building up a knowledge-based expert system – both the database and the means of access to it.

lan local area network.

land The smooth raised region between two pits in the surface of a video or compact disc.

land line A telephone cable between two points dedicated to traffic between those points only.

laser Lasers can produce high energy beams of radiation (often light) with important applications in computing and telecommunications. Laser printers are very high speed and high quality page printers. Some video disc systems depend on lasers.

laser disc See optical video disc, though some people use the term for compact disc too. Laservision is a popular type of optical video disc system.

layout The structure and appearance of material on paper or on screen, for instance.

lcd Liquid crystal display: liquid crystals do not give out light, but can switch from opaque to transparent. This feature can provide quite a legible display in suitable lighting conditions. Such displays need little power, and are used in many lap-held computers as well as in calculators and watches.

led Light emitting diode: an element of a display that gives out light when passing an electric current. Such displays are brighter than lcds, but require more power.

ledger A group of accounts with a similar function, such as sales.
library A collection of discs or tapes used by a firm, of programs and sub-programs used by a programmer, or of standard designs in software used by a designer.
light pen (wand) A pointing device which can be used to select from choices displayed on a screen, or (sometimes) to draw shapes directly on to the screen; another type is used as a bar code reader.
linear Describes material (eg program or text) through which one can pass by only one route, as opposed to branching.
line printer A high speed computer printer that prints a whole line, as opposed to a single character or a column of dots, at a time.
list processing The processing of data arranged in the form of lists; in word processing, sometimes used to describe the insertion of stored information, such as names and addresses, into mail shots.
load To copy data from a backing store (eg a disc) in to a computer's main memory.
local Describes short full-time links between those parts of an IT system that are in effect permanently online.
local area network (lan) A method for linking computers and peripherals that are nearby, usually on the same site (contrast wide area network (wan)).
local processing The use by a peripheral, terminal or networked microcomputer of its own processing power rather than that in the centre of the system.
log on To register your presence on a system, perhaps also by identifying yourself as an authorised user.
logger (Telephone) call logger, or the same kind of device used in other systems.
low resolution graphics Crude low detail pictures in which individual pixels are clearly visible, with resolution perhaps as low as 40 pixels across by 20 down, suitable for simple bar charts but not for curves.
lsi Large scale integration: method of packing a large number (100 to 1000) of electronic components and their connections on to a single chip (see also vlsi and ulsi).
luminance The part of a video signal that carries information about the brightness of each point in a television picture (compare with chrominance, that part which handles colour information).

machine code The 'language' of binary numbers in which a processor works.
machine intelligence Artificial intelligence.
machine readable Describes data held on paper, for instance, in such a form that a suitable input device can transfer a copy to a computer's memory.
magnetic (ink) character recognition (mcr or micr) Automatic recognition by machine of characters printed in special magnetic ink.
magnetic media Media on which a system can store data in the form of a magnetic record, in particular tape, disc and stripe.
magnetic stripe See stripe.
mailbox Space in the memory of a computer reserved for a user's incoming messages.
mail merge A word processing facility where details from a file of names and addresses are merged into spaces in standard letters.
mainframe A large powerful computer with many users, often spread over a distance, sometimes running a variety of languages and software at the same time (see time sharing).
Maltron An experimental keyboard

with a more efficient layout than the standard (QWERTY) arrangement.
man Metropolitan area network.
man/machine interface (mmi) The actual point of contact between a hardware system and its human user.
MAP Britain's Microprocessor Awareness Project: a government scheme to aid the introduction of IT into business.
MB Megabyte.
mcr Magnetic character recognition.
medium resolution graphics Pictures of medium quality, adequate for diagrams but unable to show good curves, technically around 300 pixels across by 200 down.
megabyte (MB) Usually taken to mean a million bytes (actually 2^{20} or 1,048,576), just enough to hold the text of this book a couple of times.
megahertz (MHz) A measure of frequency in millions of cycles per second.
memory A computer's memory is a device (or a series of devices) capable of storing information temporarily or permanently. Internal memory contains standing instructions and temporary working space. External (backing) memory stores larger volumes of information for less frequent access.
menu driven A style of program in which the user controls the system by choosing options from a menu, as opposed to typing in commands (contrast command mode).
Mercury A newly set up competitor to British Telecom.
message switching A form of transfer of electronic messages by a telephone system, storing the message at any point if all the lines to the next stage are in use, until a line is free. Packet switching is similar in this way.
metropolitan area network (man) A network that covers an urban area – an extended local or a restricted wide area network.
micr Magnetic (ink) character recognition.
microcomputer or **micro** A fairly small computer that is used by only one person at a time.
microfiche A rectangle of film, usually around 150 mm × 100 mm, carrying tiny photographic images of pages of text or drawings. A microfiche can hold between 60 and 300 pages, depending on the reduction.
microfilm A roll of film on to which tiny photographic images of pages of text or drawings are arranged in sequence.
microfloppy A floppy disc less than five inches (12.5 cm) across, generally between three and four inches.
microform General term for miniaturised storage of documents using a photographic process, eg microfiche and microfilm, with users needing a special projector to be able to read the documents.
microphone A sensor with a sound input and an electrical output.
microprocessor A computer processor on a single chip.
microsecond A millionth of a second.
microviewdata Local (or closed circuit) viewdata, even perhaps on a single micro.
microwave Very short wavelength radio waves used in some telecommunications systems (and radar navigation, burglar alarms and ovens).
Microwriter A hand-held word processing device with its own system for coding characters using only five fingers of one hand.
minicomputer (mini) Cheaper and more compact than a mainframe, but more likely than a micro to have several users at once. It is becoming increasingly difficult to see a dividing line between the power, speed and

memory of top range micros and bottom range minis.

mips Million instructions per second: a measure of the speed of a computer processor (see ips).

mix In video production, a shot can be dissolved gradually into another by mixing the two: the proportion of the second shot increases as the first one fades. A mixer is a device for mixing two or more input signals in to a single output, as above or in a range of other ways.

mmi Man/machine interface.

mobile switching centre (msc) The equivalent of an exchange in a mobile (cellular) telephone system, handling the calls of a number of base stations.

mobile telephone An instrument that can be carried around and used in different places, either within a small area (cordless telephone) or throughout a cellular network. The data transfers in each case involve radio.

modem Modulator/Demodulator: a device that allows digital devices like computers to transfer information to and from an analogue system. Modems can be built into computers or connected to them separately. An acoustic coupler is a modem.

modular A module is a self-contained unit that can readily be added to or built on. Computer hardware, telephone systems and program sections are all modular in this sense.

modulation The encoding of an information signal on to a carrier by changing the carrier in some way. For instance, amplitude modulation (am) depends on changing the size of the carrier; frequency modulation (fm) works by varying its frequency.

monitor A high quality display screen giving a steadier clearer display than a television set; a type of operating software.

monochrome One colour only, as with a black and white television set or an amber or green monitor.

mouse An input device roughly the size of a pack of cards, which the user rolls around on a desk top to control the movement of a pointer on a screen. Action choices are made by pressing buttons on the mouse.

mp/m A multi-user operating system derived from cp/m.

msc Mobile switching centre.

ms-dos A 16-bit operating system first commissioned by IBM for its Personal Computer (on which it is known as pc-dos) but available on many other machines; its main rival is cp/m-86.

multi-access Multi-user.

multi-addressing Such a technique allows a given message to be sent (by telex, for instance) to a number of different addresses.

multiplexer (mux) A device allowing more than one signal at a time to be transmitted through a single channel. One method is to split up the frequency band available into several narrow bands and allocate one to each source; this is frequency division multiplexing (fdm). Another is to allocate the whole channel to several sources in turn by dividing up each second into short slots; time division multiplexing (tdm).

multi-programming A system, offered by some operating software to make processor usage more efficient, which runs more than one program during a given period by switching attention between them from moment to moment.

Multistream A British Telecom service which gives access to the pss at local call rates by use of the same telephone number in all parts of the country.

multi-tasking Describes a 'concurrent' system – one that can deal with two or more programs at a time.

multi-user Describes a system that can work with more than one user at a time.

mux Multiplexer.

nano- Prefix for a thousand millionth, as in nanosecond, 10^{-9} second.

narrowband General term for a communication channel with restricted bandwidth and thus limited capacity for information transfer, sometimes used for channels restricted to 300Hz, and sometimes extended to those able to carry telephone conversations (up to 3000Hz or more) (contrast broadband).

narrowcast The transmission of signals intended for a specific and relatively small audience, using cable, satellite or radio waves, likely to be financed differently from broadcasting, perhaps by subscription and/or by charges related to connection time.

network System for linking one or more computers and terminals so that they can communicate with each other and share facilities like disc drives and printers (see also local area network, metropolitan area network, and wide area network).

nexus A point in a system, such as a network, at which there are interconnections.

nibble Half a byte – a group of four bits.

node A junction or data forwarding point on a network (also called switch in the former case).

noise Any unwanted signal that reduces or alters the proper one.

ntsc The video colour standard, established in the US, that applies to systems that handle colour in a certain way and use a 525-line screen running at 30 frames (60 fields) a second. Used throughout North America and Japan.

numeric Describes data that consists of numbers only (compare with alphanumeric).

nybble Alternative for nibble.

ocr Optical character recognition.

octet A group of eight bits, normally the same as a byte.

oda Office documentation architecture: a set of standards that allow the exchange of documents in electronic form between IT systems.

office of the future The shorthand term for a networked computer-based office with little call on paper, but using electronic systems for all its word and information processing, analysis, storage and communication purposes.

offline Describes a hardware device that is not at the moment linked to a computer but is resting or carrying out its own processing locally.

offset (litho) A simple but effective printing system, cheap enough to be within reach of even quite small firms.

Oftel The Office of Telecommunications, the British regulatory body for this field.

omr Optical mark reader.

online Connected to a working computer system, remotely through a standard telephone link or locally.

open systems interconnection (osi) Protocols for the exchange of data between different IT systems.

operating environment A comprehensive operating system complete with integrated software and special hardware.

operating software (os) A vital program (or suite) in overall control of a computer whenever it is operating. Without the os, the computer could not handle programs, process data, retrieve from disc or send output to a printer: it would be useless. Modern computers often have resident operating systems on rom chips; others load it from disc as needed. Many 16-bit micros give the user a choice of operating system. The characteristics of the os determine how the user perceives the computer and how easy it is to use.

operator A person with the task of keeping a large computer system running smoothly.

optical To do with light. Light waves have very high frequencies compared with radio waves, giving far greater bandwidth and information carrying capacity. The optical fibres that can carry them are very important in modern telecommunications. Some video disc systems are optical as well – they depend on the reflection or transmission of laser light. So too are compact discs.

optical character recognition (ocr) Automatic recognition by machine of characters based on their shapes.

optical disc See optical.

optical fibre A flexible strand of highly pure glass drawn out to be finer than a human hair. Compared with traditional metal communication cables, optical fibres are very light and fine, and have a much higher bandwidth.

optical mark reader (omr) A device for reading pencil marks made in certain positions on a special form.

optical publishing Publishing material in optical form, ie on video disc or compact disc in particular.

optical rom (orom) A video disc used as a computer's read-only backing store.

Oracle The teletext service provided by the Independent Broadcasting Authority in Britain.

organiser A type of business software with such features as diary, address book, and appointments database.

orom Optical rom.

osi Open systems interconnection.

output Any result which comes from a system, usually in the form of text and graphics displayed on a screen and/or printed on paper.

overwrite To record on top of; in word processing, a mode in which characters entered replace what is there already.

pabx Old acronym for private (automatic) branch exchange, pbx.

package Program or set of programs complete with documentation, designed for a particular application.

packet assembly and disassembly point (pad) A node in a pss at which the packets that form a complete message from a sender are made up from that message, or re-joined to go to the receiver.

packet switching A method of transmitting information involving splitting a message into units, each of standard size (maybe half a kilobyte) and format and labelled with source and destination. The packets then each transfer by the route that makes most efficient use of the network concerned; the system reassembles them into the original message at the other end. Very short messages go in a single packet and therefore pass through the system more quickly (contrast circuit switching; see also message switching and the last entry).

pad Packet assembly and disassembly point: unit of information in a viewdata system with a unique page number to allow routeing and direct access. It may, however, consist of a linked sequence of single frames (screensful).

paddle Joystick.

page printer A fast, quiet printer in effect producing output a page at a time, the laser printer being a common type. It is rather like a photocopier with an electronic input.

pal Phase alternating line: colour video standard.

paperless office Another name for the office of the future.

parallel interface A connection between two devices that is capable of parallel data handling, ie passing information more than one bit at a time.

parity check A method of checking data for simple input or handling errors.

password These secret codes are to prevent unauthorised use of a system. Passwords can give different categories of user access to different levels of privileged information.

payroll The name for programs that work out a firm's wages and salaries, print the pay slips, and prepare for payment.

pbx Private branch exchange.

pc Personal computer.

pcb Printed circuit board.

pcm Pulse code modulation.

pel The same as pixel, but used in the context of fax.

peripheral Any computer hardware other than the processor – an input/output device or backing store in particular.

persistence of vision The inability of our eyes to follow very rapid changes in what we see. Thus a light that flashes rapidly enough – more than about 40 times a second – will appear steady. This is the effect on which tv and movies depend.

personal computer A computer that is small enough or cheap enough to be used mainly by one person.

photo-cell A sensor with optical input and electrical output.

photo-typesetter A processor-based system that prepares fully edited and laid out documents for printing, being rather like an advanced text and graphics processor (see also desktop publishing).

pin Personal identification number: a password to identify the user of a cash dispenser or computer system.

pixel Picture cell: one of the tiny squares of light that make up pictures on a video screen; the more pixels, the higher the resolution (see also pel).

plotter An output device for drawing and lettering in which a computer controls the movement of one or more pens directly.

plug compatible A device made by one manufacturer that can be plugged straight into something made by another, then working without any adjustments.

pointer A symbol on a wimp screen under mouse control that lets the user point to the icon that represents a task to be done; a link in computer memory between two related data items.

point of sale (pos) The place where a purchase transaction usually takes place, such as the checkout in a shop.

polling A technique whereby a processor continually checks the channels to its peripherals to see if there is data to be transferred. Automatic polling can also be carried out by some terminals, in telex for instance, to see if there are messages at other terminals.

port A point of access to a processor.

portable Easy to carry, like a small microcomputer; also capable of running on other equipment, like a standard cp/m program.

pos Point of sale.

power line transfer A system which allows data transfers to pass through the normal electric mains wiring of a building or the power lines of the grid.

Prestel A British public viewdata system which contains vast amounts of information in page format. Subscribers can order goods and catalogues as well as getting up-to-date information and sending electronic mail and telex messages. Prestel subscribers with micros need only a modem and communications software to be able to access, save and print Presetel frames.

printed circuit board (pcb) A plastics sheet that carries printed metal wiring and sockets for chips and other circuit elements, a module in a hardware unit's overall design.

print engine The part of a page printer that does the actual printing (as opposed to making up the image).

printer Looking rather like typewriters without keyboards or photocopiers, and designed to produce computer output on paper. Dot matrix and daisy wheel printers print one character at a time; line printers print a complete line as one unit; page printers work much like photocopies.

printout Output from a computer printer – same as hard copy.

private branch exchange (p(a)bx) A firm's own telephone exchange (switching centre), installed on its own premises and run by its own staff for the benefit of the users of its extensions.

process camera A special camera used to prepare printing plates, especially for offset litho.

process control The automation of a process involves feedback from the system's output to its input and a program that carries out the tasks involved.

processor The part of a computer that actually does the arithmetic and makes the decisions, sometimes called the central processing unit (cpu). In a micro, it is often a microprocessor.

program An ordered list of instructions for a computer to follow to carry out a given task, written in a special language (see below).

programmable Describes a general purpose device or system (compared to a dedicated one) which can be programmed for any of a range of tasks.

programming language There are hundreds of such special languages for giving instructions to computers. All programs written using them have to be translated into machine code before the computer can obey the instructions.

project scheduler An advanced form of critical path analysis software package.

Prolog A high level programming language devised by artificial intelligence workers, and suited to developing expert systems.

prom Programmable read-only memory (rom): a memory chip that, once loaded with data, can be read but never written to again (compare with eprom).

prompt Any sign given by a computer (a symbol on screen or an audible beep) to show that it awaits a response from the user.

proportional spacing A way of printing text (as in this book) so that the space taken up by each character depends on its width – compare the spaces used for i and m in minimum.

protocol A set of rules about the format of messages that allows them to be exchanged.

pseudocode A way of writing algorithms in a form rather like that of a generalised programming language.

pss Packet switching service: a network dedicated to computer communications that gives higher speeds and lower error rates than the pstn. The charges for use of a pss often reflect the length of a message rather than its destination. For overseas communication pss is often far cheaper than mail or telephone.

pstn Public switched telephone network.

public switched telephone network (pstn) The ordinary telephone system, which can be used to transmit data as well as speech using a dial-up connection and charged as for an ordinary telephone call.

publishing Preparing material (pure text or with pictures) for others to use – on paper, on microform, on magnetic or other kind of disc (eg optical publishing), or within a viewdata system (electronic publishing).

pull-down menu Computer displays sometimes show reminders of the various facilities available, perhaps as icons along the top of the screen. The user positions the pointer suitably, and then presses a key or button to 'pull down' the full menu. For instance, the reminder might concern shading, and the menu would show the shading styles that are available.

pulse code modulation (pcm) A method for sending analogue information in digital form, in which the system samples the analog signal frequently, and converts the readings into binary numbers.

punched media Cards or paper tape punched with holes in patterns which represent data that a suitable computer input device can read – rarely used now.

query language A high level language specially designed for interrogating (asking questions of) a database.

QWERTY The standard arrangement of keys on a typewriter or computer keyboard, known by its top row of letters: QWERTYUIOP or QWERTY for short.

Quinkey A hand-held word processor without a screen into which characters coded by patterns of presses of half a dozen keys are typed. Quinkey can also be used as a direct input device with a computer.

ram A form of memory used in computers, the data in which can be changed as well as accessed.

random access Direct access.

raster Pattern of lines on a television screen.

read A drive reads information from a disc when it retrieves a copy of it (and writes when it records data on to it).

read and write memory (ram) The storage space inside a computer where data is stored while it is in use. Its contents are constantly being overwritten as different programs run, and may be lost altogether when the computer is switched off.

read only Describes anything that can be read from but not written to, such as a protected disc or rom.

read-only memory (rom) Part of a computer's internal memory that stores software in frequent use. Unlike ram, the contents of rom are not lost when you switch off (see also *eprom*).

real time Describes a system that reacts to each input as soon as it receives it, eg in interactive use or when controlling events as they happen. A real-time clock in a computer system keeps a tally of day, date and time for use or display when needed.

record Each file in a database consists of a number of records, each of which contain various fields for storing units of information. For instance, a firm's customer file might contain details of thousands of companies, with a separate record for each one. To record information on a disc or tape is to store it for future access.

redundancy The extent to which parts of a message can be predicted from a knowledge of the other parts. A large proportion of a highly redundant message can be destroyed without loss of meaning. In general, redundancy means duplication.

refresh rate The frequency with which a system renews the content of a screen or memory. If the rate is too low in the former case, a flicker may result.

reflective Depends on light being reflected (bounced) from a surface.

regenerator A device that detects, boosts and retransmits an input digital signal (compare with repeater). Because digital signals suffer from interference less than analog ones, regenerators can be further apart than repeaters.

relational Describes a database management system that represents some of the complicated relationships that exist in the real world between the items of information that it stores.

relay As a verb, to pass on information; as a noun, an electromagnetic switch.

remote Not permanently online, non-local.

repeater A device, placed in a long cable, that strengthens passing signals. Without repeaters, the signals would be too weak to detect at the end. Repeaters work on analog principles, and tend to amplify noise as well as signals (contrast regenerator).

report A user-defined summary of, or extract from, information held in a database, a report generator being a program that can extract, sort and collate information for this purpose.

resident Permanently fitted in a computer, eg held in rom.

resistance The way a wire will oppose the passage of an electric current, thus reducing its size.

resolution A measure of the quality of printout and of computer displays and graphics, for instance. The higher the resolution, the finer the detail (see also pixel).

rf Radio frequency: electromagnetic waves of frequency suitable for radio transmission (roughly in the 10kHz to 10MHz range).

rgb Red-green-blue: describes a colour monitor which handles the three primary video colour signals separately. It gives excellent displays of colour computer graphics compared with a colour tv set.

rigid disc Another name for hard disc (as opposed to floppy).

ring A network design where all the devices form a closed loop. Data goes the same way round the ring all the time, with only the device addressed taking a copy of a given chunk; the source device removes the data when it gets back to it.

robot A machine that can be programmed to drive motors to do a variety of jobs automatically, often being controlled by a microprocessor.

robust Describes environment-proof hardware, software that is unlikely to crash (fail), or signals unlikely to be corrupted.

rom Read-only memory.

routeing The system by which other paged viewdata frames can be accessed from a given one.

RS232 A standard, developed for telecommunications equipment, that concerns serial information transfer at one of a standard range of speeds. The standard has been adopted widely by computer manufacturers, so that many computers have an RS232 or similar port for connecting them to peripherals.

satellite A major use of artificial earth satellites is for the transfer of signals, although monitoring (traffic or weather, for instance) is also relevant. Modern communications satellites are active: they pick up and boost radio and tv signals before retransmitting them, rather than acting as simple reflectors (see also direct broadcast (by) satellite and geostationary satellite).

satellite tv The relay of tv signals by communications satellites.

save To copy data from a computer's main memory to backing store (usually in magnetic form, eg on to a disc).

scan To pass across a page cell by cell, and down row by row, perhaps to produce a digital version. A scanner is a digitiser used in this way.

scout A message sent through a network to check whether a terminal at the far end is ready to receive data or not.

scramble To disguise a message (for instance) so that only authorised people can access it.

screen Output device, such as a monitor, tv set or flat lcd; a method of shading printed text and the effect produced.

screen dump The contents of a screen (text and/or graphics) printed as a whole on to paper.

scroll When output material is larger than a screen, the processor makes the text seem to move up so that the display can show it 'page' by 'page'. Most systems scroll up and down when required; some (such as spreadsheets) also need to be able to scroll from side to side.

scvf Single channel voice frequency.

search To hunt through a file or database for specified types of information.

secam Sequential couleur â mémoire: a colour tv standard developed in France and adopted by Eastern European countries and parts of the Middle East and North Africa.

semi-conductor A substance like silicon, whose poor electrical conductivity is very easy to vary in order to build up complex circuit elements.

sensor A device that detects touch, temperature, sound, acidity or some other similar (analog) physical or chemical information, with a corresponding electrical output, thus able to allow computers and robots to react to their environment.

serial access When something must be searched through from the beginning (as with a cassette tape) instead of being able to jump to any part of it directly (as with a floppy or compact disc).

serial interface Connection between two devices that transfers information only one bit at a time (compare with parallel interface).

server A hardware and software unit with the function of looking after the needs of a single peripheral – thus a file server works with a drive.

shared logic When a number of terminals share the same processor, the system may be called shared logic (or shared processing). Now that processor power has become so cheap, networked micros are often preferable instead.

shared processing See shared logic.

short wave Describes radio signals with short wavelengths and high frequencies.

shredder Machine that shreds paper (for instance, computer printout) after use so that it cannot be read.

signal Any energy transfer that carries information from place to place, such as a radio broadcast, speech in a telephone system, or computer data on its way to a peripheral.

signal to noise ratio A signal always picks up noise which affects reception. The higher the signal to noise ratio, the clearer the signal will be at

the receiving end.
simplex Describes a communication channel in which messages can be sent in only one direction (contrast half-duplex and duplex).
simulator Device or software system that accurately represents something that is too large, expensive, dangerous or difficult to practise on direct; used for training and sometimes also for research.
single channel voice frequency (scvf) British Telecom's new-style telex system.
16-bit systems Such systems work with information in 16-bit chunks (words), ie they process two bytes at a time. In theory, 16-bit processors can operate faster and address more internal memory than 8-bit systems (typically 256K instead of 64K). In practice, what happens depends to a great extent on the operating software. Bigger and more modern systems work with 32-bit words, or even larger ones.
skew Data skew.
slow-scan tv Involves tv pictures shot at one frame every few seconds instead of 25 or 30 a second. The effect is like a rapid succession of still photographs, but the output takes far less bandwidth to transmit than normal tv signals. Slow-scan tv is useful for security purposes, and in situations where the cost of transmitting true moving pictures is not justified, such as a business videoconference.
smart card A type of credit card, for instance, which carries a chip to provide processing power and memory.
smart device Intelligent device (as opposed to being dumb).
software Includes programs and associated data. A software generator is a program that reduces the labour of routine programming. A software tool is any utility that helps to make programming faster and easier.
sort To re-order the contents of a data file on the basis of the user's needs at the time.
source program Instructions written in a programming language before they have been translated by a compiler into an object program for a processor to obey.
spc Stored program control.
speaker A device with an electrical input and a corresponding sound output.
special effects unit A system able to produce special video effects in programme making, such as shaping a sequence over the surface of a sphere or mixing shots by apparently turning pages.
speech recognition The use of software to allow computer input of speech; currently only with a restricted vocabulary of words which must be spoken clearly and separately.
speech synthesis The artificial production, by hardware and software through a speaker, of sounds that resemble human speech.
spelling checker A program that checks the words of processed text against its list, and takes appropriate action about those it can't find.
spreadsheet A software package that displays a set of entries (such as a firm's accounts) and allows the user to define and redefine the relationships between those entries, showing the effects of any changes automatically.
sprite Complex computer graphic units that a user or a program can control and move as a whole easily. Some games computers have colourful sprites of animals and people built in; others allow users to define or adapt their own.
stand-alone A system used on its own as opposed to being part of a

network, mainframe system or telecommunications link.

standard A set of rules and conventions about hardware, software or communications that allows easier links between systems that adopt it.

star A network in which each device or node links only to the central switching and control unit.

still frame A picture or diagram presented as a single static image rather than as moving footage (compare with freeze frame).

stock control Describes business software able to handle changing stock levels and reordering needs.

store See memory and backing.

store and forward A form of electronic communication in which a message does not go directly to its destination but is stored in a central (host) computer's memory and forwarded later, this being the way many electronic mail systems work.

stored program concept A major aspect of the modern computer – it can store the instructions it needs to carry out.

stored program control (spc) Describes (modern digital) telephone exchanges controlled by computer software rather than by permanent wired connections.

string A sequence of any keyboard characters.

stripe card A card (eg a credit card) with data held in a stripe so that it can be accessed by a magnetic or optical reader.

structure chart A diagram that displays the structure of a hardware or software system using boxes on a number of different levels; lower-level boxes detail the actions of higher level ones.

structured programming A method of programming whose sections consist of clearly defined and labelled units, each of which one writes, tests, and revises independently.

supercomputer Loosely applied to the most powerful and fast working types of system.

superconductivity The lack of resistance to passing current found in a number of materials at low temperatures.

supervisor A type of operating software.

switched star A network layout for cable tv that is specially suitable for interactive services, but tends to be expensive to build.

switching centre A telephone exchange is a switching centre – it switches signals between different lines.

synthesiser A device for producing artificial speech or music from electronic impulses.

system A set of hardware, and maybe software, or a set of working procedures that can carry out a given task.

systems analysis A skilled task involving analysing an information handling need and preparing reports that detail which systems would be suitable for meeting it most efficiently. Systems analysts often have professional programmers working with them.

systems software Software such as the operating system and programming languages that a computer needs to allow it to do anything useful.

System X British Telecom's high speed, high capacity, digital telephone network.

tailor To modify a hardware system or software package to meet a given user's needs.

tape Magnetically or optically coated plastics tape used for holding information – audio, video and computer – accessed by a suitable drive unit.

tdm Time division multiplexing.

telebanking Process of instructing payments and getting account information from a distance, often using viewdata from a terminal in office, shop, or home.

telecommunications Transfer and reception of information over a distance.

telecommuting Doing one's job from home using IT links to other people's workplaces.

teleconference A meeting between people linked by telecommunications, either audio (using telephone lines) or video (using cable).

telegram A message sent by telegraph.

telegraph Early electric method of transmitting signals using simple on/off codes.

teleshopping Ordering goods at a distance, often using viewdata from a terminal; of value for the busy, elderly, disabled and housebound, as well as in business.

telesoftware Software downloaded into a computer's memory over a distance, using telephone lines or broadcast waves.

teletex The international standard system for transfer of text and data between terminals using the public telephone network, likely to supersede telex.

teletext Information broadcast as part of a television signal, in Britain by Ceefax and Oracle, received on special tv sets with teletext decoders.

teletype(writer) A terminal that consists of a keyboard and a printer.

television (tv) The transfer of video picture signals, usually with sound, to a screen – either broadcast (mainly by short radio waves) or by cable (mainly in local distribution and closed circuit tv systems).

telex A world-wide telegraphic service that allows communication between special printers, by modern standards slow (50 baud), costly and inflexible, but well established and widely available.

terminal Equipment combining input and output hardware to allow the user to communicate with a remote system; it may be dumb or intelligent.

thimble The printhead of a type of printer; its shape is much like that of a thimble, and its outside carries raised characters. The thimble turns and nods to bring each character into contact with the paper.

tight beam Describes signals sent by radio (for instance) to a single destination.

time division multiplexing (tdm) A method of sending several messages down a single communications channel by giving each source a time slot in turn.

time sharing A method of allowing a processor to work on several jobs at once, by sharing its time between them.

touch screen A touch sensitive screen allowing the user to make choices by pointing with a finger, thus making the screen act as an input device as well as displaying output. Some touch screens detect pressure; others sense the interruption of a criss-cross grid of infra-red beams. Used in computer and interactive video systems aimed at the general public, and anywhere the traditional keyboard may present a barrier.

tracker ball A computer input device consisting of a ball set in a socket; as you turn the ball with the palm of your hand a pointer moves over the screen. The tracker ball is much like a mouse or joystick in its effect.

transborder data flow The transfer of information (as text, broadcast signals or data) across national borders.

transportable More accurate adjective for microcomputers that are too big and heavy to be truly portable; also used to describe software that will run on different computers to some extent.

transputer A very powerful 32-bit processor on a chip with a ram store that can be linked to others to provide parallel processing.

tree A method of arranging data, viewdata pages, or cable tv networks that resembles the trunk, branches, and twigs of a tree.

turnkey system A computer system supplied in a complete and customised form so that the user need only 'turn the key' to start it.

tv/monitor A display that can either display tv pictures or act as a monitor. Some can do both jobs at once and show computer text and graphics on top of a video picture.

typesetter An advanced form of word processing system that lets one prepare fully edited and laid-out pages of text and perhaps graphics for printing; also called desktop publisher.

uhf Ultra high frequency; usually applied to electromagnetic waves.

ula Uncommitted logic array: a type of chip which contains circuits not yet connected. Its manufacturer can add different final layers containing the interconnections to suit different purchaser's requirements. The result is much cheaper than making a fully customised chip.

ulsi Ultra large scale integration: a method of packing a very large number (more than 1,000,000) of electronic components and their connections on to a single chip (compare with lsi and vlsi).

Unix A popular and sophisticated operating system for 16-bit microcomputers that allows multi-users and multi-tasking.

upgrade The process of improving or adding to hardware or software. A good system will have a well planned upgrade path, so that software can be transferred on to expanded hardware without wasted effort.

upper case Describes capital letters.

upstream Messages sent by cable system users towards the centre are said to go upstream. The transmission speed needed for upstream messages depends on their nature.

user friendly Describes IT systems believed by their designers to be easy to use. In practice many turn out to be user hostile.

user interface Front end, or man-machine interface – the mode of interaction between a system and a user and its associated hardware and software.

utilities Programs that allow users to do useful jobs like copying discs or recovering deleted files.

van Value added network: one that provides subscription services like electronic mail and viewdata in addition to basic telecommunications facilities.

vcr Video cassette recorder.

vdu Visual display unit.

verification The process of checking computer input or action for certain types of mistake. To verify means to check whether saving a file, formatting a disc, or entering data to a system was successful.

vertical markets Software designed for a particular client group (eg solicitors or cocoa factories) rather than to perform a particular function (eg spreadsheet or word processing).

vhd Video high density: a form of video disc.

vhf Very high frequency: usually referring to electromagnetic waves used for tv.

video Describes hardware and systems working with vhf signals.

video camera A device whose electronic output represents the scene that it scans.

video cassette Cassette containing video tape.

video cassette recorder (vcr) A machine that records and plays back video tape packed in cassettes.

videoconference A 'meeting' between people in different places using video links for the transfer of speech, data and pictures.

video disc A plastics, metal, or glass disc that can store large numbers of moving or still video pictures with sound. Unlike video cassettes, data can be quickly accessed at random on some video discs. As they can also store digital information, this gives them great potential as a medium for computer memory because of their enormous capacity. At present, however, video discs cannot generally be recorded on to by the user.

video high density See vhd.

video phone A telephone which can transmit an image from a camera and put one received on to a screen, as well as handling speech in the normal way.

video tape High density magnetic tape on which video pictures and sound can be recorded.

videotex Electronic methods of receiving certain types of information from a distance and displaying it on a screen; may use broadcasting signals (teletext) or telephone lines (viewdata). Teletext is often referred to as one-way or broadcast videotex, and viewdata as two-way or interactive videotex. Videotext is an alternative spelling sometimes used in the US.

viewdata A two-way transfer of electronic information using telephone lines and tv sets. Local users can not only retrieve information from large databases but also send messages and instructions. Prestel was the world's first public viewdata system.

visual display unit (vdu) A device that displays computer output on a screen; also used loosely to mean a combined screen and keyboard unit.

vlsi Very large scale integration: a method of packing a very large number (1000 to 1,000,000) of electronic components and their connections on to a single chip (see also lsi and ulsi).

voice bank A public telephone answering service.

voice grade Describes a communication channel suitable for the transfer of speech.

voice mail See digital voice messaging.

voice recognition unit A computer input device that can be 'trained' to identify spoken words.

voice response systems (vrs) Users can telephone messages, orders and questions to these computer-based information systems. The computer responds immediately in a high quality synthesised voice, delivering information or confirmation in the appropriate language.

voice traffice The use of a telephone system to carry conversations as opposed to data.

volatile Describes computer memory whose contents are lost when you switch off.

vrs Voice response systems.

wan Wide area network.

wand Light pen.

wavelength The distance between two peaks (or troughs) on a wave; the larger the wavelength, the lower the frequency.

wide area network (wan) A method for linking computers and terminals that are widely separated, often using public or private telephone lines. Transmission speeds may be lower than in a lan, but wans often span immense distances.

wideband Same as broadband – describing a communications channel with a large bandwidth, at least 10 kilobaud.

wimp Windows, icons, mouse and pointers (or pull-down menus): describes a modern, flexible and friendly type of user interface.

Winchester A type of sealed hard disc unit very popular for use with microcomputers. Originally 350mm in diameter, Winchesters have become progressively smaller, yet give ever greater capacities and faster access time.

windows The effect of splitting a display screen into two or more separate sections, each able to hold different types of data to be interacted with and processed separately.

wired society A catchphrase to suggest the social implications of improved modern communications.

wood Write once optical disc.

word Processors do not deal with individual bits of information; they group them into uniform 'words' and process each as a single unit. Many older personal computers have a word length of eight bits; newer machines work on 16-bit or even 32-bit words.

word processing (wp) A system for editing, storing and rearranging text so that it can be perfected before being finally printed out. Word processed text can be produced easily and without errors to give (for instance) 'personalised' letters containing variations on a standard text. Any computer can word process if it has suitable software and peripherals.

word processor Strictly, a machine dedicated to word processing, but loosely used to describe any computer that is running word processing software.

worksheet A database or file set up in the form of a spreadsheet, with a row for each record and a column for each field.

workstation The place where an individual user interacts with an IT system; loosely, a terminal.

worm Write once, read many times: describes a type of optical disc.

wp Word processing.

write To write to a disc, for instance, is to copy data to it for storage (compare with read).

write once optical disc (wood) A type of video disc on which the user can record, but from which information cannot be erased.

wysiwyg What you see is what you get: describes a word processing system whose display of text is somewhat like a printout would be.

X25 An international standard protocol for packet switching.

xerography The technique behind modern photocopiers and some page printers which charges a drum electrostatically in the pattern of the original material, the charge attracting a plastics dust (toner) which then bakes on to the paper.

Appendix 2
Finding Out More

Information technology does not yet extend to the ability to help people find just what they want from the many thousands of books available. This appendix will point you towards some of the books you'll find most useful and readable, and a few other avenues you may wish to explore.

It is more important to keep abreast of IT with a constantly updated general knowledge than to become an expert in one small field of it, at least at the beginning. Some good tv programmes add to that general picture from time to time, while magazine programmes like *Tomorrow's World* and *Micro Live* can help a great deal with snippets. A number of companies publish video cassettes in various areas of IT, probably the consistently best being the following (in descending order):

Video Arts (68 Oxford Street, London W1N 9LA)
CFL Vision (Chalfont Grove, Gerrards Cross, Bucks SL9 87N)
TV Choice (27 Swinton Street, London WC1X 9NW)

At the heyday of the explosion of personal, business and home computing a few years ago, the number of periodicals in the field went well into three figures. Since then, things have settled down somewhat, and the best are (early 1987) as follows:

General

Ed-IT World (aimed at education, but generally up to date, thorough and thoughtful).
IT Focus (an excellent, though costly, abstracts journal on IT in practice).
Personal Computer World (primarily for the home user, but good on news, reviews and comment).
Practical Computing (aimed at business, but almost exclusively computer oriented).
Which Computer? (worth keeping an eye on for its occasional outstanding material).

Specialist

AI Business (a newsletter for aficionados of AI, so probably of little general interest – but it may grow).
Audio Visual (for its coverage of video and interactive video).
Desktop Publishing Today (very new at the time of writing, but showing the

potential to become the leader in the field).

Industrial Computing (cad, cam, robotics, and integrated manufacture).

The quality press also carry regular features on advances in technology in general, and so cover IT to a useful extent. Check, in particular, *The Times*, the *Guardian* and the *Sunday Times*. Of the weekly magazines *New Scientist* usually has material of interest, while *The Economist* sometimes does.

Three organisations are particularly able to keep themselves, and others, abreast of changes in this rapidly changing field. They are:

Council for Educational Technology (3 Devonshire Street, London W1N 2BA) – its concern is training as well as formal education.

National Computing Centre (Oxford Road, Manchester M1 8DX) – the nearest we have to a watchdog (but all competitors are *very* far away).

National Interactive Video Centre (27 Marylebone Road, London NW1 5JS) – somewhat staid, but still a leading light in this crucial field.

The other main way to keep in touch is to visit – and study – a couple of major exhibitions each year. The National Exhibition Centre has the best large ones in IT, but smaller and more specialised exhibitions and conferences take place in most major centres of the country.

Now for that book list. This *must* be a personal selection – to repeat, there are hundreds of relevant titles out each year. All the same, some of the volumes noted here will be very helpful indeed. The list includes single topic titles as well as more general ones, but, at the time of writing, in many of the fields looked at in this volume there have been no useful books published at all.

A-Z of business computing Adrian Stokes; Heinemann, 1986.
Sometimes superficial, and restricted to computing, this is a usefully detailed dictionary to computers in the office.

So you think your business needs a computer? Khalid Aziz; Kogan Page, 1986.
Aziz deals almost exclusively with the stand-alone micro in the small firm, but in that restricted area he goes wide and deep without loss of readability.

CD-ROM Steve Lambert and Suzanne Ropiequet, eds; Microsoft, 1986.
An outstanding account of the theory and practice of cd-rom as a database medium. This is in fact a large number of separate articles, so can be repetitive.

Computer aided design Paul Barr; Prentice-Hall, 1985.
This is a superb introduction to the subject, and includes detailed accounts of some popular systems.

Computers mean business Jacquetta Mergarry; Kogan Page, 1984.
A highly structured course in office computing, this thick book also includes many useful case studies.

Dictionary of computing and new information technology A. J. Meadows *et al*; Kogan Page, 1984.
Much more than a straight dictionary of definitions, this includes some lengthy articles and a number of good clear illustrations. It covers the whole field very well.

The electronic office Malcolm Peltu; BBC, 1984.
This is becoming a little dated now – but as a classic rather than fit only for the bin.

The electronic office in the small business David Harvey; Wildwood, 1986.

Sometimes slick and superficial, but an interesting and pleasant read, this covers most aspects of office IT dealt with in this book.

Informagic Jean-Pierre Petit and Ian Stewart; Murray, 1982.
This delightful comic strip book for adults describes an adventure inside a computer, where the hero and his companions learn a great deal.

Information unlimited Ian Somerville; Addison-Wesley, 1983.
Rather dated now, and not appealingly presented, this volume is all the same a useful survey.

Inside information Jacquetta Megarry; BBC, 1985.
A highly readable and very well illustrated coverage of IT theory and practice for the non-specialist, this book is associated with radio broadcasts and audio tape.

Interactive video Eric Parsloe, ed; Sigma, 1985.
Parsloe's is still the only readable guide to the subject, and also contains plenty of material on video and video discs.

Managing with micros Colin Lewis; Blackwell, 1986.
This is a rather dry and sometimes superficial account, but it is generally up to date.

The microelectronics revolution Tom Forester, ed; Blackwell, 1980.
A collection of readable and important papers on many relevant aspects of IT, Forester's is a pivotal and still highly valid book.

Handbook of new office technology John Derrick and Phillip Oppenheim; Kogan Page, 1986.
In providing thorough buying guides to 15 types of office equipment, this book – or 90 per cent of it – also provides a superb account of IT in practice.

Selecting business software E. Berman and Leslie Dewhirst; Pinter, 1985.
Each useful chapter leads to criteria and checklists for the purchase of office software packages.

Supervising the electronic office Catherin Blaazer and Eric Molyneux; Gower, 1984.
Despite its title, this book is just a guide to office management in general. It is a nice little one, though, and does occasionally consider relevant aspects of IT.

Typesetting for micro users Belinda Naylor-Stables; Quorum, 1986.
If you decide to try typesetting from disc, the book tells you exactly how to go about it, at least if you plan to work with any firm that sets type with aspic.

The videotex revolution Alan J. Mayne; October, 1982.
This book is just beginning to date. However, in that it provides thorough accounts of videotex theory and the development of systems (with a wealth of further references), it is worth scanning at least.

Word processing for the modern business Alan Davies; Prentice-Hall, 1984.
One of the best of very many treatments of this important field, this book remains largely up to date.

Appendix 3
Personal Data Protection

Most Western countries have regulations designed to protect the privacy and reputation of individuals whose details may be held in computer-readable form. The British Data Protection Act makes it illegal for almost all people and organisations to hold personal data in this form unless they have formally registered that fact.

The definitions as to the data which must be registered are fairly complex, but ignorance is not accepted as an excuse for not registering.

If you use, or plan to use, computer-readable personal data with your system (even if for someone else), and if you aren't registered, you should *immediately* ask for registration details from

The Data Protection Registrar
Springfield House
WILMSLOW
Cheshire
SK9 5AX
Telephone 0625 535777

Index

Entries in italic refer to the most detailed coverage. See also the Glossary, starting on page 211, which is not indexed.

accounts 38, *79*, 82, 103
acoustic coupler 93
ai *see* machine intelligence
air conditioning *see* energy management
alarm 97
algorithm 204
alu 17
amateur radio 148
analog *15*, 26, 51, 127–8, *139–40*
answering machine 144
applications software 27, 30, 31, 32, 96
appointments 79
archive 162, 186
arithmetic and logic unit *see* alu
artificial intelligence *see* machine intelligence
artist software *70*, 173
aspic 177
atm 13, *148–9*
audio media 158, 200, 207
automation 82, 97
autonomy 101, 103
autoteller *see* atm

backing store *18*, 20, 46, 104, 105, 118, 161, 163
balance sheet 38, 64
banking 12, 13, 23, 81, 148–9, 189, 192
base station 152–3
Basic 32
batching 133
Baudot code 130
binary 16, *18*, 31
binding 182
bioelectronics 207
bit *18*, 31, 130
bleeper 97, 145
booking 13, 149, 150, *192*
bridge 108
British Telecom 48, 130
bulletin board 192
bundled software 84
business 101
business software 34
byte *18*

cable 14, 95, 102, 104, 140, 148, 163, *167*, 195, 206, 207
camping 144
car 14
car phone *see* cellular phone
card, Drexon 202
card, punched *see* punched media 18
card, stripe 202
carousel 197
cash 13, 39, 150
cassette, audio 18
cctv 97, *157*, 169

cd-i 201
cd-rom 161, *200*
Ceefax *see* teletex
cellular phone 94, 139, 148, *152*
central processor (unit) *see* cpu
chat 52, 133
chip 19, 24, 26
choice 110
chrominance 156
clock 17
closed circuit television *see* cctv
closed user group 198
cluster 101
Cobol 31
colour 70, 116, 123, 156, 182
com 187
communication, corporate *see* corporate communication
communications 26, *38*, 41, *46*, 76, 84, 85, 93, 132, 133, 140, 146
compact disc 161, 164, *200*
compatibility 30, 105, 123, 159, 162, 163, 201
computer 12, *14*, *26*, 49, 93, 110, 140, 203
computerisation 110
concurrency 87
consultant 115
consumables 24, 124
control program 27
control unit 17
corporate communication 157, 170
cost 26, 27, 37, 86, 106, 124, 146
couriers 133
cpa 76
cpu *17*, 23, 24, 26, 27, 100
critical path analysis *see* cpa
cspdn 142, *148*
cut and paste 85, *120*, 173, 180

daisy chain 107
data *16*, 18
data capture 98
data processing 15, 23
Data Protection Act 247
database *38*, *57*, 68, 76, 90, 120, *185*, *and see* relational database
dedicated 15
desktop publishing *see* dtp
diary 79
digital *15*, 26, 51, 127, 140
digitisation 162, *179*
disc, magnetic *18*, 21, 104, 105, 202, 206
disc publishing 175
disc, video *see* video disc
display 19, *116*, 207
Drexon card 202
dtp 41, 84, 85, 121, *171*, *178*
dumb 20, 100

eds 162, 201
efficiency 28, 94, 97, 110
eft 149
8-bit etc systems *19*, 106
electronic 15
electronic document storage *see* eds
electronic mail *see* mail
electronic publishing 41, 85, 170, 185, 199
email *see* mail
energy management 95
ergonomics 122
exchange 126, 140, 152
executive software 27
expert systems 204

facsimile transfer *see* fax
fax 56, *134*, 140, 162
feedback 98
fibre optics 140, 147, 167
field, video 156
file 118
filing 36, 38, 57
finance 12, 13, 39, 65
fire 97
firmware 24
floppy disc *see* disc, magnetic
Fortran 31
frame, video 156, 157
frame, viewdata 199
future 11, 124, 162, 206, *and see* global village

gateway *108*, 147, 196, 198
generations, 15, 26
gigabyte 19
glass fibre *see* fibre optics
global village 14, 108, 170, *206*
graphics *38*, *69*, 76, 83, 85, 94, 124, 155, 157, 173, 183
graphics pad 179

hands-free phone 143

hard disc *see* disc, magnetic
hardware 23, 122
hdtv 155
health and safety 122
heating *see* energy management
heuristics 204
highlighting 44
history 15, 23, 31, 33, 127, 130, 159
home and office banking *see* banking
host computer 48, 55, 107, 191
hybrid network 102

icons 87
information 10, 12, *16*, 35, 83
information technology *see* IT
input unit 19
insurance 124
integrated circuit *see* chip
integrated services digital network *see* isdn
integrated software 39, *80*, 91, 114, 120
intelligence *see* machine intelligence
intelligent device *20*, 100, 101
interaction 98
interactive compact disc 201
interactive tv 167
interactive video 164, 170
intercom 143
Interstream 134
intruders 97
inventory *see* stock control
isdn 141, *147*
IT *12*, 25, *37*, 101, 142, 165

joystick 88, 117
jukebox 163

K 19
key system *142*, 144
keyboard 19, 28, 87, 116
kilobyte *see* K

lan *see* network
landline 25
language, programming 31
laser printer *see* printer
laservision 159, 160, 200, 202
lcd 19, 92, 144
leisure 14
library, software 18, 29
liquid crystal display *see* lcd
liveware 24
local area network *see* network
log, computer 28
logging on/off 52, 101, 103, 188
logging systems 131, 144, *146*
logic 17
Logo 31
luminance 156

machine intelligence 16, 28, *203*
magnetic disc *see* disc, magnetic
magnetic media 18
magnetic tape *see* tape, magnetic
mail 13, 26, 35, 53, 85, 135, *146*
mail merge 59, 120, 192, *199*
mail shot 57, 60
main frame *23*, 28, 48, 100, 104
mains data transfer 95
maintenance 122, 124
manuals 24, 31, 115, 124
megabyte 19
memory *see* store 17
memory phone 142
menu 25, 55, 88, 189, 195
Mercury 48, 130–31
micro(computer) *20*, 29, 100
microelectronics 15, 26
microform 162, 171, 175, *186*, 201
microphone 140
microviewdata 55, 196
microwave 22, 147
mini(computer) *20*, 47, 100, 104
miniaturisation 26, 207
mobile phone *see* cellular phone
mobile switching centre 153
modem 13, *25*, *50*, 93, 136, 147
modular computing 86, 114
money *see* cash
monitor software 27
monitor, video 19, *157*
mouse 70, 88, 117
mp/m 103
MS-DOS 30
multi-addressing 132
multiplexing 127, 153, 168
multiprogramming 29
multi-tasking 87
multi-usage 102, 105

network 21, 24, 48, 54, *98*, 155, 188
nibble 19
ntsc 154

office 10, 14, *34*, 111
office planning 102
offset printer 182
operating software 18, 19, 22, *27*, 86, 103
optical publishing 201
Oracle *see* teletex
organiser 79
output unit *19*, 97

packet 104, 107, *150*
packet assembly/disassembly *see* pad
packet switching *see* pss
pad 107, 138
page printer *see* printer
painting software *see* artist software
pal 154
paper 37, 57, 88, 172
paperless office 37, 39, 85
parallel processing 26
password 54, 103, 188
payroll *80*, 82
pbx 107, *140*
peripheral 18, 19, 23, 24, 26, 27, 121
personal computer *see* micro
personnel management *see* payroll
phone 13, 25, 48, 93, 107, *126*, *139*
photocopier 182
pixel 157
plotter 78
pointer, screen 88
polling 95, 138
portable computer 18
power line transfer 95
Prestel 13, 14, 25, 38, 52, 54, 155, 171, *188*
printer 21, 45, 70, 85, 93, *122*, 180
printer switching 104
private branch exchange *see* pbx
process control 82, 95
processing 16
processor *see* cpu
program 15, 17, 23
program language *see* language, programming
programmability 16, 120, 143
programming 31, 59
programming language *see* language, programming
project control *see* cpa
project scheduler *see* cpa
protocol 108
pss 137, 142, 150
pstn 142
publishing *see* disc publishing, dtp, electronic publishing, optical publishing
punched media 18

radio 13, 48, 148, 151
radio paging 145
ram 19
random access memory *see* ram
read and write memory *see* ram
read only memory *see* rom
regenerator 127
relational database 89
repeater 127
report 57
ring 101
robots *97*, 206
rom 19, 24
route planning 13

satellite 14, 163, *166*
scanning 162
scvf 131
searching 59
secam 154
secondary store *see* backing store
security 54, 71, 97, 103, 108
sensor 95, 97
shared logic 100
shopping 13, 168, 192
single channel voice frequency *see* scvf
slides 94
slow scan television 169
smart card 149
society 14
software 23, *27*, 114
sorting 59
sound *140*, 156
speaker 140
speech *see* voice input/output
speed 15
spelling check 43, *120*
spreadsheet *38*, *63*, 76, 80, 92
staff 23, 24, 28, 29, 100, 125
standards *see* compatibility
star 109, 122, 168
Star system 145

stock control *79*, 82
storage 15, 17
store and forward *see* mail
stripe card 202
supercomputer 23
superconductor 127, 207
supervisor 27
support 122, 124
surveillance 97, 157, 169
switchboard 52, 133
systems analysis 110, 113

tape, magnetic 18
tape, paper *see* punched media
telebooking *see* booking
Telecom Gold 38, 52, 254, 146, *199*
telecommunications 25, 48, 52, *107*, 141
telecommuting 14, 26, 56, 85, *94*, 153, 208
teleconference 85, 143, 153, 168
telegraph 130
telephone *see* phone
teleshopping *see* shopping
telesoftware 194
teletext *132*, 140, 146, 148, 168
teletext 191, 193
teletypewriter 130
television *see* tv
telex 13, *53*, *130*, *192*, 200
terminal 22, 48, 92, 99, 100, 188
text processing *see* word processing
tracker ball 88, 117
traffic 13
training 30, 157, 164, 170
transport 13
travel 13
tv 14, *155*, 165, 192
tv, closed circuit *see* cctv
typesetting 173, *175*

user-friendliness 86, 115
vhd 159
video 97, *154*, 170
videoconference 153, 168
video disc *158*, 170, 200, 202, 207
videophone 14, 85, 167, 168
videotex 168, 193
viewdata 25, 192, 193, 199, *and see* Prestel, Telecom Gold
vision, machine 206
voice input/output 26, 206
voice link 138
Voicebank 145

wan *see* network
what if 66, 68
wimp *86*, 180
Winchester 104
windows *86*, 120
wired society *see* global village
word, data 19, 130
word processing *38*, *39*, 76, 84, 86, 103, 116, 172, 183
work station 21, 101
wyswiyg 41, 44, *117*

X25 108